The Working of Social Work

of related interest

Learning and Teaching in Social Work
Towards Reflective Practice
Edited by Margaret Yelloly and Mary Henkel
ISBN 1 85302 237 3

Social Work with Children and Families
Getting Into Practice
Ian Butler and Gwenda Roberts
ISBN 1 85302 365 5

Competence in Social Work Practice
Edited by Kieran O'Hagan
ISBN 1 85302 332 9

Handbook of Theory for Practice Teachers in Social Work
Edited by Joyce Lishman
ISBN 1 85302 098 2

Boring Records?
Communication, Speech and Writing in Social Work
Katie Prince
ISBN 1 85302 325 6

Staff Supervision in a Turbulent Environment
Managing Process and Task in Front-line Services
Lynette Hughes and Paul Pengelly
ISBN 1 85302 327 2

Performance Review and Quality in Social Care
Edited by Anne Connor and Stewart Black
ISBN 1 85302 017 6

The Working of Social Work

Edited by Juliet Cheetham
& Mansoor A. F. Kazi

Jessica Kingsley Publishers
London and Philadelphia

First published in the United Kingdom in 1998 by
Jessica Kingsley Publishers Ltd
116 Pentonville Road
London N1 9JB, England
and
1900 Frost Road, Suite 101
Bristol, PA 19007, U S A

Copyright © 1998 Jessica Kingsley Publishers

Library of Congress Cataloging in Publication Data
A CIP catalogue record for this book is available from the Library of Congress

British Library Cataloguing in Publication Data
The working of social work
1. Social service
I. Cheetham, Juliet II.Kazi, Mansoor
361.3

ISBN 1 85302 498 8

Printed and Bound in Great Britain by
Athenaeum Press, Gateshead, Tyne and Wear

Contents

Acknowledgements

As editors we would like to thank and to congratulate the contributors to this volume who met our deadlines so diligently and our requests for amendments with such good humour.

We would also like to thank the service users, practitioners and social work managers who contributed to these studies in numerous ways, including their attendance at the conference at Huddersfield University in 1995 where the research described in this book was first discussed.

Finally, we are indebted to Catherine Simpson who dealt skilfully with the often eccentric disks of different word processing systems and the idiosyncrasies of the editors. Her excellent editorial assistance turned miscellaneous manuscripts into a book.

Juliet Cheetham
Mansoor A. F. Kazi
June 1997

CHAPTER I

The Evaluation of Social Work
Priorities, Problems and Possibilities

Juliet Cheetham

The Working of Social Work, the title of this book, is deliberately ambiguous. It prompts at least two rather basic questions commonly asked by people who are not usually themselves social workers: first, does social work work; and second, how does it work? The second question encompasses several others, for example about the legal and social functions of social work and about its methods.

Social workers and researchers would certainly want to refine the first of these questions and would point out that similar enquiries in other fields, for example 'does health care work' or 'does education work?' would be regarded as so large as to have no meaning. More appropriate questions would be: 'what are the effects of this drug/this type of surgery?'; 'what proportion of the population does this immunisation programme reach?'; 'does reading scheme A help children attain certain levels of competency more quickly than scheme B?' Nevertheless, perhaps because the noun 'work' can easily prompt the verb, the question 'does social work work?' is often in the minds of those who receive its services, or make referrals to them, or who pay for them directly or through taxation. Increasingly social workers acknowledge that they should attend to this general curiosity as part of their efforts to improve their own practice and accountability. Increasingly too, social workers – as practitioner researchers as well as full-time professional researchers – are becoming more adept in carrying out a range of studies, large and small, which explore both the impact of social work and its methods and contexts, as this book shows. Indeed, it can be forcibly argued that a sophisticated understanding of social work, and indeed all the human services, should now be informed by these two rather different kinds of knowledge – in the jargon, about outcome and process – and seek to connect them. Several chapters illustrate this central question, especially those by Stanley and her co-authors, Dowling, and White (Chapters 4, 8 and 9).

Encouraging Research-Minded Practice

This book is intended to encourage thinking both about social work research and about ways of carrying out evaluative studies which are relevant to policy and practice. The chapters by White, Thyer, Kazi and Shaw (Chapters 9, 10, 11 and 12) each provide a refreshing and challenging perspective on the purposes of evaluation research on social work and the ways this may be approached. However, the book is in no way a substitute for a standard methodological text; rather it is an invitation to consider the place of evaluation in social work and some ways in which it may be carried out. If readers are tempted to consider further involvement in evaluative research as sponsors, participants or researchers, as we hope they will be, then the following chapters suggest possible ways forward.

Because examples are often the strongest and most helpful form of encouragement a major part of this book consists of accounts of recent studies of a wide variety of social work practice. A further encouragement is the fact that several of the studies were undertaken by practitioners, by those very closely associated with them or by people who had recently been social workers. These are described in the chapters by Badger, Farnfield, Furness, Williams and White (Chapters 2, 3, 5, 7 and 9). This closeness to practice ensures a real understanding of the complexities of social work, indeed the very complexities which can be a deterrent to evaluative research. The studies also demonstrate methods of coping with some formidable challenges that can be encompassed within the modest enquiries which are often all that is feasible for people with many commitments other than research.

Some of the studies have also been chosen because they illustrate the way in which research questions, and ways of trying to answer them, are closely linked with high quality social work practice: that which seeks a holistic understanding of the problems it confronts and devises ways of dealing with those difficulties, or parts of them, within the resources of the practitioner or the agency. Social work practice and research both often deal with matters which are but a small part of individuals' experience; and they do so in the knowledge that, just as a small amount of well-focused help can give a person the encouragement and energy to cope with other and larger problems, so can the illumination from one or two well-formulated research questions spur further enquiry and cumulative understanding. So, for example, Badger's study points to a number of matters which may be connected with the impact of work with sex offenders, including their age and the intensity and duration of the help they receive; Furness's work invites us to think further about the nature of the abuse of elderly people in residential care; and Farnfield, through the voices of the children in his studies, highlights their competence as commentators on their lives and their priorities for help.

Several of the studies are also remarkable because their empirical enquiries have grown from and contributed to strong theoretical foundations. Badger, for example, relates his work to concepts of career. Farnfield sets his studies in the context of child development. White discusses different approaches to the analysis of 'reality' and Shaw explores and challenges theoretical traditions which can, in his view, hold research methodology in inappropriate strait-jackets. All this illustrates very well the fruitful relationship between theory, concepts and empirical social work research which is often criticised for being atheoretical.

Taken together the major purposes of this collection of papers are to contribute to critical, reflective thinking about the working of social work and to promote practice which seeks evidence about its impact. This evidence can take a variety of forms, and can often only be tentative, but its pursuit is a hallmark of responsible social work. This pursuit is increasingly being seen as both an obligation and a rewarding activity in the UK and internationally (Cheetham *et al.* 1992; Connor 1993; Everitt 1996; Everitt and Hardiker 1996; Fook 1996; Fuller and Petch 1995; Hess and Mullen 1995; Shaw forthcoming).

Twenty years – or even a decade – ago evaluation studies of the working of social work of the kind identified in this book were extremely rare. In part progress was hampered by concerns about what could count as acceptable research methods and designs; and there were several dimensions to acceptability. These included philosophical debates about the nature of evidence, which were often at the heart of arguments about the contributions of qualitative and quantitative research methods and hesitancy about the worth of small studies, particularly when the researchers were close to the fields of study. There were also considerable doubts about the willingness of social workers and their managers to expose themselves to outside enquiry, and scepticism about their readiness or ability to turn a searchlight on themselves.

Happily, these arguments continue as is evident from some of the chapters in this book; if they did not the relatively youthful activity of social work research would become ossified before it had acquired the wisdom of experience. The difference today is that methodological debate is seen as a natural part of social work research, encouraging its development in general and critical scrutiny of the lessons to be drawn from a flexible and inclusive approach (Cheetham *et al.* 1992). This approach, well established in the UK and illustrated by the studies in this book, argues that evaluative research in social work requires the disciplined use and adaptation of research methods and designs chosen to suit the matters to be studied. There is therefore no one research method to be preferred above all others; the matters to be studied drive the methodology, not vice versa. One advantage of this practical approach is to make possible evaluative research, however modest and however difficult the subject in hand, by encouraging creative thinking about feasible, systematic enquiry. This approach should also encourage, as several chapters in this book illustrate, critical debate about methodological limitations and about experiment and development. For example the chapters by Kazi and Williams illustrate some of the difficulties practitioners find in using single-case design, so enthusiastically advocated by Thyer, and give their perspectives on the limitations as well as the advantages of this method of evaluation. White and Shaw both question the wisdom and feasibility of an exclusive or predominant focus on specified outcomes and Dowling shows how accounts of social workers' activities which do not include actual observations of their behaviour can be gravely wanting.

The activities and debates which the chapters in this book illustrate point therefore to significant developments in evaluative research; but what is the contemporary context and standing of evaluation in social work in the UK and what might be its future priorities?

Audiences and their Interests

The present position of evaluative research in social work can in part be gauged by reviewing those groups with interests in it. Research funding for social work, the organisation of its programmes in universities and agencies, policy papers and a wide variety of publications from academic journals and books to practitioner broadsheets and summary fact papers are all evidence of the contemporary diverse audiences for evaluative social work research. These include, of course, policy makers, managers and practitioners, but also other professionals who make referrals to social work services. Service users are another potential audience but so far one which has been little included in researchers' activities. Then there are ordinary citizens whose well-founded understanding of the scope and impact of social work is crucial for its legitimacy as an institution to be preserved, promoted and funded as a public good.

Interests in the evaluation of social work may be defensive, developmental or merely curious. It is widely recognised that when welfare programmes are no longer regarded as self evidently worthwhile, and when public spending is being curtailed, that a necessary (but not sufficient) weapon in preserving their existence is evidence about their beneficial impact and their value for money. At the very least those responsible for welfare services, in their diverse forms, must be prepared as part of their accountability critically to review their operation and outcomes. There is also growing interest, as this book and many others indicate, in using research to illuminate and improve practice (Connor 1993; Everitt and Hardiker 1996; Fook 1996; Fuller and Petch 1995; Hess and Mullen 1995; Schon 1983; 1995).

Further evidence of interest in research can be found in the expanding research programmes in most university social work departments, an experience which has been supported by substantial funding from government and research foundations and by universities themselves. The review of research in British universities carried out by the UK Higher Education Funding Councils in 1996 showed that university social work research encompassed a broad range of theoretical and applied enquiry with energetic attention to users and often strong local involvement. It also showed that between 1992 and 1996 there had been substantial improvement in its quality (Cheetham and Deakin 1997).

How are agencies involved? The pattern appears to be a mixed one. Many local authority research departments which were active and influential in the 1970s and 1980s have either been disbanded or had their functions directed towards the determination, inspection and enhancement of service quality. At their most sophisticated such activities have strong relationships with evaluative research although they can sometimes be accused of being instruments of managerial blame for poor quality rather than vehicles for developing better practice. As an alternative to conducting in-house evaluation many agencies contract with their local universities for relevant studies to be carried out. These relationships offer several advantages including research which is specifically designed with the agencies' interests in mind but which provides an independent perspective and opportunities for researchers to explore the immediate concerns of policy makers and practitioners in the context of other conceptual or empirical work. The chapter by Stanley *et al.* provides one example. Agencies are also crucial facilitators of research by allowing access to their users, staff and records, without which there could be very little evaluative research. Negotiating the ground rules for such research and the exchanges of information and dissemination are essential and skilled activities if practice-focused research is to have benefits for all the parties. The studies by Dowling and Badger illustrate this very well.

Government research policy now underlines the status of the various users of research, echoing arguments in the White Paper *Realising Our Potential* (HMSO 1993) that the utility of research must be a foundation for its public support. Social work as an essentially practical activity should have little quarrel about such a rationale for research, although there are important debates to be had about the various uses of research in social work. For example, an immediate practical use is knowledge derived from various measures, perhaps using single-case design, about the changes – personal or material – which follow some kind of social work intervention. The chapters by Thyer, Kazi and Williams describe these very well. A further use of research comes from the light it can throw on the shape and delivery of social work and the influences organisations bring to bear on this. Dowling's account of social workers' responses to people requesting financial help and Furness' study of residential staff's understanding of the abuse of elderly people are examples. They invite further enquiry, particularly within the organisations concerned, about what scope there is for improved service delivery.

There is utility too in research, more broadly focused than that included in this book, which enquires, for example, into the social and political worlds which social work inhabits and the problems its confronts. One possible consequence of such enquiry is some assessment of those problems which lie within and beyond the scope of social work. Such research draws heavily on the social sciences and helps social work to fulfil its potential and to know its place (Cheetham, forthcoming).

Are social workers flattered, frightened, intrigued, challenged or indifferent to this potential level of interest in their activities? No doubt there are some who fit each of these descriptions; and the same would be true of every professional group. Some social workers, and particularly their managers, are aware that major changes in policy and legislation affecting social work have had some foundation in research. Much of this has been funded by large, long-term Department of Health research programmes focusing on community care (Robbins 1993) and child protection. The 1992 Children Act provides a good example of the interaction between research, professional expectations and policy (Hallett 1991), as does the shift of emphasis on procedural approaches to child protection to welfare and family support from major concern about children *in need of protection* to children *in need* (Gibbons, Conroy and Bell 1995).

Major changes in the delivery of community care through care management were also in part prompted by research carried out by the Personal Social Services Research Unit at Kent University, although much actual implementation has not been consistent with the conclusions of these studies (Lewis *et al.* 1997; Petch *et al.* 1996). Increasingly social workers are becoming aware that research may provide an important foundation for policy change, and that this may be necessary, but certainly not sufficient, to counter political preference and fashion and ideological commitments which are now such an important well-spring of welfare and social policy. The shape of penal policy in the last two decades provides the most startling evidence of this last phenomenon, with the relentless increase in custodial penalties which have been shown repeatedly to be no more effective than community based programmes and much more expensive (Mair 1997). Experience shows, therefore, that social workers need to be both research literate and politically wary.

A final example of interest in evaluation is increasing reference to research- or evidence-based practice. In part this is a product of the move towards empirical practice, which Thyer and Shaw discuss in their chapters, but it also reflects the growing expectation of the UK Department of Health that health services, both hospital and community, should be evidence-based. This department's Review and Dissemination Unit at York University exists to promote evidence-based medicine, and a unit at Exeter University, in collaboration with neighbouring local authorities, has also been established to promote similar awareness and practice within social work.

This interest is, however, far from universal. Shaw illustrates the ambivalence and even hostility of some social workers towards evaluation, particularly when such enquires are perceived, as they easily can be, as an unhelpful and intrusive management tool more likely to punish than reward. Further evidence of social workers' disinterest in and alienation from research can be found in the Department of Health's enquiry into practitioners' involvement in social work (Department of Health 1994).

How can positive interest in evaluative research be encouraged and strengthened and fears about its risks reduced? Practical possibilities include reviewing the place of users in research, counting users as both the receivers and providers of services; widening understanding of what should count as evidence; drawing more social workers into the process of research, either as practitioner researchers or as contributors to research studies; and making evaluation, in its many forms, a mainstream component of practice and its management.

The Contribution of Users

The fact of different audiences for – or, to use contemporary jargon, users of – social work research (and that relating to many other public and human services) is generally accepted. Less explored are the questions of whether any audience should have primacy; of the possibility, within any one study, of dealing adequately with the interests of several; and – perhaps the issue of greatest contemporary interest – the extent to which audiences can move from being more or less passive spectators to being actors.

Service users as research subjects

In social work research service users may well be seen as the ultimate beneficiaries of research in that its conclusions are intended to promote good practice. However, despite this often only implicit aspiration, in many studies these users seem somewhat remote, appearing only as research subjects. In qualitative studies service users may speak with a distinct voice but they often appear more anonymously, simply as respondents to research instruments which can seek data on matters ranging from people's social supports, contacts and activities to their capabilities, mood, attitudes and quality of life. One problem for contemporary social work research is that any single instrument from the huge and growing array of those available can seem to trivialise the complex realities of the individuals being studied. A consequence is that social workers can often be reluctant contributors to research which requires them to administer such instruments (and it is a pity that this word has such sharp, surgical connotations), perhaps because they do not see how this material can be incorporated into their routine contacts with service users (Cheetham 1997 and forthcoming; Nocon and Qureshi 1996). Service users can thus become almost invisible and so attempts to assess the actual impact of help offered end up being filtered through the perceptions of providers or others in contact with users. Such proxy assessments have their place but they should not be the sole or the most usual evidence of what social work has or has not achieved.

Small studies, especially those involving practitioners, may avoid these problems, perhaps because research represents only one part of the practitioner's activities. He or she can set the evidence derived from research into a wider understanding which is informed by data but also enriches it. In at least six or seven chapters in this book clients have centre stage, either informing social workers about what matters in good practice (for example in the studies of Dowling and Farnfield) or as the source of information about whether their circumstances have been changed following the help they have received (see the chapters by Badger, Kazi, Thyer and Williams). Despite the criticisms in Shaw's chapter that the use of single-case design can reinforce the passivity of service users there is some practice and research experience which shows that they like the chance to review their progress and appreciate the fact that this is being taken seriously by social workers. In short, using well-chosen research instruments in the context of wider practice can underline service users' status. It may also give them some authority on which to comment on the sense or otherwise of the help they are receiving.

Another important priority for social work research, which could also receive some pioneering boost in practitioner research, is the blending of a variety of ways of collecting data, including that which comes from standardised research instruments. The practice aim is to incorporate review into mainstream social work activity; the research aim is to ease the collection of a range of data to allow as holistic a picture as possible of people's needs, the help they receive and the progress achieved. The studies by Badger and Stanley *et al.* provide examples.

If the protection of service users' needs and rights is really the ultimate rationale for research then many of the studies described here which have been so close to practice, can, to use Shaw's words 'keep social work honest' by illuminating the relationship between needs, services and their outcomes and, in one or two instances, as in Dowling's study, casting an uncomfortable searchlight on what social workers *really* do in contrast to their claims and hopes. These practice-focused studies can also keep the researchers' eyes on the ball, reminding them of the primacy of service users' interests. These are positive achievements, but if research is to deal with the real concerns of those who receive social work they need to have larger roles in influencing research agenda. This matter is now more talked about than acted upon but it is worth remembering that, about a decade or so ago, involving users in setting research agendas and shaping the research process would have been considered, if it was considered it all, a bizarre idea, at best patronising and at worst a waste of time. Opinion and practice is changing and there is now a steady flow of accounts of research involving children and disabled and elderly people, including those with learning disabilities, in which they have played a variety of influential roles (Oliver 1992; Silburn, Dorkin and Jones 1994; Tozer and Thornton 1995; Whittaker 1994). Contributions have included shaping research agendas through giving priority to service users' perspectives on key issues for evaluation, and users' membership of advisory groups and users acting as co-researchers. Indeed some researchers who are committed to advancing social action through research regard the views and interests of community members or service users as the essential starting point for any research. Furthermore, as partners in the research process they can be expected to play important roles in collecting and interpreting data and then disseminating conclusions. It is argued that this approach maximises the focus on the interests of ordinary citizens and enhances their ownership and use of the research and its conclusions (Dyson and Harrison 1996).

The chapters in this book do not address these issues in great depth but there are some which give some insight into the contribution of service users to research. For example, the children in Farnfield's studies give some perhaps unexpected indications of what matters to them in service delivery and therefore what should be on evaluative agenda. And in modest ways service users who select the points of focus for single-case designs and who keep the records themselves are also contributors to research. Furthermore, in reaching agreement about the focus of work they may also influence the assessment of their problems and so indirectly help develop understanding about feasible social work priorities. Certainly Williams and her colleagues thought that using this method of evaluating ongoing practice enhanced the partnership between the workers and service users which is so often extolled and so hard to achieve.

The involvement of service users in research now needs much more practical attention if we are to advance beyond rhetoric and good intention. Here practitioner researchers, because of their proximity to service users, could be pioneers. In addition to accounts of partnerships between users and researchers we need some sober assessment, from all the parties, of their practical consequences. These could include attention to hitherto neglected topics, easier access to and a greater contribution from research subjects, more sophisticated conclusions, greater public understanding of research and enhanced legitimacy for such enquiry and what it seeks to illuminate (Cocks and Cockran 1995; Stalker forthcoming). Service users may also be a very important research audience because those who are properly informed about the impact of social work interventions can, through their questions and expectations, exert a significant influence on practitioners.

The roles of other research users

It is not always possible or appropriate for service users to be the main focus of social work research studies, even though they may have influenced their design. The roles of other research users – those who provide or fund social work services – include being the subject of research, shaping its focus and receiving and acting upon its conclusions. Since the process of social work is a key area of interest then the way services are delivered and the roles social workers and others play are important subjects of enquiry and a possible vehicle of change if the content and conditions of good practice can be better understood. White writes powerfully about this and her chapter underlines the importance of understanding and exploring 'ways of conducting business as usual' in social work.

Such studies are often resisted as an intrusion or because it is feared, not without reason, that they will bring bad news about service deficiencies. There are some examples in this book of social workers apparently behaving in ways in which they and their managers would deplore. Indeed, it seems a common-place research conclusion that, whether through social workers' own accounts or through their records or through the eyes of service users and, perhaps most of all, when they are observed, social work practice is often found wanting. Not surprisingly, as Dowling's study shows, this is not welcome news, particularly when a profession as a whole – or a department or a group within it – feels demoralised or under attack, a common experience in social work. However, such research is some of the most important that can be done if it is a means of improving service delivery and not simply an occasion for denial or defensiveness and a prompt for recrimination and penalties. The following are necessary but not sufficient conditions for research to be a stepping stone to service improvement: there must be some ownership of research by its subjects; managers must see identified deficiencies as opportunities for improvement; there must be some consensus about remedies.

Ownership includes not just consent to participate in the research but some part in its planning. Ownership is also enhanced by opportunities to learn about the research conclusions as they emerge, contribute to their interpretation and to consider the reasons for service deficiencies, all of which are attempted by Stanley and her colleagues and by Dowling and Badger. These are stepping stones to agreement about remedies which are not just the often unwelcome recommendations of researchers but shared agreements about feasible changes on the one hand and irremovable obstacles on the other.

All this is far more easily said than achieved, as Dowling's chapter shows, but potentially research undertaken by practitioners, or in close collaboration with them, is more likely to embrace these three conditions. Topics are often those known to be close to colleagues' preoccupations and the intimacy of working relationships require not just consent but feedback and agreement about implications. Research of this kind can therefore be an important vehicle for change and – cumulatively – can provide knowledge about effective practice which is embedded in agencies and not just regarded as remote often misunderstood external judgement.

What is being described here is a subtle and not yet well-understood relationship between researchers, service providers and users in which each party influences the other in trying to determine a research agenda which will be regarded as useful, its utility perhaps having various interpretations. Research ideas can come from several sources. Schon (1983, 1995) has emphasised the role of practitioners in this process who 'in knowing more than they can say or is said about them' can spur and enrich research agendas and be the crucial conduit in turning research conclusions into mainstream thinking and action (1995, p.39). Other examples of this interaction on a larger scale can be found in some of the policy-orientated research programmes funded by the UK Department of Health which are focused on community care, child protection and child care. As the recent assessment of research in British universities shows this funding has supported very high quality research (Cheetham and Deakin 1997). In these programmes, which may extend over many years, policy makers, research funders, practitioners and researchers respond to each other's ideas and, through research and the related policy and practice developments, knowledge and understanding accumulates which in turn prompts further research and changing practice. A good example is the Department of Health's 'Looking After Children' programme which is intended to provide social workers with the means of assessing the needs and progress of children, for whom they are responsible from infancy to adolescence (Ward 1995, 1996). In such a context social workers and researchers are absolutely interdependent in developing their ideas, achieving their goals and being clear about each other's strengths, skills and shortcomings.

These triangular relationships between research, policy and practice, which are reflected in several chapters in this book, are far removed from the simple formula in which funders commission exactly the research they want and researchers carry it out. This arrangement, which experience shows is more imagined than real, puts researchers in a passive role and can raise critical questions about the independence and creativity of evaluative research. An alternative and equally undesirable model, and one which is usually unrealistic in practice, is that in which the researchers are the sole source of topics for study and seek to impose their agenda on the subjects of their enquiry.

In the evaluation of social work the tasks of the researcher are to help turn ideas and worries about policy and practice, from whatever source, into researchable questions. This is a skilled and highly practical endeavour. Researchers must also ensure that no one perspective is heard to the exclusion of others. Stanley and her colleagues deliberately planned their study with this in mind. My colleague Roger Fuller has written about researchers' obligations 'to tell the truth' (Cheetham *et al.* 1992), a tall order and one which often entails dealing with different 'truths' and sticking with conclusions which are unpopular or unfashionable. Dowling's chapter illustrates this often uncomfortable juggling act. It is this independent judgement which is a major justification for research; and although these judgements can (and sometimes should) cause discomfort they are also highly valued. This was the firm view of the users of research who were consulted by the Social Policy Social Work panel in the 1996 review of research in British universities. As Albaek (1995, p.97) crisply observes, such research 'may not please the court and the king but it benefits public debate. And it safeguards the self-respect of research'.

This notion of partnership between researchers and the various users of their labours is still breaking new ground and its possibilities and limitations need further testing and sober assessment. As a start the following questions are therefore worth asking in the early stages of thinking about a research study.

- For whom is this research being conducted?
- Who are the research users likely to be affected by this study?
- Is there agreement about a priority audience or beneficiary?
- How might users – in their various guises – contribute to shaping its focus and methods?
- Why should they be included – or excluded – from different stages of the research process?
- What are the particular tasks of the researcher in designing, conducting and reporting on the study?

Evidence and Social Work Practice

Evidence-based practice, or at least talking about it, is becoming a fashionable slogan and – like all fashions – it attracts enthusiasts and detractors. The merits of such an approach – the pursuit of effective practice, legitimacy, accountability and openness – hardly need rehearsing and so, since they seem so laudable, why does the notion of evidence-based practice also attract such scepticism? The chapters by Shaw and White helpfully illuminate this resistance by reminding us that much, indeed perhaps most, social work practice does not consist of components in which carefully specified problems are tackled with discrete forms of help producing clearly identifiable outcomes. And Williams and her colleagues remind us that even when an individual's or family's difficulties are tackled in such a way surrounding and confronting problems may be left untouched. There are also fears that crude measures of evidence will be used inappropriately by managers as indicators of social workers' performance.

These are legitimate concerns but, rather than polarising debate about evidence-based practice, they should encourage thoughtful exploration of what counts as evidence and therefore its various manifestations in social work. The essential point is: what evidence is needed to answer or to illuminate what questions? The *Oxford English Dictionary* helpfully reminds us of the several meanings of 'evidence':

> an approach from which inferences may be drawn…an indication, mark, sign, token, trace…grounds for belief, testimony or facts tending to prove or disprove any conclusion.

These possibilities are taken further by the *Chambers Dictionary* where 'evidence' can be:

> information that gives grounds for belief...that which points to, reveals or suggests something.

Plain English therefore allows, indeed requires, an interpretation of evidence which is consistent with a range of social work and research activities: drawing inferences from observations; exploring grounds for belief; gathering and analysing data to see what it suggests. This is – or should be – a painstaking and disciplined process in which several minds are brought to bear: those of service users, social workers, managers, other professionals and lay people. Their often different interpretations must be compared and tested against established knowledge, where this exists, and observations of circumstances and behaviour where appropriate. White describes all this very well in her discussion of assessment in which lively awareness of theoretical influences, competing explanations and the frequency of significant events can be seen as evidence-based practice. She, Badger and Shaw also refer to testing researchers' hypothesis or social workers' presumptions against data and other interpretations 'if necessary to destruction'. This is an essential mindset for research-led practice in which both emerging ideas and treasured beliefs are open to justification, no mean task when social workers often have to think and act almost simultaneously. Shaw rightly describes this process of asking 'how we may best know whether we have good grounds and evidence, what conclusions can probably be drawn, and what plausibly justified action should be taken' as a moral calculus.

This testing of hypotheses and critical scrutiny of theory and 'practice wisdom', pursued energetically and with discipline, are as much part of evidence-based practice as 'empirical practice' which seeks to capture particular outcomes, often using some standardised measurement tools. Evidence is therefore not confined to empirical data which emerge from experiments, which are rare in social work. In these wider interpretations evidence-based practice is a necessary, worthy and feasible cornerstone for social work. Indeed its components – careful observation, analysis and synthesis of data, the testing of judgements – are, or should be, part of a social worker's repertoire. They are also, of course, the essential tools of research, and in both activities reference has to be made to what has emerged from a range of enquiry, including critical reviews of policy and practice and empirical studies, especially those which include service users' views about the essentials of helpful social work which reveal a substantial consensus (Howe 1993; Rees and Wallace 1982; Sainsbury *et al.* 1982; Sinclair 1992).

This is a time-consuming and complex task, often beyond the resources of the individual practitioner and taxing too for the professional researcher. The role of agencies and training organisations in disseminating such knowledge needs far greater attention. So too does the time and space practitioners will need if they are to be aware of and integrate into their work – an altogether more complicated venture – the accumulating knowledge about the impact of social work. Social workers are not alone amongst professionals who practice often in the dark and sometimes contrary to clear evidence; health service reviews show this happens in medicine and is extremely difficult to tackle. However, compared with teachers, nurses and doctors social workers now have one of the shortest periods of professional training and the most limited opportunities (or obligations) for further education and training. To talk about promoting evidence-based practice in this context could be described as a fantasy. I talk about it none the less in the hope that encouraging interest in the nature of evidence, its origins in and its contribution to practice will, little by little, help transform this fantasy into reality.

Practitioners and Research

> Those of us who do or have done social work practice 'know' – perhaps in vague or unformed terms – that practice combines enquiry and authority in its attempt to make sense of the moral, value laden, spiritual and other elusive often untidy dimensions of living. (Goldstein 1994, p.49)

An essential first step in this journey is promoting the involvement of practitioners in research. Lest this should seem a grandiose aspiration it is important to be clear about the various meanings of research and to call in aid, once again, the *Oxford English Dictionary*. Here 'research' is:

> the act of searching...a search or investigation directed to the discovery of some facts by careful consideration or study of subject...a course of critical and scientific enquiry.

These definitions imply several activities: observation, inquisitive questions, persistent enquiries, reflection, recording and analysis. These are not simply the tasks of social scientists; they are at the heart of social work practice. I do not wish to imply that every act of social work is a research act, far from it; but the characteristics and qualities of research enterprise included in the *Oxford English Dictionary* definition are familiar to social workers and, indeed, to many other practitioners. They are rooted in their mindset in asking questions, in careful observation of complicated behaviour and communication – from service providers and users alike – and in making sense of partial or conflicting information. These are the foundations of research-minded practice, just as they are the cornerstone of fully paid up researchers' skills. This is a good beginning for the relationship between research and practice. All this echoes the earlier discussion about the nature and place of evidence in social work.

There are conflicting views about practitioners' interest in research. A recent Department of Health report (1994) argued that while policy makers had established relationships with the research process practitioners had little interest in this, partly because they felt excluded from it. A rather similar analysis of American social workers was made by Austin (1992) who found that many felt quite alienated from the institutions, particularly universities which were largely responsible for social work research. More cheerful conclusions can be drawn from the growing involvement of practitioners in many countries in conducting their own research and their preparedness, despite many pressures on their time and energy, for various kinds of involvement with research (Connor 1993; Everitt and Hardiker 1996; Fook 1996; Fuller and Petch 1995; Hess and Mullen 1995; Smith 1995). This more optimistic account is supported by the work reported in this book, and my own recent experience as a director of a social work research centre confirms that it is appropriate now to presume practitioners' interest in research, to expect some resistance and anxieties and to devise, with practitioners, collaborations between researchers and practitioners who take these into account.

An important first step is to distinguish between different kinds of involvement. A key role is as an attentive but critical audience; without this social work research can have little impact on practice. However, as the earlier discussion indicates, this is a problematic role and one which cannot at present (perhaps ever) prosper in a *laissez-faire* context which presumes that social workers will pick and choose from an increasingly rich and diverse research menu. Qualifying and post-qualifying educational institutions, professional organisations and social work management have to devise clear expectations of and arrangements for information about and review of research.

Experience of the health services' approach to research use is relevant here, as will be the strategies of the Department of Health Social Work Dissemination Unit at Exeter University. The Joseph Rowntree Foundation is also leading an initiative to promote knowledge-based change in the social services which will involve collaboration between local authorities, voluntary agencies, educational institutions and user organisations in promoting research-based policy and practice in key areas.

Experience shows that a guiding principle in such initiatives must be the distinction between getting research 'out' in clear and accessible formats and getting it 'in' as an appropriate influence on policy and practice (Phillipson and Williams 1995). This is because in social work most evaluative research does not and should not – given its focus and methods – present unequivocal prescriptions for actions. More often it provides a basis for critical review and reflection, perhaps including comparison of different ways of providing similar services, an analysis of factors which influence quality and a pointer to unintended or unexpected outcomes. The 'integration' of such material into the practice of individuals and groups is a subtle and often lengthy process, subject to both organisational influences and professional judgements. In Britain the National Institute of Social Work, with sponsorship from the Department of Health and the Joseph Rowntree Foundation, have pioneered programmes in which research findings, for example in relation to hospital discharge or key workers, are presented to policy makers and practitioners who then devise action plans which are appropriate to their agencies to take account of these findings (Neill and Williams 1992). The implementation and progress of these plans are then reviewed by researchers and agency staff. Such programmes have yet to be evaluated but their key component – that research findings are interwoven with actual policies and practice in specific programmes – deserve attention for their potential to increase researchers' and social workers' understandings of their respective work and roles in promoting research-based practice.

Practitioners as Research Actors

In such initiatives practitioners become a highly interactive audience but they can also be important research actors. This can be as collectors of data for other people's studies, a not unproblematic role given some of the limitations of research instruments but one which experience shows can, with skill, be usefully incorporated into practice. Practitioners can also contribute directly as respondents to research enquiries, perhaps most usefully in qualitative studies. Although requests for interview time may often be resisted because of practitioners' many obligations, again experience shows that they often enjoy such opportunities to reflect on their work while making a crucial contribution to a subtle understanding of the process of social work.

Practitioners move to the centre of the research stage as evaluators of their own work, either as part of regular review of their cases, perhaps using single-case design, or as architects of their own small agency-based studies. These are often at their most successful when carried out in conjunction with sympathetic university departments which offer some basic training in evaluative methods (Fuller and Petch 1995). Such enterprises probably represent the largest contribution practitioners can make to research-led social work. In these roles they are 'no longer passive consumers of an outsiders' expert investigation but take on responsibility for testing and documenting their own activities – what they know best and what they deem as significant' (Goldstein 1994, p.50).

In the light of these several research roles I conclude with the optimistic expectation that evaluative research in its various forms can be a mainstream social work preoccupation and that increasingly it will become so. The following chapters show that this journey is well underway; like all worthwhile explorations its risks and frustrations add it its achievements and excitement and reassure us that the destinations and arrivals are worthwhile.

References

Albaek, E. (1995) 'Betweeı. ınowledge and power. Utilization of social science in public policy making.' *Policy Sciences 28*, 79–100.

Austin, D. (1992) 'Findings of the NIMH task force on social work research.' *Research on Social Work Practice.* (Special Issue: *Research and Practice: Bridging the Gap) 2*, 3, July, 311–322.

Cheetham, J. (1997) 'Evaluating social work: progress and prospects.' *Research on Social Work Practice 7*, 3, 291–310.

Cheetham, J. (forthcoming) 'Disciplinary research agendas and institutional arrangements for evaluation research.' *Scandinavian Journal of Social Welfare.*

Cheetham, J. and Deakin, N. (1997) 'Assessing the assessment: some reflections on the 1996 research assessment exercise.' *Social Policy Association Newsletter*, February/ March, 1–4.

Cheetham, J., Fuller, R., McIvor, G. and Petch, A. (1992) *Evaluating Social Work Effectiveness.* Buckingham: Open University Press.

Cocks, E. and Cochran, J. (1995) 'The participatory research paradigm and intellectual disability.' *Mental Handicap Research 8*, 1, 25–37.

Connor, A. (1993) *Monitoring and Evaluation Made Easy*. London: HMSO.

Department of Health (1994) *A Wider Strategy for Research and Development Relating to the Personal Social Services*. London: HMSO.

Dyson, S. and Harrison, M. (1996) 'Black community members as researchers: working with community groups in the research process.' *Groupwork 4*, 2, 203–3220.

Everitt, A. (1996) 'Critical evaluation.' *Evaluation 2*, 2, 173–188.

Everitt, A. and Hardiker, P. (1996) *Evaluating for Good Practice*. Basingstoke: Macmillan.

Everitt, A., Hardiker, P., Littlewood, J. and Mullender, A. (1992) *Applied Research for Better Practice*. London: Macmillan.

Fook, J. (ed) (1996) *The Reflective Researcher*. NSW: Allen and Unwin.

Fuller, R. and Petch, A. (1995) *Practitioner Research: The Reflective Social Worker*. Buckingham: Open University Press.

Gibbons, J., Conroy, S. and Bell, C. (1995) *Operating the Child Protection System*. London: HMSO.

Goldstein, H. (1994) 'Narrative accounts in social work research.' In E. Sherman and J. Reid (eds) *Qualitative Research in Social Work*. New York: Columbia University Press.

Hallet, C. (1991) 'The Children Act 1989 and community care: comparisons and contrasts.' *Policy and Policies 19*, 4, 282–291.

Hess, P. and Mullen, E. (eds) (1995) *Practitioner–Researcher Partnerships: Building Knowledge From, In, and For Practice*. Washington DC: NASW Press.

HMSO (1993) *Realising Our Potential: A Strategy for Science and Technology*. London: HMSO.

Howe, D. (1993) *On Being a Client*. London: Sage.

Lewis, J. with Bernstock, P., Bovell, V. and Wookey, F. (1997) 'Implementing care management: issues in relation to the new community care.' *British Journal of Social Work 27*, 1, 5–24.

Mair, G. (ed) (1997) *Evaluating the Effectiveness of Community Penalties*. Aldershot: Avebury.

Neill, J. and Williams, J. (1992) *Leaving Hospital: Elderly People and their Discharge to Community Care*. London: HMSO.

Nocon, A. and Qureshi, H. (1996) *Outcomes of Community Care for Users and Carers*. Buckingham: Open University Press.

Oliver, M. (1992) 'Changing the social relations of research production?' *Disability, Handicap and Society* (Special Issue: *Researching Disability*) 7, 2, 101–14.

Petch, A., Cheetham, J., Fuller, R., MacDonald, C. and Myers, F. with Hallam, A. and Knapp, M. (1996) *Delivering Community Care*. Edinburgh: The Stationery Office.

Phillipson, J. and Williams, J. (1995) *Action on Hospital Discharge*. London: National Institute for Social Work.

Rees, S. and Wallace, A. (1982) *Verdicts on Social Work*. London: Edward Arnold.

Robbins, E. (ed) (1993) *Community Care: Findings from Department of Health Funded Research 1988–92*. London: HMSO.

Sainsbury, E., Nixon, S. and Phillips, D. (1982) *Social Work in Focus: Clients' and Social Workers' Perceptions on Long Term Social Work*. London: Routledge and Kegan Paul.

Schon, D. (1983) *The Reflective Practitioner: How Professionals Think in Action.* London: Temple Smith.

Schon, D. (1995) 'Reflective inquiry in social work practice.' In P. Hess and E. Mullen (eds) *Practitioner – Researcher Partnerships: Building Knowledge From, In, and For Practice.* Washington DC: NASW Press.

Shaw, I. (forthcoming) *Doing Evaluating in Social Work Practice.* Wrexham: Prospects Publishing.

Silburn, L., Dorkin, D. and Jones, C. (1994) 'Innovative practice.' In S. French (ed) *On Equal Terms: Working with Disabled People.* Oxford: Butterworth Heinemann.

Sinclair, I. (1992) 'Social work research: its relevance to social work and social work education.' *Issues in Social Work Education 11,* 2, 65–80.

Smith, J. (1995) *Social Workers as Users and Beneficiaries of Research.* University of Stirling Social Work Research Centre.

Stalker, K. (forthcoming) 'Some ethical and methodological issues in a study of choice making by people with learning disabilities.' *Disability and Society.*

Tozer, R. and Thornton, P. (1995) *A Meeting of Minds: Older People as Research Advisers.* York: University of York, Social Policy Research Unit.

Ward, H. (1995) *Looking After Children: Research into Practice.* London: HMSO.

Ward, H. (1996) 'Constructing and implementing measures designed to assess outcomes in child care.' In M. Hall and J. Aldgate (eds) *Child Welfare Services.* London: Jessica Kingsley Publishers.

Whittaker, A. (1994) 'Service evaluation by people with learning difficulties.' In A. Connor and S. Black (eds) *Performance Review and Quality in Social Care.* London: Jessica Kingsley Publishers.

PART ONE

Studying the Content, Process and Outcomes of Social Work

Researching the Effectiveness of a Small-Scale Community-Based Project for Sex Offenders

Douglas Badger

This chapter provides an account of the process of researching the effectiveness of a newly established small-scale sex offenders programme. The research methodology was based on the notion of a sex offending career and the method involved experts making year ahead predictions for each offender. These predictions were based on what was most likely to happen to each offender in the absence of a sex offender programme. After one year the predictions were compared with the actual outcomes and hence a measure of effectiveness obtained. The chapter includes a discussion of the theoretical underpinning for the methodology because it is believed to be the first time this methodology has been applied to research into sex offending. The actual process of the research is also fully described for similar reasons.

In early 1994 I was invited to help with monitoring and evaluating a community-based project for sex offenders in its first year of operation. The project, a small-scale experimental programme run by a local probation service, was funded for the first year by a Home Office grant of £10,000. It was a condition of the grant that the programme be monitored and an independent report of its effectiveness supplied. The number accepted on to the project was estimated to be in the order of ten men per year with referrals likely to be spread over the year. The proposed methods of intervention included psychiatric counselling, psycho-sexual counselling and groupwork, and for some offenders a requirement to abide at a local housing association.

A Methodological Challenge

Through discussion with project staff it became clear that the need was to evaluate the total impact of the programme and to establish if it was more effective than traditional probation supervision. The amount of money available for research was modest – £1000. Given the range of sex offenders being targeted, the small numbers involved, the variety of treatment approaches on offer and the need for some sort of global measure of effectiveness, there seemed little point in using traditional clinical research methods.

These methodological problems have been rehearsed by Fuller (1992) in his report on the MARS project, a unit for young people and their families in the city of Dundee. That project sought to provide a service to young people and their families whose difficulties had been tackled unsuccessfully by conventional agencies and approaches. The resolution of this research challenge that Fuller devised was one based on the idea of the 'career' that each young person was likely to follow unless some other intervention was attempted or offered.

Using the idea of a career, a group of experts looked at a profile of each young person as they were at the time of referral and predicted what they thought was the most probable outcome for that person a year hence. This was then compared with the actual outcome and hence a measure of effectiveness was obtained. With the MARS project this methodology was applied retrospectively: predictors were asked at the end of the year to look at the information that had been available at the beginning of the year. An adaptation of this methodology, but with predictions made prospectively at the time of referral, was adopted for this study.

The Career Concept

A plea for the career concept to be opened up as a research approach to mentally disordered offenders who move between the criminal justice and psychiatric systems has recently been made by Watson (1993). However, Watson does not closely define the concept in his discussion. The everyday notion of career is that related to employment, but for the social scientist it is more likely that Becker's notion of the criminal career will come to mind (Becker 1963). This analysis has been successfully applied in the field of social work, most strikingly in relation to interventions with young offenders. For example, the work of Thorpe (1976) and Tutt (1978) alerted social workers and probation officers to the danger that their efforts to do preventive work could escalate the young person up the sentencing tariff. This definition of career has also been influential in the establishment of divert to treatment schemes for mentally disordered offenders (Vaughan and Badger 1995).

This sociological understanding of career is less attractive or convincing as a basis for working with sex offenders, for two reasons. The first is that Becker's approach removes the spotlight from the offender and his behaviour and places it instead on the institutions such as courts and psychiatric hospitals that society expects will deal with the problem. This conflicts with a recurring issue in working with sex offenders which is to encourage them to accept responsibility for their past actions and for controlling their future behaviour.

A second reservation relates to practice wisdom that much sex offending is undetected and that it is this invisible or hidden career that is the focus of concern and treatment rather than the labelling process. It seems that another definition or understanding of career is required if it is to fit with the field of sex offending and with research based on the idea of a career as a predictable path.

Farrington (1992) provides a helpful review of criminal career research in the UK. The framework that he describes is one based on an epidemiological approach with a central focus on statistical analysis of large-scale longitudinal studies. This leads to discussion of key concepts such as incidence, prevalence and frequency of offending. However, the reality that there are few longitudinal studies of offenders in general and even fewer of sex offenders in particular means that this approach is currently rather limited. In the long term it is likely that such research will develop further and one can imagine a time when strategically important groups such as sentencers will be able to draw on such statistical data to make choices between community-based and custodial disposals. At present the only relevant conclusion drawn by Farrington was that sex offenders' careers were highly specialised compared to other offenders. It would also appear from his review that sex offenders' careers do not feature the early adolescent peak of many other criminal careers, nor do they tail off by the late twenties. Ultimately it should be possible to bring together large-scale studies such as these with small-scale studies such as that reported here.

Another source of definitions and concepts of career can be found in the field of vocational guidance. My own review of this literature revealed a range of approaches from those emphasising personal psychology, the life cycle and individual decision making (Super 1968), to those embracing a degree of social determinism which left the individual as merely the product of social structures (Watts *et al.* 1981). More recently Hodkinson and Sparkes (1997) have evolved an interesting synthesis of these polarities through the concept of careerism.

A polarisation between sociological and psychological models would seem to be unhelpful. It is interesting to note that Becker's original concept of career development in an article entitled 'Careers, personality and adult socialisation' (Becker and Strauss 1956) incorporated the concept of the life cycle. In fact the only reference that he cited in that article was to Erikson (1950), the founding father of the life cycle approach! There is instead a need for a psychosocial notion of career to be developed which takes more account of clinical understanding of sex offending in particular and other forms of deviant behaviour in general.

The concept employed in this research design involved 'experts' making judgements about the likely paths to be followed by a particular sex offender. In doing this the experts were drawing on typical patterns of sex offending that they had identified from their professional knowledge and through their experience of working with offenders. That meant that they were attempting to apply objective patterns to the experience of an individual.

This definition of career can be translated into two propositions:

1. In any field of human activity people with knowledge and experience will be able to identify a number of career pathways that recur and are typical. These pathways represent an interaction between the life cycle of the individual and the opportunities and choices available to the individual. These pathways are likely to reflect the opportunity structure of that society in terms of wealth, gender, age, race and ethnicity, sexual orientation and disability.

2. These pathways are unlikely to fit perfectly with any one person's experience. However it is possible to locate the majority of individual experiences within the broad band of each ideal pathway.

The Process of the Research

The research was carried out between March 1994 and November 1995 and it took place as the sex offender project was itself developing and changing. The project was based in a probation day centre and operated initially one day a week. The staffing was built around the female probation officer for the day centre and the male psychiatrist, with a number of female probation officers being involved as co-workers in both groups and counselling sessions. The male senior probation officer took a leading management role but was less involved in the everyday running of the programme. A female psychosexual counsellor was also employed initially but when she left after some months she was not replaced. All the staff and all the offenders in the first year were white. By the end of the research period the project had grown to two days a week and there was also a relapse prevention group for 'graduates'. The treatment approach, which was eclectic, was based on weekly groupwork and individual sessions usually with the psychiatrist and a probation officer.

In the first month I met with staff of the sex offenders project to discuss the research methodology. It was agreed that predictors would receive all the information available to the project; confidentiality would therefore be extended to predictors. This information would include committal forms, victim statements, pre-sentence reports, summary of evidence, Crown Prosecution statements, judge's directions, previous convictions sheet, psychiatric reports and depositions (all subject to availability). I arranged to visit quarterly to discuss developments at the project and to identify if the research approach needed modification. It was also clarified that I would be the research director but would not be a predictor.

A month later the three predictors were invited to take part in the research by myself. I was responsible for their selection; however, the senior probation officer for the project approved the names before any approaches were made. The group consisted of a clinical psychologist, a senior probation officer and a psychotherapist/social worker. Two were male and one was female; all were white. All three had considerable experience in the management and treatment of sex offenders. They were paid for their time in attending meetings and making predictions. None had a prior involvement with the project.

When the study had run for about eighteen months the eleven men had all either completed a year on the project or left during that time. It was therefore possible to test the predictions made about them. There was a seminar for project staff, supervising probation officers and predictors to discuss the progress of offenders. This was the point at which actual outcomes were compared with predicted outcomes. It was also the first time that the predictors had met since the start of the research. Probation officers were asked to report on any life events which might have affected the offenders' behaviour during the year; for example, one offender had been investigated for a suspected recurrence of cancer of the bladder. The significance of this was that he linked the start of his offending career to the onset of the cancer.

The seminar acted as a useful deadline for all involved in the research. The predictors had to complete and return all their paperwork, as did the project staff. I had to collate the material and find a clear way of sharing it with others. It was also a complex event to manage as sufficient time had to be allowed for each offender to be properly discussed.

Later that month there was a presentation of findings to an invited audience from the probation service, a judge, local magistrates and other interested parties. This was a well-attended event and included presentations by project staff on their work. An interesting component to the programme was a couple of tape recorded interviews with offenders who were asked what prediction they would have made for themselves had they not come on the project, which, though not part of this research, this did provide a nice example of another approach to the career concept. This is discussed briefly at the end of the chapter.

The Prediction Process

At the beginning of the research the three predictors met with me to discuss the methodology and agree a way of working. A proforma for predictions was agreed after amendment to include a longer term prediction as well as that for one year (see below). The procedure was that information was sent out to the predictors when the men had been accepted on to the programme. They independently completed a year prediction for each sex offender and sent it to me. These predictions were not shared with the project workers until the end of the research year, when a comparison of actual and predicted outcomes was made.

The Prediction Proforma

This started by posing the question 'what is most likely to have happened in this case during the next year?' It was suggested that predictors might find it helpful to approach this question by structuring their answer around the following questions:

1. What is the sex offender and/or family at risk of in this situation?

2. What kind(s) of intervention would be likely to prevent that?

3. What would be the likely consequences of it not being provided?

4. Are there any comments you would like to add about this case?

5. Long-term prediction (timescale of up to four years). What is the likelihood of this person committing further sexual offences within a year of supervision ceasing and thereafter?

The first four questions were based on those employed by Fuller (1992) but the fifth was included because the predictors were of the opinion that some offenders would cease offending for the duration of any form of supervision, whether that was provided by the project or through normal probation arrangements. For that group the telling measure of effectiveness would be after supervision ended. It was felt that this might be where the project would be found to be more effective. Obviously this finding would not be available in the one-year time span required but it was still felt to be worth pursuing.

Comparing Predicted and Actual Outcomes

At the seminar held at the end of the year I circulated a summary of the referral data that had been sent out to the predictors and the predictions made for each offender. These were read by the twenty professional staff present and I then summarised the areas of agreement between predictors. This was followed by the written progress report from the project staff and the probation officer's verbal report. There was then a discussion of whether the offender's career had shown no change, some change, or considerable change from the predicted pathway. The group came to an agreement in each case and this was recorded. There also had to be agreement that the treatment which predictors identified as necessary to bring about change was available through the project and had been taken up. This was a necessary check in considering whether any changes that had taken place could be attributed to the project and not to other factors such as life events. With a small sample (inevitable in such a study) and without a control group receiving alternative intervention (impossible in these circumstances) it is not possible to conclude with certainty that any changes recorded in this study were a product of the project's activities. The role of prediction methods in evaluation research is discussed later. However, if this project's activities were simply *intended* rather than real (a not uncommon feature of social work practice) then not even tentative claims about impact could be made.

Results

Profile of sex offenders

A summary of the profiles of the eleven men included in this study can be seen in Table 2.1. It will be seen that their ages range from 19 to 54 with an average of 37.8 years. Six were single at the time of their most recent offence and five were married. Two were on licence with the majority being on probation orders with a condition of psychiatric treatment. The group was made up of six men with offences against children and five men with offences against women. Seven of the men had previous criminal convictions, only two of which were reported to not be sexual offences. This compares with a 50 per cent rate of previous sexual offences and 70 per cent rate of other previous criminal offences in a project reported by Lewin *et al.* (1994). However that group of twenty-seven sex offenders attending a community service in Watford were seen as having an unusually high rate of prior criminal offending compared to other studies.

Outcomes

Of the eleven men three were considered to have made no changes which could be attributable to the project, two were thought to have made some change, and six to have made considerable change. These categories emerged from the end of year seminar when project staff, supervising probation officers and expert predictors met to review and discuss the predicted and actual outcomes for each offender.

The following case studies illustrate each of the three categories.

NO CHANGE – CASE NO. 5

Pen picture. This 32-year-old single man was on licence after a two-year sentence for six offences of indecent assault on two sisters aged ten and eight. He had a conviction for possession of an offensive weapon at the age of 21 but no further offences. He attended the project for 25 individual and about 30 group sessions over a seven-month period.

Table 2.1: Offender profile summary chart

No.	Age at time of this offence	Marital status at time of this offence	This offence	Sentence	First sexual offence – age and offence	Criminal record other than sexual offending	Abused as a child	Bullied as a child
1	53	Married (2nd time)	Taking indecent photographs of children	1 year probation order with condition of treatment	44 years old Self report – indecent photography	None	No	No
2	37	Single	Indecent assault; criminal damage	3 year probation order with conditions of treatment	18 years old stealing woman's coat	None	Yes, physically by father	Yes
3	44	Divorced, living with new partner	Gross indecency; taking indecent photos of girls under 16	9 month imprisonment; voluntarily started project	36 years old Taking indecent photos of girl under 16 years.	None	Yes, sexually by neighbour	No
4	36	Married	Improper use of telecom system	1 year probation	19 years old Indecent assault	None	Yes, physically by father	No
5	32	Single	Indecent assault (6 times) of girls of 10 and 8	2 years of prison – licence	This offence	21 years old Possession of offensive weapon	No	Yes
6	19	Single	Indecent assault on woman of 19	2 year probation	18 years old Indecent assault of women over 16 (3 TICS)	None	No	Yes

Table 2.1: Offender profile summary chart (continued)

No.	Age at time of this offence	Marital status at time of this offence	This offence	Sentence	First sexual offence – age and offence	Criminal record other than sexual offending	Abused as a child	Bullied as a child
7	26	Married	Rape; indecent assault; ABH (Wife)	30 months prison – licence	This offence	None	Yes sexually by father	No
8	54	Married (2nd time)	Indecent assault girl under 14, under 13, 2 TICS	3 year probation order with condition of treatment	36 years old Indecent assault on daughter	None	Yes, sexually by neighbour	No
9	22	Single	Breach of the peace; found in enclosed premises	1 year probation order	20 years old Nuisance telephone calls; indecent exposure	None	No	No
10	46	Single to 3 girls aged 13 years	Gross indecency	2 year probation order; voluntary attendance	This offence	13–44 years old Dishonesty and violence	No evidence	No
11	47	Single	Indecent assault of three children, two 7-year-old girls and one 6-year-old boy	2 year probation order with conditions	20 years old Confessed (not charged) to indecent assault on children (parents of whom he recently was convicted of assaulting)	None	Yes	No
	Average age 37.8 years	**6 single 5 married**	**6 offending against children 5 offending against women**	**2 on licence 1 voluntary 8 probation order**				

Predicted outcome. All three predictors saw this mans as continuing to present a threat to vulnerable families with pre-pubescent girls. To change this career path it was agreed that he would need groupwork in relation to his sexual motivation and cognitive distortions and psychotherapy related to his childhood experiences. It was also agreed that he needed to work on his adult relationships and change his lifestyle so that he reduced his access to vulnerable families.

Actual outcome. Though these forms of help were available and he attended individual and group sessions regularly there was little or no change in the areas indicated. He did gain limited insight into his paedophilia and alcoholism but remained totally egocentric and manipulative. He left the project when his licence expired and made no subsequent contact. It was agreed that there remained a moderate to serious risk of him offending again within one to four years.

Conclusion. This man's career as a sex offender was well established when he came to the project and there was no evidence that this career path had been altered by the help available.

SOME CHANGE – CASE NO. 3

Pen picture. This 44-year-old divorced man was found guilty of gross indecency and taking indecent photographs of children under the age of sixteen. He received a nine-month prison sentence for this offence and attended the group voluntarily for three months after leaving prison. He was then charged with offences which dated back four years and resumed attendance, again on a voluntary basis. He had a conviction for taking indecent photographs some eight years prior to this conviction. He was still attending the project at the end of the research year and had attended twelve individual and nineteen group sessions in total.

Predicted outcome. There was very close agreement between predictors that this man presented a continuing risk to young girls and of the danger of escalation to violent penetrative assault. He was seen as likely to re-offend within the year and as a very difficult case.

Actual outcome: Although the offender was charged with further offences these had not been committed in the previous year. He was seen to have made progress in that he came to admit his offences and told his co-habitee about them. He also changed his attitude to women. However he remained a fixated paedophile in that his sexual fantasies were still centred on children.

Conclusion: This offender made some changes in that he gained insight into his paedophilia and made good use of the group sessions. Doubts remained about his motivation to change and the situation was clouded by the court case that was pending at the end of the research year. The risk of his re-offending was seen as moderate to high unless he could make further changes in relation to his fantasies about children. His known career was eight years long but it is highly likely that his sexual interest in young girls extended further back than that. His time on the project allowed him to review his career but there was no change in his paedophile fantasies. However the help available did appear to have improved the chances of his exercising greater control of his sexual behaviour in the future.

CONSIDERABLE CHANGE – CASE NO. 2

Pen picture: This 37-year-old single man was on a three-year probation order with condition of treatment for indecently assaulting a woman and damaging her car. He had a 20-year history of committing this type of offence which involved incapacitating the cars of young women, then coming to their rescue with a view to engineering an opportunity for kissing or touching. He was still on the project at the end of the research year and had attended 35 individual sessions and 40 group sessions.

Predicted outcome: The predictors agreed that he was highly likely to continue with his existing pattern of offending and that escalation to rape was a possibility. The crucial change needed to alter this pattern was for the offender to gain understanding of his sexual needs and to improve his social skills.

Actual outcome: In fact the individual committed another criminal damage offence soon after starting on the project, one of only two men known to have re-offended during the year. Ironically this experience occasioned the breakthrough in his use of the project. Thereafter he made good progress, gaining significant insight into his personality and understanding of the dynamics of his offending. He showed a marked increase in his self-confidence, motivation and desire for stability. He obtained full-time work and established a relationship with an adult female.

He also re-established contact with his family of origin and discussed his offending with them. He was considering independent living after more than twenty years in a variety of hostels. Most significantly he had not offended in the subsequent eight months, whereas his previous pattern had been to offend about every eight weeks. Though this was based on self-report it was corroborated by the local police who knew this offender and his pattern of offending very well.

Conclusion: This offender made considerable changes in his time on the project. Although he offended once in the year his pattern of offending changed radically, he developed insight into his sexual needs and offending, and made changes in his way of life. The risk of his re-offending moved from high to low though the need for long-term monitoring remained. In summary, he started at the project with a well-established career as a sex offender, a career in which his offences were frequent and becoming more serious. The outcome was a change in that pattern and significant changes in his way of life which made it less likely that he would re-offend.

The full results are summarised in Table 2.2. This repeats some details from Table 2.1 and additionally includes length of known career of sex offending (produced by subtracting age at first sexual offence from age at this offence), number of individual and group sessions attended and time on the programme.

Analysis and discussion of results

There are always dangers in an over-detailed analysis when numbers are small and it is not known how representative the sample is. Nevertheless there are some patterns in the data which are worth highlighting.

LENGTH OF TIME ON PROGRAMME

It is evident that those who stay longest are most likely to appear in the considerable change group. However, two of those in the no change group attended for six to twelve months so there is no clear and obvious correlation between time and effectiveness.

NUMBER OF GROUP SESSIONS

Caution needs to be exercised in relation to this variable as groupwork was not initially available on the programme. It is nevertheless clear that while everyone in the considerable change group had at least 20 groupwork sessions there are examples in both the no change and some change groups of individuals with similar numbers of sessions. It would appear that groupwork is a necessary but not sufficient basis for considerable change.

Table 2.2: Results

		Age at this offence	Length of career in years	Offences against women/children	Individual sessions	Group sessions	Time in months on project
No change	No. 5	32	0	Children	25	30	6–12
	No. 6	19	1	Women	11	0	1–6
	No. 10	46	0	Children	19	4	6–12
	Total	97	1		55	34	
	Average	32.3	0.3		18.33 sessions	11.33 sessions	
Some change	No. 3	44	8	Children	12	19	6
	No. 7	26	0	Women	11	6	6
	Total	70	8		23	25	
	Average	35	4		11.5 sessions	12.2 sessions	
Considerable change	No. 1	53	9	Children	30	44	6–12
	No. 2	37	19	Women	35	40	6–12
	No. 4	36	17	Women	26	37	6–12
	No. 8	54	18	Children	28	44	12+
	No. 9	22	2	Women	32	44	12+
	No. 11	47	27	Children	19	20	12+
	Total	249	92		170	229	
	Average	41.5	15.3		28.33 sessions	38.16 sessions	

NUMBER OF INDIVIDUAL SESSIONS

From the outset individual sessions were a mainstay of the project but frequency of appointments was effected by both the needs of the individual and the availability of staff. Numbers of sessions was closely linked to the length of time spent on the programme.

OFFENCES AGAINST WOMEN OR CHILDREN

There were no significant differences in response between the two groups with examples of both appearing in all three categories.

LENGTH OF KNOWN CAREER OF SEXUAL OFFENDING

A clear pattern is evident of those with the longest career being most likely to appear in the considerable change group. This is an unexpected finding as psychotherapy and counselling are often thought to be more effective with younger adults. The presence of one young offender in this group suggests that offenders may be most open to help at the beginning and later stages of their careers and least likely to change at the 'peak' of their careers. That older offenders are able to change is encouraging in that it suggests that therapeutic optimism is justified even with men who have well-established patterns of sex offending. However it is a concern that younger sex offenders may find it harder to change their ways.

AGE AT THIS OFFENCE

Again there is a pattern of middle-aged sex offenders being more amenable to change than those in their 20s and 30s. However, the considerable change group does include one man of 22 years old who seemed to use the programme to establish a more adult sexual identity.

OTHER POSSIBLE FACTORS

The information about marital status, abuse as a child and being bullied all produced inconclusive patterns in relation to change.

RECIDIVISM

The problem of using recidivism as a measure of effectiveness within a one-year timescale was rehearsed earlier in this chapter. In fact two men re-offended during the research period and the differences between them outline further difficulties of using recidivism as an outcome measure. Case no. 2, which was described earlier, provides a pleasing illustration of a man who re-offended but went on to make considerable change. In fact he appeared to have broken a compulsive pattern of offending and remained clear of offences for the remaining eight months of the research period.

Case no. 6, who appears in the no change group, was a young man who left the programme when he was charged with a number of sexual assaults. The likelihood that he was responsible for these was drawn to the attention of the police by the project staff who were becoming aware of the dangers that this offender presented. The ability and confidence to make such assessments and to act on them is likely to be enhanced by staff working in specialist projects; the project was unsuccessful in changing this man's offending but partially successful in protecting the public from him.

LICENSEES

Three of the eleven men were attending the project after a period in prison. Two of these were on licence and the third attended on a voluntary basis (nos. 5, 7 and 3 respectively). None of these appears in the considerable change group and their average attendance was 16 for individual sessions and 18.3 for group sessions. This compares with the average for others attending the Project of 25 for individual sessions and 24.1 for group sessions. However number of sessions of itself is probably not as significant as motivation. Case no. 5 illustrates well that it is possible for an offender to attend for many individual and group sessions but still show no change. Licensees are a group which requires further research. It is possible that a period of imprisonment makes the offender less open to individual and group therapy, something that clearly needs to be thought about when relatively low sentences are being considered by the courts. This is an important issue as the licence group is likely to increase in the future.

Conclusions

The research demonstrates that this project had considerable impact on six men – more than half of those who participated. There was some impact for a further two men with no change being recorded for three – less than a quarter – of the participants. This rate of success is encouraging to staff and good enough to attract the interest and support of the police, magistrates and judges.

The sample included all the men accepted at the beginning of a new project, a time when treatment approaches and methods of assessing referrals were still being evolved. This group and their treatment experience may therefore be atypical. A similar study at a later stage could well produce better results. Improved assessment would be likely to exclude inappropriate referrals and treatment approaches would probably improve with experience.

Of the variables considered a clear pattern was often not evident. Length of time on the programme and number of groupwork sessions both seemed to be important but were not of themselves conclusive. Older offenders and those with long careers were unexpectedly over-represented in the considerable change group. It is possible that the older men were at a stage of their careers as sex offenders when they were more willing to exercise control over their behaviour and to take responsibility for it.

Methodological Discussion

Why not a control group?

There were a number of reasons why a control group seemed neither necessary nor feasible. The first was logistics. Matching the members of this project with other sex offenders who were not being dealt with in this way would have been difficult and time consuming with the numbers and timescale involved.

There was also a technical problem that the project users did not all receive the same service. Services were made available on the basis of what was thought appropriate for a particular offender. Also it is inevitable that the services available will evolve in the light of experience, staff changes and the nature of referrals made to the project. One obvious example of this is that groupwork clearly could not be offered until sufficient numbers had been accepted. There would therefore have been a problem of consistency of treatment within the experimental group.

Having control groups who do not receive a service that they may have benefited from has always posed an ethical problem for the researcher and those practitioners who are co-operating with them. This problem is avoided with this methodology which improves the acceptability of the approach to staff whose support is essential.

A final point is that it is Fuller's view that the group acts as its own control group. He makes the case for viewing the treatment group as its own perfectly matched control group, using the phrase 'Its own control group in an alternative universe' (Fuller 1992, p.77). This alternative universe is one in which the sex offenders project did not exist and the only help available was the supervising probation officer. In effect this was what the expert predictors were assuming in making their predictions. Fuller's rather startling claim takes one to the heart of the methodological assumption that it is possible to identify an alternative scenario for each offender had he not attended the project.

Why not a standardised measure of change/success?

Sex offenders are a disparate group both in terms of their offences and of the stage at which they are in the criminal justice system; for example some will be first offenders whilst others will be on licence following a period in prison. Success or failure therefore needs to be measured in relation to the individual's circumstances. This methodology, a multi-case study approach, allows this.

Reliability

This was tested by examining the similarities and differences in predictions between the three predictors. At the beginning of the research it was agreed only predictions supported by two out of three predictors would be used. This judgement was initially made by myself but was shared and validated with project staff, supervising probation officers and two of the three predictors at the end of year seminar (one predictor was unable to attend). The predictions all met these requirements, although in two cases there were only two predictions available.

The amount of agreement between predictors from different professional backgrounds was quite striking. Although they often expressed their views in different language it was not difficult for all those attending the end of year seminar to identify a strong shared view of the likely career paths of each offender and what would be needed to change these. There were some differences in relation to the timescale of a few predictions, and also some variations in therapeutic optimism. The only major difference centred on the issue of whether an actual or potential rapist could be effectively treated in a group where paedophiles were in the majority.

As the views of the project staff and the predictors were all written down before the seminar it was possible to establish whether these two groups agreed on the criteria for making progress. In most cases there was full agreement and the no change and some change groups held no surprises for the predictors. This is encouraging and suggests a greater validity for practice wisdom than it sometimes receives.

Conclusion

The methodology described allows effectiveness research to be done on small-scale, experimental, low-budget projects that are normally seen as unresearchable. Despite its limitations it offers a sensitive approach that is acceptable to staff, is economic in terms of data collection and is ethically unproblematic. It is also in many ways an unobtrusive measure.

The results produced by this approach are inevitably crude and any conclusions must be tentative. However, the over-representation of older offenders in the considerable change group is interesting and can be usefully understood in terms of the career concept. The hypothesis that receptiveness to help or treatment varies in relation to the sex offender's career stage is worth exploring both clinically and in a larger-scale research study.

The research also offered the opportunity to review and refine the concept of career. The research process brought together career projections from project staff and research predictors and an encouraging degree of agreement was found. The possibility of enriching the understanding of career using the offenders' perspective was also briefly illustrated and that needs to be retained as a research avenue. Finally the reader is reminded of the challenging methodological goal of linking this material to models based on longitudinal studies of cohorts of sex offenders.

References

Becker, H.S. (1963) *Outsiders: Studies in the Sociology of Deviance.* New York: Free Press.

Becker, H.S. and Strauss, A.L. (1956) 'Careers, personality and adult socialisation.' *American Journal of Sociology* LXII 3, 253–263.

Erikson, E.H. (1950) *Childhood and Society.* New York: W.W. Norton.

Farrington, D.P. (1992) 'Criminal career research in the United Kingdom.' *British Journal of Criminology 32,* 4, 521–536.

Fuller, R. (1992) *In Search of Prevention.* Aldershot: Avebury.

Hodkinson, P. and Sparkes, A.C. (1997) 'Careership: a sociological theory of decision making.' *British Journal of Sociology of Education 18,* 29–44.

Lewin, J., Beary, M., Toman, E., Skinner, G. and Sproul-Bolton, R. (1994) 'A community service for sex offenders.' *Journal of Forensic Psychiatry 5,* 2, 297–316.

Acknowledgements
To Edith Brown, Ian Caren and Dr Barry Stone and all the staff of the North Hampshire Sex Offenders Project for their enthusiasm for being researched.
To Dr Roger Fuller, Stirling University, who had the idea first, and for his encouragement and support.

Super, D.E. (1968) 'A theory of vocational development.' In B. Hopson and J. Hayes (eds) *The Theory of Vocational Guidance.* Oxford: Pergamon.

Thorpe, D. (1976) 'Punishing juveniles – social workers to blame.' *Social Work Today 8*, 6, 2.

Tutt, N. (ed) (1978) *Alternative Strategies for Coping with Crime.* Oxford: Blackwell and Robertson.

Vaughan, P. and Badger, D. (1995) *Working with the Mentally Disordered Offender in the Community.* London: Chapman and Hall.

Watson, W. (1993) 'Future directions for research.' In W. Watson and A. Grounds (eds) *The Mentally Disordered Offender in an Era of Community Care.* Cambridge: Cambridge University Press.

Watts, A.G., Super, D.E. and Kidd, J.M. (eds) (1981) *Career Development in Britain.* Cambridge: Hobson's Press.

CHAPTER 3

The Rights and Wrongs of Social Work With Children and Young People

Steve Farnfield

Introduction

Children's rights, and their views as consumers, are now an important issue for welfare practitioners, generating new questions about the appropriateness or otherwise of involving children in processes designed to help them. As well as reporting what some children think of social work services, this chapter explores the problems encountered when trying to interview children as consumers, and the light this sheds on the power relationships between children and the adults trying to care for them. It also highlights the very real constraints that social workers face when trying to talk to children in the early stages of child protection, and the ways in which children's views are, inevitably, influenced by the quality of their attachment to carers.

The material is drawn from three research projects plus the less formalised reflection on everyday practice with children and families. One of the projects, referred to as the Mental Health Survey (Farnfield 1995), was a commissioned survey of the views of forty-eight children and young people, aged seven to nineteen, of mental health services. This covered a wide selection of professions from fourteen different sites including social workers from a variety of settings. The second study is an ongoing action research project, referred to as the Involvement of Children Project (Farnfield a), into how social workers represent children's views at protection conferences and what children make of their efforts to protect them. The third study, referred to as the In Care Study (Farnfield b), is a personal project asking middle-years children (age seven to twelve) who have been in care for more than six months to talk about their experiences.

Where children's names occur in this account these are pseudonyms chosen by the children themselves.

Ethics and the Research Bargain with Children

Some professionals are anxious about asking children for their views on sensitive issues such as the experience of being protected from abuse or of being in care. The younger the child, the more likely are the adults in charge to resist efforts to interview them on the grounds that it will upset or damage them.

Resistance from social workers is compounded by a lack of ethical guidelines. Whereas educational and medical settings have a clear and practised approach to the ethics of research involving children, no such clarity has been evident in three local authority social services departments which have participated in this research so far. This appears to reflect a general neglect of ethical issues in social research (Gallagher, Creighton and Gibbons 1995; Morrow and Richards 1996) and, despite some important initiatives in the voluntary sector (Alderson 1995; National Children's Bureau 1993), the lack of a protocol for operationalising research in social service departments in particular.

Furthermore, the case of children in care poses a different set of ethical problems to those involving children as patients or pupils. For those children who have lost touch with their parents, or where contacting their parents may be inflammatory, the line taken in these studies has been that the local authority is asked to give blanket consent and the interview proceed, or not, according to the wishes of the child. However, despite support for this position from senior managers, many social workers have not been happy with it and maintain that parental consent should pass to themselves as the social worker to a particular child. The result is that the younger the child the more likely the social worker is to say no.

Does consumer research damage children? The experience of interviewing eighty children shows that the vast majority of children, of seven and upwards, are perfectly able to decide whether or not they want to talk to a research worker and probably do so for the same reasons as many adults: they want to help; they are curious and they like talking about themselves.

In addition, the notion that it is necessary to have a relationship with a child before asking them for their opinions about sensitive matters (Ireland and Holloway 1996, p.156; Morrow and Richards 1996, p.101) has not been borne out by these studies. The research bargain in consumer opinion studies is very clear and can easily be shared with both child and adult participants. Honesty, clarity of purpose and sensitivity to the feelings of the interviewee are readily appreciated by children who, not surprisingly, are suspicious of grown-ups who go through arcane rituals in the name of 'relationship building'. Finally, the quality of the research worker's relationship to children is strikingly different to that of the practitioner: in the latter the relationship is of itself important whereas in research the child frequently gives the impression of doing the interviewer a favour.

The Social Construction of Childhood

The context within which ethical debates take place is invariably shaped by the question: 'What do we mean by a child?' This is reflected in the growing literature on the social construction of childhood (Aries 1962; James and Prout 1990; Stainton Rogers and Stainton Rogers 1992) which highlights the problem of locating what needs are intrinsic to children and what are socially constructed. As Shemmings puts it: 'Are "children" mini-adults…or are they "qualitatively separate" from adults…typically described with words like "innocence", "purity", "uncorrupted" and "naivety"?' (Shemmings 1996, p.2). That there is no easy answer to this question is evidenced by the agonising of the social workers in the Involvement of Children Project over the age and understanding of children in relation to their attendance at case conferences.

The children themselves were much clearer. For those who did attend their protection conference, attendance was overwhelmingly a rights issue; they believed they had a right to hear what people were saying about them even though they sometimes found the conference distressing (see also Shemmings 1996).

When the social workers were asked if it was possible to define an age at which most children could attend their conference, only eight out of twenty-five said yes, and the ages at which they believed a child could attend varied considerably, from seven to fifteen. In addition, nineteen out of forty-one said that in making protection plans, they had never or only very occasionally disagreed with the child over what was in the child's best interests. While the extent of professional experience did not appear to influence these views, there was a suggestion that people with no children of their own were less likely to disagree with the child than those who were parents. This suggests that how professionals view the capabilities and rights of children is determined by a very complicated set of personal and social constructs, of which developmental psychology, itself not a strength of child care workers, plays only a small part.

The Approach to the Studies

The sampling in all three studies was broadly that of theoretical sampling developed by the sociologists Glaser and Strauss (1967; Wells 1995). That is, rather than trying to make statements about the numbers of children who do or think X, the research aims to build models of X or examine the process of X or the conditions under which it occurs. For the cottage industry research worker, what matters is that small samples can yield meaningful results provided developing hypotheses are tested to destruction on the available data.

This approach is probably familiar to practitioners as good practice has some similarities with qualitative research. In particular, Schon's model of the reflective practitioner emphasises how both agency procedures and the classroom knowledge taught on social work courses only take the practitioner so far when confronted with messy cases that have no obvious solution. The latter require what Schon called reflection in action (Schon 1983, Chapter 5): the ability to reflect on the material of the case while the interview is actually in progress. This locates practice as a form of ongoing qualitative research whereby the reflective practitioner draws on previous interviews and client interactions to inform how he or she might act in this particular instance. While there is a symbiosis between practice and research they differ in aims; the former setting out to help, the latter to understand.

There are also similarities in the interview techniques used with children. However, the more prescribed the collection of data becomes, the more the investigator is steered towards procedures which are familiar to those, such as psychologists, who carry out tests on children. This can produce a sense of trying to get the child to fit the interview schedule rather than the other way round.

At the other extreme are attempts to facilitate children in the telling of their core story. In its ideal form the interviewer explains what the research is about and the child tells his or her story with a minimum of prompts (see Main 1991). A second interview can then usefully fill in the gaps according to the themes emerging in the project as a whole.

Rather than doing research on children, the aim here is to facilitate research with them. This means that a decision has to be made about the degree of help each child will need in telling his or her core story.

Explorations of narrative are currently popular in research on adults (see the attachment literature, Fonagy *et al.* 1994; Howe 1995, Chapter 14) and worth extending to children. While Main contends that a reasonably secure ten-year-old is able to 'tell the story of your life' with the minimum of prompts (Main 1991, pp.148–50), securely attached children do not appear very often in at risk samples. Indeed, some unhappy children, with very insecure and damaging attachments, are unable to process their experiences to the point where they can think about them or tell the story at all. That said, the three studies outlined here included many children with traumatic life experiences who were able to tell their stories with the help of some simple facilitative techniques. Their transcripts indicate that the middle-years child (aged seven to puberty) is far less dependent on non-linguistic methods of communication than is generally supposed (Ireland and Holloway 1996, p.156). In other words, given a bit of help, even emotionally disturbed children can actually tell us more than we sometimes give them credit for.

The facilitative techniques recommended here are based on the premise that once in school the majority of children are socialised into sitting down at a table with a grown-up and doing activities using paper and felt tips. Using that model, some simple techniques have proved consistently reliable in facilitating a great deal of information in a surprisingly short time. For example, flow charts asking where and with whom children have lived and whether it was a happy or a sad house have proved extremely effective and universally applicable. A similar chart looking at the schools the child has attended has been equally reliable. Eco-maps, plotting the people the children love and who love them are more specific but equally successful, as are sentence-completion books. Conversely, asking children to draw has not guaranteed success. The idea that all children love drawing seems to be an adult myth; some do not like it or feel they are no good at it (for further information on techniques see Farnfield 1996).

Reflective practice is, needless to say, the opposite to the rigid application of techniques and, if these approaches are to succeed, the interviewer must feel comfortable with children and receptive to what they have to say.

Some Findings from the Three Studies

The following sections outline some of the findings from the three studies introduced at the beginning of this chapter. Although two of the projects have been externally financed they have all been small scale, employing usually one and no more than three interviewers, with one person coding and analysing data and two others typing up transcripts from the interview tapes. All three projects have made productive use of the Australian NUDIST computer programme (see Fielding and Lee 1993; Miles and Huberman 1994). To date eighty children have been interviewed using the approaches and techniques discussed above.

Most of the interviews have been conducted by one or two men, although on the Mental Health Survey it was possible to offer children the choice of a man or a woman to talk to. As it turned out they had no particular preference but young adults (fifteen to twenty) of both sexes were more likely to request a questionnaire than a personal interview.

As well as personal interviews with the children and their social workers, the Involvement of Children Project has used a variety of approaches including questionnaires and focus groups for professionals. Albeit based on very limited experience, there seems to be great potential in consumer surveys like these both for children to interview each other and to use focus groups for children.

Family dislocation and abuse

Practitioners are faced every day with children who have had wretched experiences and, perhaps as a way of managing our own feelings, we tend to think in terms of one case at a time. The research experience involves placing cases together, so that even a small sample is enough to underline just how destructive the lives of some children really are. When reading their stories the severity of trauma, and mistreatment by adults, is only less striking than the resilience displayed by many of the children.

Along with the trauma comes a high level of family dislocation. This was most marked for the children in care, few of whom knew or had ever met their fathers and who exhibited great confusion, in some cases, as to who was who in their families. For example, Laura (aged ten): 'Well Mum sort of had two Mums because there was Nan J. and Nan D., so she sort of had two, but I don't really know who's her real one'.

The difficulty children have in telling

Professionals are well aware that it is very difficult for children who are frightened to tell someone what is happening to them and these studies reinforce that. In the Mental Health Survey, bullying was a real problem for the majority of special needs children while they were in mainstream school, but few of them had received any help and three had attempted suicide following persistent verbal or physical abuse from other children. Of sixteen children in the Involvement of Children Project, only one had been able to tell someone directly that she was being abused.

The helpful professional

It is possible to go with the less specific emotional aches and pains to a wide variety of professionals but the Mental Health Survey found that the profession of the person offering help mattered very little. Whether you see a psychiatrist, a social worker, an art therapist or a community nurse seems less important than the application of core skills and the degree to which they discharge the role of the helpful professional.

The model of the helpful professional, which emerged from the children's accounts of the help they had received, was universal and is given here with the utmost confidence (for a full analysis see Farnfield and Kaszap, in press).

The ideal type of a helpful professional for children is:

- empathetic
- available
- confident
- eager to listen
- understanding
- able to talk to children
- able to help them make decisions
- open and trustworthy
- powerful enough to make things happen
- someone who has the child in mind.

If there is nothing surprising about this model there were some interesting omissions. Although one or two young adults talked about kindness and sympathy, these virtues were not made explicit by the sample as a whole, whereas considerable emphasis was placed on listening and on genuineness. Children seemed to sense very early on when a professional was genuinely interested in them and when they were just going through the motions. But listening on its own does not always change very much. The second order of helpful professional is the adult who makes things happen, exemplified by the ideal type model of the helpful solicitor.

Solicitors are used predominately by children in care, and they have been singled out because, by virtue of their role, they are the only professional who, for a child, does exactly what you want. The helpful solicitor takes your instructions and carries them out. The helpful solicitor defends you, not so much against the law when you have done something wrong, as against the vagaries of the adult professional world. The helpful solicitor is seen by the children who use him or her as the perfect foil against the unhelpful adult; the one who doesn't listen, doesn't care and doesn't understand what you want.

Together with core skills and the adult who makes things happen, it was also possible to add a third order to the role of the helpful professional: the adult who has the child in mind. Its key components are identifying the silent, suffering child, and having the child continually in mind, rather as a parent might do. This is a peculiarly 'adult' responsibility in that it may be independent of the wishes of the child and goes beyond a study of consumer views.

If the helpful professional is important to children, parents and friends are crucial. The Mental Health Study made it clear that if a child has one secure base attachment figure, and the ability to make and keep even a few friends, then the chances of needing professional help are reduced dramatically.

The model of the helpful professional is important because it applies to all caring professionals; the next sections discuss the role of the social worker.

Some Constraints that Child Protection Workers Face in Communicating with Children

The Involvement of Children Project strongly suggests that, in the initial stages at least, the main focus of intervention for the majority of social workers is not the child but the child's mother. There appear to be two reasons for this: the modification of parental behaviour is frequently seen as the key to improving the life of the child, and, without a statutory order, most social workers are keenly aware that parents have rights which makes isolating their offspring for direct work not only difficult but, perhaps, unethical.

A useful concept here is what Dingwall and colleagues (Dingwall, Eekelaar and Murray 1983) termed the rule of optimism. That is, in monitoring the way parents look after their children, the worker feels obliged, if he/she is to go on doing it at all, to think the best of a family unless there are severe indications to the contrary. The reluctance to isolate children in work with families would seem to be an extension of this rule.

There are two notable exceptions to this. The first concerns the use of joint police–social service investigations into alleged abuse, which were experienced by eleven of the children. At the time of a joint investigation the rule of optimism breaks down and the child is suddenly the subject of massive individual attention from the professionals involved. Children's accounts of these interviews vary, but there is a strong suggestion that talking to people you do not know in the circumstances of an investigation is very difficult, and the methodology adopted by the investigators is not always understood by the child. Although children found the investigative phase arduous, some of them still went on to form useful and trusting relationships with their field social worker.

The second exception involves the minority of social workers who have developed an interest and expertise in direct work. These supplementary skills are likely to have been developed on courses run by the British Agencies for Adoption and Fostering, or courses on bereavement counselling, and used, not in everyday practice with children deemed to be at risk, but in particular pieces of work that are seen as an extra to child protection duties. This fits with a general consensus among the social workers that they would like to do more direct work with children, that this is a necessary part of their job but there is simply not enough time to fit it in. Eliciting children's views does not, on this evidence, appear to be in the repertoire of the average child protection worker.

The Independence of Children's Views

When they do meet the field worker, how easy is it for children to express an independent opinion? Children are, inevitably, products of their family, and the data from these samples of children at risk suggests that, for children up to puberty, it is extremely difficult to isolate their views from those of the family they live with.

A simple discourse analysis, in the context of attachment theory, suggests that a child's views may be:

- *Enmeshed*: seen through the same eyes as their parents. A child who is enmeshed with, for example, her mother, has a mind which is not independent from that of her mother's.

- *Idealised*: there is a strong tendency for children to idealise attachment figures who are not, in reality, protecting them. This idealism means that the child goes to great lengths to deny that their parent is not to blame for any abuse even though, to an outsider, this is obviously not the case.

- *Derogatory*: the opposite to idealism (unrealistic optimism) is derogation (extreme pessimism) about a parent. This seems to be rare.

- *Avoidant*: this category refers to children with a very insecure attachment, who have suffered high levels of neglect, and who are no longer protecting parents from blame nor blaming them. They seem to protect themselves by avoiding emotional issues and putting on an air of toughness. Whatever approaches are used, eliciting their views is often difficult.

Children's Views of Child Protection

The experience of being protected is generally described by children as a massive intrusion into normal life. Paradoxically, it seems that proximity to danger may actually lessen the effect of feeling unsafe. If so, this would go some way to explaining why eight out of sixteen children said they did not feel at risk either before or during their conference; a perception that was clearly at odds with the view taken by the professionals. Idealisation of an attachment figure may also lead children to deny that they themselves are at risk.

The Involvement of Children Project supports much of Shemmings' study (Shemmings 1996). Children go to conferences to find out what is being said about them and to try to influence decisions, particularly about where and with whom they should live. However, curiosity may be cancelled out by a sense of shame and this is most likely to occur when the child, rightly or wrongly, feels implicated in events or that their behaviour is on trial.

Being in Care

In the Mental Health Survey the world of local authority care was qualitatively different to that of the special schools, the child guidance clinics and surgeries. The eco-maps of children from the last three told a story of mums and dads, nans, grandads and friends. The eco-maps of thirty-one children in care (drawn from two studies) were a stark contrast to those living with their 'real' families: one example, in order of closeness, is: boyfriend, my dog, foster mum and dad, best friend, my real Dad.

Their sentence completions told a similar story:

> My life would have been different if only my Mum had been shot. (Wesley, 16)

The stories of children in care were not about 'mental health' so much as entire childhoods. Autobiographies were punctuated by helpful and unhelpful professionals, but particularly social workers who were often described in either glowing or highly derogatory terms. This suggests that the job of the social worker may be qualitatively different to that of other 'mental health' professionals.

The Power of the Field Social Worker

Both children and adults in the Mental Health Survey tended to personalise agencies to a high degree; there was a clearly defined view that personalities did matter and that the efficacy of a particular service depended on there being enough helpful professionals to carry out the work with clients. This emphasis on the personal qualities and core skills of the professional means that, for children in care, enormous power is vested in the individual field worker or foster parent.

Joe Davis was fourteen and in foster care. His stepmother contacted a psychologist when he was twelve:

> I talked to him quite a lot and it didn't do much good and he said well I think it would be a good idea to get a social worker in... She suggested things. She controlled it from there...I think the social worker's the main person who sorts it all out, who gets in contact with people... She just organised lots and lots of things... What was going to happen and stuff like that.

The field worker here appears as the adult who makes everything happen. Joe liked his social worker and found her very helpful but what is noteworthy is the power she has. A power that shapes Joe's career in care.

Social workers also have the power to make nothing happen, even to the extent of Paul (age fifteen) who had no social worker at all for two years and lived with a foster family who 'just stopped speaking to me'.

Unfortunately the children in care exhibited a deep distrust of the social services in general, even if they had formed a good relationship with their social worker. There were also an alarming number of entry into care stories like Laura's (aged ten):

> Well the social worker Ken took us there [foster home] and then Mum had to go as soon as we got there, she didn't even get a chance to step outside the car door, and Ken said that Mum would be up in a minute, then by the time we come back downstairs after we had unpacked, Mum had gone.

What the above examples indicate is that the field worker appears to actually be the care system; she or he actually can make things better or worse in a way that other professionals may not.

Resistance as Data

In the same way that a client's attitudes to the worker may be considered as data by the practitioner, so the attitudes of gatekeepers to research can be treated as data also. An example of this is the high number of refusals from social workers asked to grant access to children in care for a research interview (see also Schein 1987, p.29).

There are a number of possible explanations for this. One possibility is that protecting children evokes attachment behaviour whereby social workers are filling the 'perceived' gap left by the failure of the child's own parents to protect them. Another is that social workers, constrained by procedures that actually discourage reflective practice, feel guilty about how little direct work with children they are free to do and want to hide this from researchers and, possibly, even themselves. A further possibility is that social workers see themselves as the sole keeper of the child's story. Such an emphasis on individualisation, as Mayer and Timms (1970, p.16) pointed out, can lead social workers to assume ownership of their clients.

Whatever the cause of the resistance, attempts to unravel it take the research worker deeper into the care system itself. If, for research purposes, the social worker of a child can say yes or no to an interview, this suggests that considerable power is held by the individual practitioner. The role of the individual worker is no doubt crucial in the public care of children, and few would argue that children in care should be brought up by a committee. However, the power of this individual does seem to have been significantly underrated.

Compared to, say, France, social workers in the UK have little authority in child protection, faced as they are with a highly legalistic frame of reference to work in. Once in care, however, from the child's point of view, the balance of power seems to shift dramatically. In crucial decisions about everyday life events the social worker seems, to the child, omnipotent. Mindful of François Ewald on Foucault (quoted Sheridan 1980, p.221), that there are three not two parties to every power struggle – those who have it, those who want it and those upon whom power is exercised – it is possible to posit the following equations:

$$\text{Power in child protection} = \frac{\text{social services v. parents}}{\text{child}}$$

$$\text{Power once in care} = \frac{\text{social services v. child}}{\text{parents}}$$

Foucault emphasised that power can be productive, but social workers have never been eager either to embrace power or admit to its ownership. This puts us in a curious position. As a profession we currently socialise students into anti-oppressive practice that draws heavily on sociopolitical concepts of power, coupled with skills in the empowering of clients. But personally we are more likely to be frustrated, feel powerless and identify with client experiences that speak of victimisation and failure (Barford 1993; Stanford 1995). Meanwhile an excursion into the views of children in care reveals us as having great power over fundamental things like where and with whom they live and even whether they see their mothers.

Concluding Observations

A dilemma, familiar to practitioners and researchers alike, is whether to go 'inside' for the meaning the world has to the actor, or 'outside', for meanings put together by the worker and of which the actor may be unaware (Agar 1986, p.44). Children's views of social work reveal much about the belief system of the subject but they cannot provide an 'objective' explanation of a system. The task of both practitioners and researchers is to negotiate the meanings of these views (see Everitt *et al.* 1992, p.122) in the context that interests them.

The 'in' and the 'out' are not, of course, always reconcilable, nor do the practitioner and the researcher have the same aims. For this reason ethically sound procedures on access to children in care for research purposes are a matter of urgency for social work in the United Kingdom.

From the professional end of the telescope how much weight we want to give to children's views is still unclear. What is clear, listening to the stories of the children in these studies, is that the current emphasis on children's rights does not relieve the professional from the task of holding the child in mind. Unfortunately it is still too easy to find children bullied for years and nobody helping them; children drifting through an alarming number of unsatisfactory foster placements and children's homes with no apparent boundaries or sanctions, in which woolly notions of young people's rights are used to cover a lack of clarity about the task in hand.

The enquiries into the deaths of abused children have underlined the need for social workers to look at and listen to the child. But the Involvement of Children Project indicates just how difficult child protection work is, and how the procedural framework resulting from those enquiries omits the crucial processes that inform what really happens when the social worker visits the family. Finding out what the child thinks, in the early, grey, stages of child protection, is subject to a variety of real constraints. The task is not therapeutic and does not, indeed cannot, entail building a relationship with the child. It requires risk assessment based on good information including the views of the child; in obtaining the latter, the methodologies outlined in this chapter have, in a research environment, proved remarkably successful.

In these studies social workers appear to have relatively little power in sociopolitical terms but in the eyes of children in care they are omnipotent. Children themselves are clear that they want the services of a 'helpful solicitor' which lends support to the existing advocacy schemes (e.g. Scutt 1995). Given the experiences of some of these children in care, and the current wider concern about the abuse of children in institutions, there is a strong case for all children in care to have access to an independent advocate as a matter of right.

The word 'child' has been used somewhat indiscriminately in this chapter and there is a real need for a developmental perspective in research and practice methodologies which purport to engage with children's worlds. Likewise, if the constructionist thesis is correct, the crucial research area is to work out ways of evaluating how social constructions of childhood are actually used by professionals.

Hopefully the examples here have shown that daily practice with child clients and small-scale qualitative research can inform each other, thereby making Schon's reflection in action more conscious and hence more accessible to scrutiny. And if the model of the helpful professional seems obvious, then maybe the social work task is to do the obvious as best we can. For that we need core skills. It is a traditional message but, whatever the current reorganisation is doing to the office, probably still the reason most practitioners get out of bed on a Monday morning.

References

Agar, M. (1986) *Speaking of Ethnography*. (Sage University Paper series on Qualitative Research Methods, Vol. 2.) Beverly Hills, CA: Sage.

Alderson, P. (1995) *Listening to Children: Children, Ethics and Social Research*. London: Barnados.

Aries, P. (1962) *Centuries of Childhood*. London: Jonathan Cape.

Barford, R. (1993) *Children's Views of Child Protection Social Work*. Norwich: UEA Social Work Monographs.

Dingwall, R., Eekelaar, J.M. and Murray, T. (1983) *The Protection of Children: State Intervention into Family Life*. Oxford: Blackwell.

Everitt, A., Hardiker, P., Littlewood, J. and Mullender, A. (1992) *Applied Research for Better Practice*. Basingstoke: Macmillan.

Farnfield, S. and Kaszap, M. (in press) 'What makes a helpful grown up? Children's views of professionals in the mental health services.' *Journal of Health Informatics 3,4.*

Farnfield, S. (1996) *Can You Tell Me? Some Useful Approaches to Eliciting Children's Views*. Reading: The University of Reading.

Farnfield, S. (1995) *Report to the Southampton and South West Hampshire Health Commission: Research into the Views of Children, Young People and their Carers, of Mental Health Services*. Reading: The University of Reading.

Farnfield, S. (a ongoing) *The Involvement of Children in Child Protection Conferences*. (A three-year action research study funded by the Gatsby Charitable Trust).

Farnfield, S. (b ongoing) *Being in Care: The Experience of Some 8 and 11 Year Olds in Local Authority Care*.

Fielding, N. and Lee, R. (eds) (1993 updated) *Using Computers in Qualitative Research*. Beverly Hills, CA: Sage.

Fonagy, P., Steele, H., Higgitt, A. and Target, M. (1994) 'The theory and practice of resilience.' *Journal of Child Psychology and Psychiatry 35*, 2, 231–257.

Acknowledgements

Thanks to: the research team of Laraine Beavis, Susie Dutton, Margot Kaszap, Derek Lockhart, Marie Preston and Carole Wyatt; a wide variety of professionals in Southampton; the staff of the Social Services Department who have collaborated in the Involvement of Children in Child Protection research, and the Gatsby Charitable Trust for financing that project; Nicola Hilliard at the National Children's Bureau and Sally Barrett closer to home; all the children and their families who have responded with such commitment and frankness.

Gallagher, B., Creighton, S. and Gibbons, J. (1995) 'Ethical dilemmas in social research: no easy solutions.' *British Journal of Social Work 25*, 3, 295–311.

Glaser, B. and Strauss, A. (1967) *The Discovery of Grounded Theory: Strategies for Qualitative Research.* London: Weidenfeld and Nicolson.

Howe, D. (1995) *Attachment Theory for Social Workers.* Basingstoke: Macmillan.

Ireland, L. and Holloway, I. (1996) 'Qualitative health research with children.' *Children and Society 10*, 2, 155–164.

James, A. and Prout, A. (eds) (1990) *Constructing and Reconstructing Childhood: Contemporary Issues in the Sociological Study of Childhood.* Basingstoke: Falmer Press.

Main, M. (1991) 'Metacognitive knowledge, metacognitive monitoring, and singular (coherent) vs. multiple (incoherent) model of attachment: findings and directions for future research.' In C. Murray Parkes, J. Stevenson-Hide and P. Marris (eds) *Attachment Across the Life Cycle.* London: Routledge.

Mayer, J. and Timms, N. (1970) *The Client Speaks: Working Class Impressions of Case Work.* London: Routledge and Kegan Paul.

Miles, M. and Huberman, A. (1994) *Qualitative Data Analysis.* Thousand Oaks, CA: Sage.

Morrow, V. and Richards, M. (1996) 'The ethics of social research with children: an overview.' *Children and Society 10*, 2, 90–105.

National Children's Bureau (1993) *Guidelines for Research.* London: NCB.

Schein, E.H. (1987) *The Clinical Perspective in Fieldwork.* (Sage University Paper Series on Qualitative Research Methods, Vol. 5.) Beverly Hills, CA: Sage.

Schon, D. (1983) *The Reflective Practitioner: How Professionals Think in Action.* London: Maurice Temple Smith, Basic Books.

Scutt, N. (1995) 'Child advocacy.' In C. Cloke and M. Davies (eds) *Participation and Empowerment in Child Protection.* London: Pitman.

Shemmings, D. (1996) *Involving Children In Child Protection Conferences.* Norwich: UEA Social Work Monographs.

Sheridan, A. (1980) *Michel Foucault: The Will to Truth.* London: Tavistock.

Stainton Rogers, R. and Stainton Rogers, W. (1992) *Stories of Childhood: Shifting Agendas of Child Concern.* Buffalo, NY: University of Toronto Press.

Stanford, R. (1995) 'Creativity and child protection social work.' In M. Yelloly and M. Henkel (eds) *Learning and Teaching in Social Work: Towards Reflective Practice.* London: Jessica Kingsley Publishers.

Wells, K. (1995) 'The strategy of grounded theory: possibilities and problems.' *Social Work Research 19*, 1, 33–37.

CHAPTER 4

Researching Community Care Assessments
A Pluralistic Approach

Nicky Stanley, Jill Manthorpe, Greta Bradley
and Andy Alaszewski

'Proper assessment' of individuals' need for social care was the cornerstone of the NHS and Community Care Act 1990. This chapter examines the research methods used to explore the process of assessment in one English local authority. We begin by outlining the research context, and proceed to describe the research and present the main findings of the study. The three research methods used in the study are evaluated and issues of consent and confidentiality, as well as user participation, are discussed in some detail. Finally, the applications of this research are considered together with the strengths and weaknesses of the study.

The Research Context

The White Paper *Caring for People* (Department of Health 1989) proposed legislation to resolve the twin problems of high social security spending combined with uncoordinated and inefficient delivery of care. While the aims of improving services and restricting expenditure might appear to conflict, the policy is one familiar to other countries facing fiscal and demographic imperatives (see Wistow 1995). The NHS and Community Care Act 1990 translated these aims into legislation which transformed a pattern of community care which had hitherto developed in a piecemeal and uncoordinated manner (Ovretveit 1993).

Caring for People marked a national endorsement of care management. This system attempts to focus services on those assessed as being in greatest need. Resources are to be used more efficiently through the appointment of a named individual, the care manager, who carries budgetary responsibilities. In England and Wales, the care manager is a local government employee who undertakes the dual tasks of assessing need and designing and implementing a range of coordinated service provision.

Our research focused on the assessment process in care management. While assessment is significant in determining the nature and extent of resource allocation and exemplifying organisational priorities, it is not the whole of the care management process or cycle. The cycle includes targeting potential service users, developing and implementing a care plan where appropriate and is interwoven by processes of monitoring and review (for a description of this see Payne 1995).

Lewis and Glennerster (1996) describe the range of structures adopted by a number of social services departments in their implementation of the NHS and Community Care Act 1990. Despite an outpouring of central government guidance that was both voluminous and prescriptive, considerable choice was available to local authorities as to which model of care management to adopt. The local authority involved in this study had chosen to separate the task of assessing users' needs from that of managing care packages by creating two different posts: that of assessor and that of coordinator. The existence of a large group of staff whose function was clearly defined offered the researchers a means of focusing on assessment.

The project was devised as a way of capturing some of the implementation issues around the new patterning of social care; the focus was to be primarily on practitioners and the extent to which they had taken on board the new culture of community care and were translating it into practice. The study was funded by one particular local authority which wished to consider the further training implications of the new system of community care once operationalised and wanted an evaluation of the training provided for those social workers who conducted assessments. We were in a position to undertake such work but wished to place the study in a broader context and explore wider attitudinal shifts, cultural changes and the process of assessment itself. Such aims are complementary rather than competitive and, on the basis of an understanding of the authority's and the researchers' distinctive but overlapping agendas, we entered discussion about ways of working together on a research project that would prove mutually advantageous.

Consequently, we see two major stakeholders in this research: the first a local authority (henceforward referred to as the local authority) which required information that it considered might be more easily collected by independent researchers who could consider the effectiveness of in-house training from an outsider's position; the second, a group of university-based researchers who wanted access to practitioners in order to explore the transformation of policy into practice. The actual research design was a product of discussion and debate in which the local authority set down the conditions of its involvement and an exchange model of work developed in which those conditions were negotiated.

This ensuing agreement covered commitments to confidentiality, time limits and the focus of the research. Once an agreement had been established, the research relationship between the local authority and the university researchers was sustained by regular meetings of a research steering group that included the university researchers and a cross-section of local authority staff who acted as sounding-boards or consultants. This steering committee had *de facto* control in identifying the focus of research. In the area of research design, it examined the questionnaires and piloted early examples, checking, for example, that they could be completed in a short space of time and were understood by the staff in question. It was the steering committee which made decisions about the best ways of ensuring that questionnaires were completed and returned. Initial results from the research were communicated to local authority members of the committee and their response was assessed.

Much research in social work assumes a fairly problem-free context and is set at some distance from the internal workings of local authorities. We were influenced by work which stressed that research should be both manageable and relevant to practical administration (Booth 1988). In accepting this we undertook to meet the demands of the local authority as represented by their members of the steering committee, for data that was immediately relevant and could be communicated in non-technical, non-theoretical and brief reports. Our research agreement was negotiated on the basis of a recognised imbalance between the researchers and the gatekeepers of data: the local authority could have turned to other researchers; we recognised that our access to staff and users had to be facilitated, whichever geographical area we chose.

There is enormous advantage for academics in writing for a purpose and for an audience. It instils a discipline, a commitment to a practical or jargon-free report style and a purposeful direction to the research process. Questions are to be answered rather than proposed and a circularity of research and teaching has significant benefits for social work educators.

Whilst social work departments within academic institutions in the United Kingdom are growing, there are few dedicated social work research centres – for notable exceptions see Stirling (Cheetham 1993) and Huddersfield (Kazi 1996). For many social work educators their research must embody a dual focus and demonstrate relevance to informed practice development through academic training programmes as well as a value to purchasers of research, which is in the main funded by central or local government.

The Methodology Described

In this section we shall outline the three research methods employed to answer the research questions formulated by the researchers and the local authority. The use of a number of research methods allowed us to build up a picture of the assessment service that incorporated a range of perspectives. This approach was not adopted with the aim of achieving validity by triangulation (Denzin 1970); rather we sought to elucidate a number of player perspectives which together constituted a pluralistic image of community care assessments.

The research design included a postal survey of assessors. Its aim was to elicit their views concerning their jobs, their training needs and their aspirations for the future. In addition, the questionnaire asked for information on the range of tasks that they undertook and the skills and knowledge that the assessors felt they used in their jobs. The postal questionnaire was completed by virtually all the assessors employed by the local authority: the high response rate of 93 per cent can be attributed both to the design of the form and to the visible commitment to the research from the respondents' line managers.

Fielding and Fielding (1986) suggest that research which adopts a range of methods needs to include at least one approach that reveals the structural aspects of the area researched. We therefore incorporated into the research design a survey of those managing the assessors which aimed to illuminate planning and policy issues and highlight organisational characteristics of the service. Telephone interviews were completed with the twenty-three middle managers and four senior managers responsible for the local authority's care management service. A semi-structured questionnaire giving the managers the opportunity to discuss their work and its problems at some length was designed and pre-arranged interviews were carried out by a single researcher. The interviews explored the managers' commitment to the philosophy of care management and asked them to comment on the difficulties of implementing the new system. They were asked to identify which issues their staff regularly raised with them and to comment on the local authority's strategy for the future. The research team were subsequently able to compare the differing degrees to which practitioners and managers were wedded to the new culture. This second stage of the research also offered an opportunity to explore the extent to which the managers' perceptions of their staff's needs coincided with practitioners' views of their needs.

Hunter, McKeganey and MacPherson (1988) identify the complementarity of both interviewing and observation, arguing that 'the strengths of each approach are an antidote to the weakness of the other' (p.22). The observation or shadowing stage of the research involved contacting ten of the local authority's adult assessment teams who were asked to give access to a researcher who would observe one of their cases from the first point of contact to completion of the assessment. The teams were selected to illustrate the diversity of the region in terms of environmental, social and economic factors. We considered that ten cases would allow us to explore older people's experience of assessment in some depth. This stage of the research was the most onerous in terms of research time. Shadowing cases involved observing and recording practitioners' interviews with users and carers; conducting unstructured interviews with the assessors assigned to the cases on a number of occasions; reading and analysing all the paperwork associated with each case; interviewing the colleague to whom the case was handed on and interviewing the user and carer once the assessment had been completed. This approach yielded a three-dimensional, dynamic image of the assessment process that allowed us to view the process in its full complexity and to identify the wide range of tasks, skills, judgments and interactions that make up an assessment.

Results

The survey of the local authority's assessors produced a wealth of quantitative data that was analysed using the SPSS package, a statistical package designed for use in the social services. We were able to build up a group portrait of these workers and to identify them as, in the main, professionally qualified workers who prior to their present appointment had been employed as social workers. Forty-four per cent considered their current posts to be less satisfying than their previous work while 54 per cent found their current work equally or more satisfying than their previous job. They identified one of the main areas of difficulty in their jobs as the amount of paperwork required of them, a point identified by Baldwin (1996). The other main problems experienced by the assessors were failures on the part of other professionals to provide information speedily (Manthorpe et al. 1996) and a lack of resources to offer users following assessment. This last point is echoed in McGrath et al.'s research (1997). Although the majority of assessors appeared to have taken on board the new philosophy of care management, some evinced sceptical or more traditional approaches to their work.

Rachman's (1995) research into the impact of community care reforms on hospital social work found that managers evinced more enthusiasm for the new culture than practitioners. Indeed, the status and power of managers is considerably enhanced by the 'New Managerialism' ethos of care management (Sheppard 1995). In comparison with the assessors, the managers interviewed by telephone in the second stage of this research project expressed a more fully developed commitment to the principles of care management, although this was tempered by a recognition of the difficulties of implementing the new policy:

> Whilst critical, I remain enthusiastic about care in the community. I think that we will get there but it will be and has been...a painful journey. (Manager)

The managers' greater involvement in establishing goals and strategy may have reduced the impact which day-to-day problems had on their overall commitment to the new system. However, the middle managers included in this study did demonstrate a keen awareness of the range of problems described by the practitioners and some were developing strategies to tackle these problems. The managers also commented on the assessors' lack of confidence in working with adult users with special needs. Over half the assessors surveyed felt that they lacked the skills needed to work with adult users with a mental health problem or a learning difficulty.

In contrast to the comprehensive nature of the postal and telephone surveys, the third stage of the research involved ten cases which were studied in depth. Nine of the ten users were over sixty-five years of age and five of this group were suffering from some degree of dementia. Such intellectual impairment has been described 'as perhaps the most demanding problem facing any community service' (Challis et al. 1990, p.43). While the assessors who participated in the research used a range of interpersonal skills in assessing these users, there was little evidence of a systematic approach to either the assessment of risk or the protection of vulnerable adults from abuse. These research findings together with the information from the postal survey on skill deficits were used to make specific recommendations to the local authority concerning the training needs of their staff (Bradley *et al.* 1996).

The policy of community care is founded on the assumption that most social care will be provided by kin. Consequently, the needs of carers have been the focus of considerable research interest in the United Kingdom (Nolan, Grant and Keady 1996; Manthorpe and Twigg 1995; Twigg and Atkin 1994). In four of the cases observed by the researchers, users were highly dependent on co-resident carers. The majority of assessors who participated in the postal survey reported assessing carers' needs separately from users, a practice which may be increased following the implementation of the Carers (Recognition and Services) Act 1995 in 1996. However, such assessments did not appear to be undertaken on a regular basis and the process of shadowing offered the opportunity to observe the extent to which assessors were able to respond to carers' needs in addition to assessing users' needs. While assessors interviewed co-resident carers on their own in two of these cases, pressures of time and circumstance combined to prevent this happening in the other two cases. One of these co-resident carers commented on the need for an individual interview with the assessor:

> I would have felt a bit inhibited talking to him [the assessor] unless I was on my own.

Here, the qualitative data derived from the shadowing was used to develop the quantitative data on work with carers which was supplied by the postal survey.

However, the findings of the third stage of the research did more than simply confirm or colour in the quantitative material collected by the survey. The process of shadowing assessments served to introduce the perspectives of users and carers into the research and to identify their contribution to the assessment of need. In contrast with the 'perceived 'passivity' of clients' reported by care management workers in MacDonald and Myers' study of community care in Scotland (1995, p.67), we shadowed three cases where the user or carer had determined that they needed a service and that view was expressed forcibly. In these cases, the assessment tended to develop as a receptive response to that expressed view. This proved to be the case even when pursuing the user's or carer's expressed needs conflicted with the principle of keeping users in their own homes whenever possible. For instance, Mrs Walker, who was admitted to hospital with a fracture, expressed a strong desire to move into the particular residential home where her husband had died. Although her main needs seemed to be related to her bereavement rather than her physical dependency, the assessor's initial interview with her moved very swiftly onto the procedures for admission to residential care. Some of the users and carers observed in this stage of the study were seen to wield considerable power in determining the outcome of assessments.

Discussion

The postal survey

The use of three different research methods in this study allows us to contrast the benefits and problems associated with each approach. The postal survey of the authority's assessors was sufficiently large-scale to yield up some definitive statements about this group of workers and the job they were doing. The survey allowed large amounts of information to be collected and analysed with relative ease. Moreover, it was possible to collect this information in a fairly short period of time (two months). This may be significant when undertaking research in local authority social services departments as policy, procedures and personnel can change rapidly. During the year it took to complete the shadowing of ten cases, the assessment forms used by the local authority were completely revised, making it difficult to compare the relationship between form-filling and social work practice in all cases.

However, while the information obtained from such a survey may be copious in quantity, its quality is limited by the researchers' interests and hypotheses. In this study, the interests of the local authority also influenced the content of the questionnaire and a number of questions on the issue of training were included at the request of steering committee members. Although it was possible to include some open questions which allowed the assessors to speak to the researchers in their own words, the information yielded by the postal questionnaire failed to convey the complexity of the range of tasks, judgments and transactions which made up a community care assessment. Moreover, there was no opportunity to explore the relationship between the assessors' accounts of their work and their day-to-day practice (see Edwards and Popay 1994). The focus on the views and activities of the practitioner excluded both the organisational context and the user's perspective.

The telephone interviews

The semi-structured telephone interviews with the service managers were also conducted over a relatively short time period (again two months). These interviews were pre-arranged so that the interviewees' attention was fully engaged. The managers had the opportunity to talk at length about their work and the following quote from a manager illustrates the way in which telephone interviewing allows respondents to develop their thinking as they talk:

> I think that this is the right approach…for those getting a service – and more are getting a service than before – it's an improved service – we are responding to what people say they need…we've put together some high quality packages to keep people at home – we wouldn't really have done that before.

This approach also enabled the managers to communicate ambivalences and uncertainties, and a more complex picture of a new service still in the process of change and subject to both political and resourcing pressures emerged. While the authentic voices of the managers were clearly communicated by this stage of the research, it was again difficult to know how their account of the service, its strengths and weaknesses, related to the experiences of the users. We were, however, able to compare the managers' views with those of the practitioners and were able to conclude that the managers seemed to have a good understanding of the problems experienced by their staff in implementing the new system.

Shadowing

Whilst the rhetoric of user consultation and choice permeates writing on care management and community care in the United Kingdom, few research projects have been able to focus on the transaction between user and care manager. Wilson's work explores the difficulties of producing meaningful consumer evaluations of community care services, especially from older users, and she has developed a methodology which was successful in eliciting critical responses to community psychogeriatric services from a group of users and care-givers (Wilson 1993). This research, together with that of

Baldock and Ungerson into the views of people who had experienced a stroke (1994), is effective in presenting the user as a critical consumer of community care, but does not portray the user as an active player in the care management process. The ethnographic approach employed in shadowing ten community care assessments allowed us to view assessment as a dynamic process in which users and their carers have key roles to play.

The main problem associated with this approach is the high investment required in terms of the researchers' time and energy. The term 'shadowing' is used here to encompass a range of research tasks including interviewing, analysis of transcripts and observation notes, analysis of assessment forms and case notes as well as the actual observation of assessments. The three researchers were all conducting the research in addition to other teaching and administrative commitments and it took a year to complete the shadowing, interviewing and analysis that ten community care assessments entailed. While ten cases were sufficient to produce a vast amount of qualitative data, some members of the steering committee used the number of cases shadowed as grounds for questioning the validity of the findings generated by this stage of the research.

As with most ethnographical research (Fielding 1993), we do not operate within a positivistic paradigm and make no claims for the objectivity of shadowing as a research methodology. This research project aspires rather towards 'pluralistic evaluation' (Smith and Cantley 1984). We would argue that there is no meta-account of the community care assessment. Instead, we have explored a number of perspectives or gazes: that of the assessors, that of the service managers, those of the users and carers (these two perspectives differ and can conflict) and that of the researchers. Howe (1994) has argued that 'The role of the social scientist and social worker in the post-modern world is…to interpret and understand one world and present it to another' (p.523). This seems a worthwhile objective for research into the practice and experience of community care.

The local authority

As a major stakeholder in the research, the local authority represents yet another perspective. Whilst the commitment of senior managers to the research ensured a high response rate to the postal survey, it also had an impact on staff's attitude to the research project. We experienced some difficulties and delays in identifying both teams and individuals who had suitable cases for us to shadow, and we speculated that, in some cases, the research might be seen as intrusive.

There was also a need for negotiation with the steering committee concerning the drafts of the project reports. The three stages of the project were written up as three separate reports which were produced for the local authority's own use and were not for external publication. It was decided to preface the main body of the report on the shadowing with pen portraits of the ten users and their carers and these heavily disguised cases were referred to by their fictitious names throughout the body of the report. The result was a report which took on a vivid and immediate quality. It was peopled by a set of characters whose words were included in the text, whose experience of assessment was detailed, life-like and convincing. For some members of the steering committee, the vivid quality of the writing when combined with evidence of varied practice raised concern. It was agreed to relegate the pen portraits to an appendix where they would have less impact on the reader, to tone down some of the descriptive detail and to stress the limited number of cases observed.

Consent and confidentiality

The issues of consent and confidentiality provoked considerable discussion both among the researchers and within the steering committee. The American Psychological Association has identified the process for establishing informed consent as:

> The procedure by which individuals choose whether or not to partici-pate in an experiment after being given information that likely would af-fect their decision. (Gallagher, Creighton and Gibbons 1995, p.305)

Gallagher, Creighton and Gibbons (1995) suggest that this definition, which was developed for use in the behavioural sciences, can be harnessed for use in social research. However, there are difficulties in identifying which information is likely to affect individuals' decisions to participate and in obtaining that information. We felt that the key information determining the decision to participate in research concerned confidentiality and the purpose of the research. Fielding (1993) argues that it may not be possible to predict accurately the uses to which ethnographic research may be put. The future uses of research become less susceptible to control when there is more than one stakeholder involved in the research project. Moreover, as Smith and Cantley (1984) note, challenges to the traditional rationalist models of planning and organisational change have succeeded in stripping researchers of any certainty that their research will be used to effect change in services.

We therefore confined ourselves to describing the purpose of the research as exploratory and investigative. The introductory letters sent to the managers and practitioners who were being invited to participate in the research introduced the research in this light:

> ...to examine the ways in which the new arrangements for assessing the needs of service users are developing;

> ...to look at the ways in which the needs of service users are being assessed.

When we introduced staff to the third stage of the research, the researchers discussed the study with the community teams in addition to talking to individuals who had volunteered to be shadowed. In these introductions to our work, we emphasised our desire to observe the complexity of community care assessments at close quarters.

In describing the purpose of the research to users and their carers we sought to communicate that our interest was in the process of assessment rather than the user's personal circumstances and we explained that 'we were interested in seeing how staff were doing their new jobs'. We experienced no difficulty in obtaining consent from users nor in obtaining their permission to record interviews. However, this was perhaps to be expected given that all but one of the users involved in the shadowing were over sixty-five and therefore members of the group of clients whom Wilson (1993) describes as 'a particularly compliant set of users'. Moreover, in some cases, the community care assessment had been precipitated by a request for services and users were therefore anxious to propitiate their visitors. The distinct functions of assessor and researcher were not always clear to users, although the researchers did explain that they worked at a university and were careful not to participate actively in interviews.

Since five of the ten users involved in the research suffered some degree of confusion and in two cases this confusion could be described as severe, we need to address the question of whether their consent could be described as meaningful. Where possible, carers or professionals were consulted as to whether it was appropriate to observe and record interviews with these users. Where this was not possible, our argument would be that those who are confused need to have their experiences as service users researched as much as any other group of users. We were also guided here by the principle adopted in health studies that research should do no harm (see Butler's discussion 1990). In these cases, we did not attempt follow-up interviews with the users on their own as we felt that these could prove confusing and threatening for them.

We had promised confidentiality to both users and professionals and while there was no difficulty in maintaining the anonymity of the responses to the questionnaire and telephone survey, some problems did arise when the research team produced the first draft of the report on the shadowing for the local authority. It had been agreed that the research findings would be made available to all those workers involved in assessment and, although we had made strenuous efforts to conceal the identities of both users and workers, it was clear that in the teams where workers had been shadowed, other staff members would be able to recognise both the client and the assessor. This issue was ultimately resolved by issuing all the ten assessors who participated in this stage of the research with a draft copy of the report and inviting them to voice any concerns as to whether their confidentiality and that of the client was preserved. In the event, no comments were forthcoming.

User participation

While the pluralistic approach adopted for this piece of research allowed users' views and experiences of community care assessment to be incorporated into the findings, it remains the case that the major stakeholders in the research were academic researchers and the local authority who managed the assessment service. In retrospect, it would have been valuable to have included users or their representatives on the steering committee. Davis (1992) examines a number of user-led research projects in both the United States and Britain and comments on the need to 'consider some fundamental issues of research siting, ownership, direction and style…with service users at the outset of our work' (p.45–46).

The arguments for involving users in the planning stage of research go beyond attempts to confer credibility upon the findings. The participation of users in the early stages of a research project can have a significant effect on the direction and focus of the researcher's attention. The steering committee for the research project included one basic grade worker who played an important role in articulating some of the major preoccupations of practitioners. While there are difficulties in identifying individuals who can adequately represent the very various views and experiences of service users, such representation needs to be attempted if different perspectives are to be given equal validity.

Applying the Research

As stated earlier, researchers cannot assume that organisations will inevitably feed research findings into the planning process. While the local authority's training department showed a keen interest in translating some of the research findings into new staff training programmes, local government reorganisation in England and Wales makes it difficult to predict the full extent to which the findings will be used to develop the local care management service. However, periods of structural reorganisation offer opportunities for change at all levels in an organisation and we have been gratified that some of our findings concerning the procedures and policies which structure and shape adult assessment have been used to inform thinking about services (Bradley 1997).

In an attempt to influence practice at the practitioner level, the researchers encouraged the local authority to make the research findings available to all assessors and their managers. We presented the research findings to practitioners and managers in workshops organised by the steering committee. These provided an opportunity to enter into a dialogue with practitioners and to observe which of the research findings attracted most interest and comment. We were heartened to hear that the picture we had painted of adult assessment was recognisable to practitioners and that many of the issues that we had identified as areas of action for the local authority were felt to be relevant and significant by the staff who attended these sessions. These workshops, together with the reports produced for the local authority, also offered a means of providing feedback to all those professionals who had contributed to the research.

It was less easy to identify appropriate ways of feeding back to the users and carers who were involved in the research and this constitutes a weakness of the project. Here again, we conclude that the presence of users on the steering committee would have been valuable. However, we do consider that the pluralistic approach adopted allowed the different groups of people participating in community care assessments to articulate their views and their perspectives. We would define the research task in this study as bringing these different perspectives together, illuminating them and exploring them while recognising their distinctiveness. In addition, our use of ethnographical research techniques allowed us to observe assessment as it happened and to identify the user as an active participant in a dynamic process. This approach represents the main strength of the project and we consider that the chosen methodology has produced a picture of a process that reflects the complexity of the web of interests, ideologies and transactions that constitutes a community care assessment.

References

Baldock, J. and Ungerson, C. (1994) *Becoming Consumers of Community Care.* York: Joseph Rowntree Foundation.

Baldwin, M. (1996) 'Is assessment working?' *Practice 8,* 4, 43–52.

Booth, T. (1988) *Developing Policy Research.* Aldershot: Gower.

Bradley, G. (1997) 'Translating research into practice.' *Social Sciences and Social Work Review 7,* 1, 3–12.

Bradley, G., Manthorpe, J., Stanley, N. and Alaszewski, A. (1997) 'Training for care management: using research to identify new directions.' *Issues in Social Work Education 16,* 2, 27–45.

Butler, A. (1990) 'Research ethics and older people.' In S. Peace (ed) *Researching Social Gerontology.* London: Sage.

Challis, D., Chessum, R., Chesterman, J., Luckett, R. and Traske, K. (1990) *Case Management in Social and Health Care.* Kent: Personal Social Services Research Unit.

Cheetham, J. (1993) *Why Research Social Work? Some Considerations for Practitioners and Managers.* Hull: The University of Hull.

Davis, A. (1992) 'Who needs user research? Service users as research subjects or participants, implications for user involvement in service contracting.' In M. Barnes and G. Wistow (eds) *Researching User Involvement.* Leeds: University of Leeds, The Nuffield Institute for Health Services Studies.

Denzin, N.K. (1970) *The Research Act in Sociology.* London: Butterworth.

Department of Health (1989) *Caring for People.* London: HMSO, Cm 849.

Edwards, J. and Popay, J. (1994) 'Contradictions of support and self-help: views from providers of community health and social services to families with young children.' *Journal of Health and Social Care in the Community 2,* 1, 31–40.

Fielding, N. (1993) 'Ethnography.' In N. Gilbert (ed) *Researching Social Life.* London: Sage.

Fielding, N. and Fielding, J. (1986) *Linking Data.* London: Sage.

Gallagher, B., Creighton, S. and Gibbons, J. (1995) 'Ethical dilemmas in social research: no easy solutions.' *British Journal of Social Work 25,* 3, 295–311.

Howe, D. (1994) 'Modernity, postmodernity and social work.' *British Journal of Social Work 24,* 5, 513–532.

Hunter, D., McKeganey, N. and MacPherson, I. (1988) *Care of the Elderly: Policy and Practice.* Aberdeen: Aberdeen University Press.

Kazi, M. (1996) 'Centre for evaluation studies at the University of Huddersfield, England: a profile of activities in social work settings.' *Research on Social Work Practice 6,* 104–116.

Lewis, J. and Glennerster, H. (1996) *Implementing the New Community Care.* Buckingham: Open University Press.

MacDonald, C. and Myers, F. (1995) *Assessment and Care Management: the Practitioner Speaks.* Stirling: University of Stirling.

Manthorpe, J. and Twigg, J. (1995) 'Carers and care management.' *Baseline 59,* 4–18.

Manthorpe, J., Stanley, N., Bradley, G. and Alaszewski, A. (1996) 'Working together effectively? Assessing older people for community care services.' *Health Care in Later Life 1,* 3, 145–155.

McGrath, M., Ramcharan, P., Grant, G., Parry-Jones, B., Caldock, K. and Robinson, C. (1997) 'Care management in Wales: perceptions of front-line workers.' *Community Care, Management and Planning 5,* 1, 5–13.

Nolan, M.R., Grant, G. and Keady, J. (1996) *Understanding Family Care.* Buckingham: Open University Press.

Ovretveit, J. (1993) *Coordinating Community Care.* Buckingham: Open University Press.

Payne, M. (1995) *Social Work and Community Care.* London: Macmillan.

Rachman, R. (1995) 'Community care: changing the role of hospital social work.' *Journal of Health and Social Care in the Community 3,* 3, 163–172.

Sheppard, M. (1995) *Care Management and the New Social Work: a Critical Analysis.* London: Whiting and Birch.

Smith, G. and Cantley, C. (1984) 'Pluralistic evaluation.' In J. Lishman (ed) *Evaluation.* Aberdeen: University of Aberdeen.

Twigg, J. and Atkin, K. (1994) *Carers Perceived.* Buckingham: Open University Press.

Wilson, G. (1993) 'Users and providers: different perspectives on community care services.' *Journal of Social Policy 22,* 4, 507–527.

Wistow, G. (1995) 'Aspirations and realities: community care at the crossroads.' *Journal of Health and Social Care in the Community 3,* 3, 227–240.

CHAPTER 5

Elder Abuse Within a Residential Setting

Sheila Furness

Recognition of the presence of elder abuse has grown slowly. There is now a substantial literature which explores its different forms, tries to determine its extent and examines policies and practices to combat it (Biggs, Phillipson and Kingston 1992; Pritchard 1995; Decalmer and Glendenning 1995; Glendenning 1993; Eastman 1984, 1994). Questions about power and dependency are crucial to an understanding of the abuse of elderly people. Ageism persists at structural, cultural and personal levels and, as the proportion of retired people increases throughout the world, old age can be perceived as a burden on the state and on individual families. Negative attitudes and stereotypes surrounding old age lead to the marginalisation and disregard of the rights of elderly people, and particularly the very elderly, who may be quite unable to protect their own interests and not regarded as any political threat. Such attitudes may encourage only minimalist stances in social policy which seek to prevent the most extreme forms of physical cruelty or deprivation but neglect to promote the life chances of elderly people.

There have been some recent efforts to alert those who are responsible for commissioning and delivering services to elderly people to the extent of abuse and to develop procedures to deal with it. Throughout the 1980s Age Concern England campaigned to highlight the problem and the Social Services Inspectorate (1992, 1993) has published practice guidelines to confront elder abuse, particularly within domestic settings. Through case studies from practice Pritchard (1995) provides some practical guidance for health and social care workers. However, as McCreadie's (1996) helpful view of current research on elder abuse indicates, there has been surprisingly little exploration of the presence of abuse within residential care, apart from some general reviews of serious problems which have identified shortfalls in standards within the institutional setting (Biggs *et al.* 1995; Clough 1988). Although the vulnerability of people living in institutions is well recognised, and there has been much concern about the quality of residential care and how this may be improved, the role of mainstream staff in identifying and combating abuse has been little discussed.

What is Elder Abuse?

In part this lack of discussion may be because there has been no generally agreed definition of elder abuse despite various attempts to provide one (Action on Elder Abuse 1994; Eastman 1984, 1994; Fulmer and O'Malley 1987; Royal College of Nursing 1991). Definitions of abuse include the quite specific, for example 'misuse, perversion, unjust or corrupt practice, insulting or unkind speech' *(Oxford English Dictionary)* to the more wide ranging proposed by Eastman in 1984: 'systematic maltreatment – physical, emotional or financial – of an elderly person…which may take the form of physical assault, threatening behaviour, abandonment or sexual assault'. Further dimensions of whether the abuse was deliberate or unintentional consequences of neglect, described by the Royal College of Nursing in terms of 'active' or 'passive' abuse and consideration as to the severity of the abuse contribute to the difficulty of defining a complex phenomena.

Fulmer and O'Malley (1987) suggest another perspective; that all cases of abuse and neglect can be classed as inadequate care. They define elder abuse as 'actions of a caretaker that create unmet needs for the elderly person'. Neglect is defined as, 'the failure of an individual responsible for caretaking to respond adequately to established needs for care'. Inadequate care could be the result of abuse, neglect, lack of resources or services or ignorance.

My interest in elder abuse stems from my work as an inspector of residential care. As a professional employed to monitor and effectively control prescribed standards of care on behalf of a local authority, an opportunity arose to carry out some research. Practitioners are in a privileged position to be able to use their knowledge and expertise to contribute to the growing body of work around good practice in health and social care: As an inspector of residential care it is essential to make judgements about quality of care and quality of life of residents. In effect, inspection officers are evaluating practice in order to comment on good practice observed, as well as identifying areas of development and in more serious cases inadequate care. However, the impact of those judgements are restricted and localised. This study is an attempt to show how research does not have to be carried out solely by researchers and the valuable contribution that practitioners can make to promoting good practice.

This chapter describes a small study which explores residential staff's awareness of elderly abuse and their responses to incidents they observed. The study indicates some inconsistencies between attitudes to abuse and action to challenge abuse. The chapter then explores the ways in which the rights of vulnerable elderly people may be better protected and the quality of residential care improved.

Background

In the mid 1980s there was a massive increase in the number of private and voluntary residential and nursing homes for elderly people. In just four years over 3000 new homes opened. This was a response to the greater demand for residential care places prompted by changes in social security regulations which allowed elderly people with little capital to claim the fees payable to the home. This expansion in private and voluntary residential care was accompanied by a steady decline in local authority residential homes for elderly people, partly because the government wanted, through its community care policies, to promote a mixed economy of welfare. It was also the case that the costs of voluntary and private residential care were usually less than that provided by the local authority. By 1995, there were 1500 voluntary run homes and 8500 private homes (Health and Personal Social Services Statistics 996).

There has been long-standing concern about the standard of residential care for elderly people. Over thirty years ago Townsend (1962) described conditions of public care which were reminiscent of the work houses of the nineteenth century and, despite legislative and other attempts to tighten regulations and inspection procedures, scandals in residential care have continued (Clough 1988). Enquiries have revealed both extreme types of abuse and also serious shortcomings in quality of care. It is now widely accepted that some of these shortcomings, for example, serious failings to respect people's privacy and dignity, can amount to abuse.

On a more positive side there have been considerable efforts on the part of government and voluntary agencies to improve standards of residential care and to try and ensure, as the Wagner Committee envisaged, that it should be a positive choice. As a result of this interest and concern about promoting and identifying good practice in residential care, a code of practice, *Home Life*

(Centre for Policy on Ageing 1984), has been adopted and, more importantly, accepted as a baseline of standard within the Registered Homes Tribunal. A companion practice guide *A Better Home Life* (1996) is also available. Another influential model outlining key standards for good practice in residential homes was published by the Social Services Inspectorate (SSI 1989) and is widely used by inspection officers and managers of residential homes.

The Registered Homes Act 1984 empowered local authority social service departments to register and inspect all private and voluntary residential homes providing accommodation and personal care to four or more adults with a wide range of different needs.

With the introduction of the NHS and Community Care Act 1990, registration and inspection units were expected to become more independent of social service departments in order to carry out new, 'even-handed' functions of inspection of public sector residential care of children and adults. The Registered Homes (Amendment) Act 1991 included the registration but not inspection of small homes, where less than four residents were accommodated. Griffiths (1988) in his recommendations had extended inspection to small homes but this was not taken up under the Act.

Health authorities have also established their own, separate units responsible for the registration and inspection of nursing homes under Part II of the Registered Homes Act 1984.

The implementation of the independent inspection required by legislation has not been straightforward, with joint working between health and social service units being long debated within the Department of Health. The Burgner Report (1996) considered a number of options, including transfering responsibility for this monitoring arm to local authorities chief executive offices or moving the relevant units to local trading standards services. A white paper on these matters is expected.

Judgements about the Quality of Care

All this has been accompanied by strenuous efforts to identify and promote quality of care which takes account of people's environment, their health and emotional well-being and which respects them as self-determining individuals. Bland *et al.* (1992) showed that excellent quality of care, measured on all significant dimensions, could be found in residential homes for elderly people in the private, voluntary and public sectors. However, this study also showed that there was a much wider range in the standards of care in the voluntary and particularly private sectors, with greater overall consistency in local authority homes. These uneven standards present major challenges for local authorities which are the purchasers of care with important implications for their registration and inspection functions.

Making judgements about quality of care is complex. In part this reflects the subjective nature of views about the needs of elderly people and what counts as good and bad care. Even when checklists are used Gibbs and Sinclair (1992) have shown that inspectors may fail to make reliable judgements about quality although the researchers also identified some general correlates of good quality care (Gibbs and Sinclair 1994).

The role of inspection not only demands inspectors to have a good working knowledge of key pieces of legislation but also to be able to interpret and apply local guidance on registration and inspection within a framework of professional knowledge and codes of good practice. Inspectors have a legal responsibility to ensure that residents receive minimum standards of good care and work with managers to promote and improve care practices.

A number of homes, in their quest for quality, have pursued a British Standard ISO 9000 certification award as recommended by the UK Registered Nursing Home Association and the British Federation of Care Home Proprietors. Although quality assurance systems contribute to improving care practices, there must be a note of caution that any quality management system cannot guarantee total excellence and an absence of abuse (Clough 1988; Secretary of State for Health 1992). Any system which relies on checking outcomes can be in danger of overlooking less tangible aspects of performance.

Furthermore, since local authorities have discretion in drawing up requirements for registration of the building and the person deemed fit to own and manage a home there are wide variations of requirements for registration between local authorities. In addition, although legislation has strengthened the role of local authorities in regulating and monitoring care homes, and the registered homes tribunal system was introduced to ease and speed up the legal processes for deregistration, there are still difficulties with enforcement of certain requirements. Experience also shows that the final sanction of deregistration can be very problematic.

This briefly is the context for understanding residential staff's perceptions of elder abuse and their response to it. First, while extremes of abuse may be easy to recognise there can be no disagreement about the continuum of good and poor quality care and the extent to which poor care should count as abuse. Second, there can be doubts about the efficacy of the monitoring and regulation procedures which may make people query the value of complaining.

The Study

As an inspector of residential care I was much aware of these problems and the various strategies that might be needed to address them. This study was the first step in identifying the level of awareness amongst staff of abuse and procedures for complaint. This study was modest in scope which meant it was feasible for it to be undertaken by someone whose main responsibilities were not for research. Several lessons were learnt during the conduct of this research which would not be difficult to incorporate in any further similar studies.

The study focused on residential homes within one local authority. The homes were randomly selected from a total of 102 registered private and voluntary homes and twenty-four local authority homes for elderly people.

The sample

Twenty questionnaires were sent to each one of eighteen private, two voluntary and six local authority residential homes. The questionnaires were sent to the manager of each home with a covering letter and enclosing a stamped addressed envelope for replies. The letter stated that the aim of the research was to enquire about staff's perception of abuse and to identify potential barriers which prevented staff from making complaints. In subsequent interviews with staff consideration was given to ways of overcoming those barriers so that staff would challenge poor practice or report their concerns.

Out of a total of 520 questionnaires sent out to care staff, ninety-nine replies were returned (17.5% of the total). All respondents could remain anonymous but forty-seven staff provided names and addresses indicating that they could be contacted to be interviewed as part of this research.

This rather low return was the consequence of a number of factors, some of which could be avoided in another study. First, as the size of homes can vary from four to forty beds, the staff team will also vary in direct correlation to the size of the home. Therefore, it is likely that within the sample were those homes only employing between eight to twelve supervisory and care staff, so one possible reason for the low response rate was that a substantial number of the questionnaires were superfluous.

Second, care staff working in residential homes tend to be female, poorly paid, and have low status (Dalley 1988). As a consequence the turnover of staff can be high. Therefore, the interest in completing the questionnaires could have been affected by staff changes.

The third factor which could have affected response was that completed questionnaires could have been read by the proprietor, manager or other staff. In fact, one member of staff completed one questionnaire which was sent with all the other responses and then sent a second separately. She had concerns about a supervisor at the home but felt unable to take this up with the home's management. She was not aware that she could complain to social services and so it was opportune that the questionnaire prompted her to take this action. Others undertaking a similar study need to consider sending each individual a separate questionnaire and stamped addressed envelope. This would ensure confidentiality and – it is hoped – a higher response rate.

Finally, although this study was supposed to be separate from the researcher's role as an inspector, some staff may not have completed the questionnaire because of fears about how the information could be used.

Experience shows that research in this area is a sensitive topic, as defined by Lee and Reazelli (1990), in that it can pose a substantial threat to staff and can be problematic for the researcher and the researched in raising questions about confidentiality, dissemination and action. Plans for such studies have therefore to be carefully made and usually a large number of interested individuals will need to be consulted.

The staff group

Over 90 per cent of the respondents to the questionnaire were female and nearly all of these were of white British origin. Nearly one-third were under twenty-one and another quarter were aged between twenty-one and twenty-five.

Nearly two-thirds of staff indicated that they held no care-related qualifications or received any formal training. About one-third had attended a range of training courses from short three-day courses to part-time courses over two-year periods. Some courses were accredited through colleges; others were for personal knowledge and skills development. Some staff named one course whereas others had attended several courses.

In terms of experience of care work, nearly a fifth – the highest number – had up to one year's experience; a nearly equal number had up to two years' experience. Only 15 per cent had up to five years' experience. The low level of experience was consistent with the age group of the sample.

The questionnaire

The questionnaire sought to identify staff's understanding of abuse and what action individuals would take when a specific abusive act occurred; the example given was a resident being slapped by a staff member. The questionnaire also enquired into staff's understanding of the complaints system. Care staff knew that the researcher was employed as an inspection officer, but that any information given was confidential unless the respondent indicated otherwise. One reply was treated as a formal complaint and investigated accordingly.

Some Findings

Recognising abuse

The relevant question was 'Can you give specific examples of the type of treatment of residents which you consider to be wrong?'

Over two-thirds of staff gave three to four examples of what they considered to be poor treatment of residents. Examples included ignoring wishes, shouting, violence, rough handling, force feeding, leaving wet, giving no choice, using restraint, neglect, stealing, invading of privacy. All the examples given fell within broad categories of physical, mental, verbal and financial abuse and were evidence of a disregard of residents' rights in terms of privacy, dignity, independence, choice and respect.

More worrying, the remaining staff – nearly a third – did not provide any examples of poor treatment of residents. If those staff, for whatever reason, are not able to identify abuse or ill treatment then they will not be able to take any action to challenge it and, in addition, they may collude or be a party to unintentional abuse.

The absence of research in the UK on the identification of abuse means that it is impossible to judge whether this level is typical. However, an American study of staff in nursing homes reported that 81 per cent of nurses had observed psychological abuse and 36 per cent physical abuse. Furthermore, 10 per cent admitted physical and 40 per cent psychological abuse (Bennett and Kingston 1993).

Another question described a specific example of abuse (slapping a resident) and gave options of the action to be taken. All staff indicated that they would take some action. The preferred option of three-quarters of the staff was to report it to the person in charge and also say something to the person concerned.

In the eight follow-up interviews with care staff, who had also completed questionnaires, all indicated that they would report any matters of concern. Of the interviewees only two admitted in the questionnaire to witnessing things which caused them concern. However, when the staff were interviewed I found that four out of eight had in fact witnessed some incident of abuse. Anxiety about the confidentiality of the questionnaire returns, referred to earlier, may account for this discrepancy.

Making complaints

Although all respondents indicated that they would report any matters of concern, in fact only one had taken such action. There appears to be a reluctance for people to complain. Pillemer and Finkelhor (1988) identified from a telephone survey in North America that only one in fourteen abuse cases had been reported. In this study, even though respondents indicated that they would complain, this had not been followed through. Another example of this discrepancy between attitudes and action can be found in the study by Dowling reported in this book (Chapter 8).

There appear to be several constraints on individuals as to whether to report concerns or not. First, the person has to recognise an abuse; this is dependent on his or her awareness of the rights of residents and understanding of good practice and correct care procedures. Second, the individual needs to have confidence that the concern will be dealt with in a proper and fair manner with due regard for all parties involved.

Complaints procedures aim to make it easier for people to voice their concerns about standards. However, in a number of recent notorious cases of abuse in institutions which have been subject to public enquiries, it is clear that those people who do speak out are often at risk of losing their jobs, facing disciplinary procedures and being ostracised by colleagues. A legal charity Public Concern at Work has been set up to advise and support employees and employers about handling concerns at work. The charity has been instrumental in pressing for legislation to protect whistleblowers. Complaints procedures devised by local authorities and other bodies generally require complainants to be named. However, this can act as a deterrent to the person making a complaint, whether this be a resident, relative, member of staff or even care professionals, usually stemming from some fear of retribution.

A further problem is the fact that some residents' or carers' complaints may be discounted because of their alleged unsound state of mind or because they are considered trouble makers. The recent exposure of alleged abuse at Ashworth secure hospital only reached media attention after the complainant sent sensitive material to an MP who alerted the Secretary of Health to the case. Apparently the complainant, an ex-patient, had made numerous complaints to hospital management which had not been investigated.

Even though there is a legal requirement under the NHS and Community Care Act 1990 for public bodies such as the health service and local authorities to institute complaints procedures, complaints can still be mishandled or dismissed by those responsible for their implementation.

Students

A further example of problems associated with the status of complainants concerns students. Students often bring a fresh perspective and are in a good position to observe poor or abusive practice. To qualify as competent practitioners of social work, students have to demonstrate their understanding and contribution to tackling oppression. Much has been written about the value base of social work in terms of respect for the individual (Biestek 1971; CCETSW 1976, 1996; Horne 1988). There is an expectation that social work students will demonstrate commitment to the value base stated in CCETSW's 1996 *Assuring Quality* document by challenging poor practice. This could arise as a result of 'a passive neglect of the principles of good practice' or 'an active betrayal of the basic values on which the organisation is supposedly based' (Wardhaugh and Wilding 1993, p.5).

Experience shows that students can identify areas of poor practice but that they often need considerable support from tutors and practice teachers to pursue those concerns. Students have a real reluctance to challenge some issues, particularly when they feel that their assessment can be affected by making complaints.

If social work students have difficulty in challenging bad practice, then it is equally likely that untrained or unqualified care staff face similar difficulties.

The Nature of Complaints

This study also reviewed complaints made to one registration and inspection unit of a local authority in 1992. Sixty-three complaints were received during this period, the vast majority in respect of private homes. However, since there is a local authority complaints procedure it maybe that other complaints were made about local authority homes which were dealt with directly by social services managers. There may also have been some further complaints to private and voluntary homes which were dealt with by the management.

The majority of people making complaints were staff and relatives of residents. Other significant groups were ex-members of staff, social workers and anonymous complainants. Analysis of the nature of the complaints illustrates some difficulty in distinguishing out of context between incidents which can truly be regarded as abusive and those indicating poor quality of care. For example, complaints categorised as psychological abuse included the few incidences of verbal abuse but also other complaints of 'poor staff attitude'. In addition, there were examples of neglect in which it is difficult to distinguish between abuse and inadequate quality of care, for example the poor physical standards of a home might include a wide range of short-comings. Complaints about food could range from subjective assessments of what is palatable to clear examples of insufficient or very poor quality meals. Complaints about violation of rights, such as lack of independence or choice of bed time, also indicate shortcomings in quality of care without necessarily pointing to specific abuse. On the other hand, complaints of physical abuse, for example beating or being hit by staff and misuse of money or property are clear examples of direct abuse.

In this study the highest number of complaints, more than a fifth, concerned lack of food or poor quality staff. The next highest category focused on the poor attitude of the proprietor or staff followed by complaints about physical standards and hygiene and then misuse of money or property. These findings are consistent with other studies which have reported a higher rate of psychological than physical abuse (Beaulieu 1992; Foner 1994; Lee-Treweek 1994; Pillemer and Moore 1989).

Instances of psychological abuse or poor quality of care deserve further attention. It is much easier for inspection officers to comment on issues such as the physical standards and cleanliness of a home as these can be readily observed. Where there is a complaint about food quality, for example, some authorities allow inspectors to take meals with residents as and when appropriate and, although judgements about the quality of food can be problematic, food supplies can be considered as can the use of fresh or frozen food, the portions, the presentation, the choice, the cook's qualifications and so on. However, it is unlikely that inspectors will witness verbal abuse during a visit and for complaints of this nature they must rely on the fact that residents or witnesses will report it. Psychological abuse may be difficult to interpret out of context, however, although judgements might be made about the overall attitude of proprietors and staff to their work and to the residents in their care.

Preventing Abuse and Improving Quality of Care

When abuse is identified as causing serious risk to the life, health or well-being of residents the ultimate sanction is an application for an emergency closure order (Section 11 of the Residential Homes Act 1984). Notice can be sought from a magistrate to cancel the registration of the proprietor or manager although this person has a right of appeal to an appropriate council committee and thereafter to a Registered Homes Tribunal.

Tribunals hear appeals from residential home's registered owners and managers against local authority social service departments (SSDs) and from owners of nursing homes against health authorities (HAs) under Part II of the Residential Homes Act (RHA) 1984.

Although the tribunal system was introduced to give easier access on a more informal basis to legal procedures, witnesses can feel intimidated and damaged by the ordeal of being cross-examined as if in a court of law by solicitors, barristers and even tribunal panel members, and this process can act as a deterrent to people making serious complaints.

Emergency closure orders are rarely sought. In the period from 1985 to 1991 there were 135 appeals heard by registered homes tribunals against SSD decisions and twenty-nine appeals against HA decisions. There appears to be a large difference between the number of homes served with deregistration notices by social services and those by health authorities and this would be worthy of further research.

It is likely that the promotion of a flourishing independent sector alongside good quality public services will remain government policy and that the private and voluntary sector will continue as the main providers of residential and nursing care. This means that it is essential that there is adequate funding to resource the regulation and monitoring of those services. The Social Services Inspectorate have found that a number of local authorities are not meeting the statutory requirements of two visits per year to homes requiring inspection (SSI 1993, 1994, 1995), which indicates that current resources are not sufficient, particularly if local authorities are to work with residential homes to improve quality of care rather than simply identifying shortcomings.

There is a debate about whether registration and inspection units should remain as a regulatory function of local authorities or become totally independent. For some time central government has been considering different options, one of which is possibly further deregulation and cuts in inspection visits. However, the number of complaints received by a representative local authority are significant enough to suggest that there is a need for a body to continue to regulate residential care. To be effective standards have to be seen to be maintained if inspection officers and the role of the registration and inspection unit are to retain their credibility. This includes strengthening the independence of the units. There is a conflict of interest with the present position of units under the auspices of Social Service Departments. The Department of Health Circular LAC (94) 16 emphasises the need for units to be structurally independent of managers directly responsible for social services. As managers of units report to directors of SSDs, then that relationship could influence decisions or action taken by the unit.

All health and social care services, whether provided by statutory or independent agencies, should be open to scrutiny. There needs to be changes in legislation to take account of this need to regulate a range of community care provision. Statutory powers of legal intervention must be granted to registration and inspection bodies so that appropriate action can be instigated as and when necessary. In the present climate of cutbacks in the provision of statutory services and an increasing reliance on the independent sector to provide care services, then there needs to be adequate regulation and monitoring of these diverse services. Domiciliary services, for example, are not required to be inspected by law; however, some authorities have taken steps to include those services within the inspection remit.

Inspectors need to be recruited for their knowledge and expertise of particular client groups and care settings. There also needs to be a closer working relationship between health and social care services. Both residential and nursing home settings should concentrate on providing a holistic approach to care (Centre for Policy on Ageing 1996) so that the social, emotional, recreational, cultural, ethnic and religious needs of residents are recognised and balanced with their medical needs and the practical assistance needed for them to carry out daily living tasks. This can be achieved through joint registration and inspection of those homes by health and social care professionals and standards from the Department of Health, which underpin all forms of continuing care (CPA 1997). There are also major implications for basic and continuing education and training for all levels of staff. The useful training materials produced by Pritchard (1995, 1996) and Biggs and Phillipson (1992) are excellent contributions.

The media continues to expose the horrifying accounts of continual abuse of both children and adults that has occurred in a number of institutions over recent years. It is now clear that the abusers were well known but that staff and victims were prevented from challenging these very serious malpractices. Responsibility for detection cannot just lie with inspectors of those services; there needs, as this study has indicated, to be much greater awareness of abuse within residential care and the ways in which it can be identified and challenged.

Legislation to protect whistleblowers could give some support to encourage individuals to speak out about their concerns. When individuals have exposed corruption in care, some have subsequently expressed regret as the toll on their families and personal health and well-being has far outweighed the rewards they perhaps envisaged for championing 'justice' issues. Many others would have remained silent and not got involved. It is crucial to foster a culture in which it is acceptable to raise concerns inside the organisation and for appropriate and responsible action to be taken to address the problems.

A change in culture is necessary not only within the organisation but also within the wider society. A passive attitude to the abuse of elderly people and the toleration of poor quality care are not acceptable. There has to be more responsibility for safeguarding each other's rights and a willingness to challenge others' actions which contribute to causing harm and distress to others. Research studies of this kind described here can be a first step in raising the awareness of responsible people and promoting debate about how abuse can be prevented and care improved.

References

Action on Elder Abuse (1994) *Working Paper No.1*. London: Action on Elder Abuse.

Beaulieu, M. (1992) 'Elder abuse: levels of scientific knowledge in Quebec.' *Journal of Elder Abuse and Neglect 4*, (1/2), 135–149.

Biestek, F. (1971) *The Casework Relationship*. London: Allen and Unwin.

Bennett, G. and Kingston, P. (1993) *Elder Abuse*. London: Chapman and Hall.

Biggs, S., Phillipson, C. and Kingston, P. (1995) *Elder Abuse in Perspective*. Buckingham: Open University Press.

Biggs, S. and Phillipson, C. (1992) *Understanding Elder Abuse: a Training Manual for the Helping Professions*. London: Longman.

Bland, R., Cheetham, J., Lapsley, I. and Llewellyn, S. (1992) *Residential Homes for Elderly People: their Costs and Quality*. Edinburgh: HMSO.

Burgner Report (1996) *The Regulation and Inspection of Social Services*. London: DoH/HMSO.

CCETSW (1976) Paper 13. *Values in Social Work*. London: CCETSW.

CCETSW (1996) *Assuring Quality*. London: CCETSW.

Centre for Policy on Ageing (1984) *Home Life*. London: CPA.

Centre for Policy on Ageing (1996) *A Better Home Life*. London: CPA.

Centre for Policy on Ageing (1997) *Achieving a Better Home Life*. London: CPA.

Clough, R. (1988) *Scandals in Residential Care*. London: National Institute of Social Work.

Dalley, G. (1988) *Ideologies of Caring*. Basingstoke: Macmillan.

Decalmer, P. and Glendenning, F. (eds) (1994) *The Mistreatment of Elderly People*. London: Sage.

Department of Health (1984) *The Registered Homes Act*. London: HMSO.

Department of Health (1990) *The NHS and Community Care Act*. London: HMSO.

Department of Health (1991) The Registered Homes (Amendment) Act. London: HMSO.

Eastman, M. (ed) (1984) *Old Age Abuse*. London: Age Concern England.

Eastman, M. (ed) (1994) *Old Age Abuse*. London: Age Concern England/Chapman and Hall.

Foner, N. (1994) 'Nursing home aides: saints or monsters?' *The Gerontologist 34*, 2, 245–250.

Fulmer, T. and O'Malley, T. (1987) *Inadequate Care of the Elderly: a Health Care Perspective on Abuse and Neglect*. New York: Springer.

Gibbs, I. and Sinclair, I. (1992) 'Consistency: a pre-requisite for inspecting old people's homes?' *British Journal of Social Work 22*, 535–550.

Gibbs, I. and Sinclair, I. (1994) 'Residential care for elderly people: correlates of quality.' *Ageing and Society 12*, 4, 463–482.

Glendenning, F. (1993) 'What is elder abuse and neglect?' In P. Decalmer and F. Glendenning (eds) *The Mistreatment of Elderly People*. London: Sage.

Griffiths, R. (1988) *Community Care: Agenda for Action*. London: HMSO.

Health and Personal Social Services Statistics (1996) London: HMSO.

Horne, M. (1988) *Values in Social Work*. Aldershot: Wildwood House.

Lee, R. and Reazelli, C.M. (1990) 'The problems of researching sensitive topics.' *American Behavioural Science 33*, 5, 510–528.

Lee-Treweek, G. (1994) 'Bedroom abuse: the hidden work in a nursing home.' *Generations Review 4*, 1, 2–4.

McCreadie, C. (1996) *Elder Abuse: Update on Research.* London: Age Concern Institute of Gerontology, King's College.

Pillemer, K.A. and Finkelhor, D. (1988) 'The prevalence of elder abuse: a random sample survey.' *The Gerontologist 28*, 1, 51–7.

Pillemer, K.A. and Moore, D. (1989) 'Abuse of patients in nursing homes: findings from a survey of staff.' *The Gerontologist 29*, 3, 314–320.

Pritchard, J. (1995) *The Abuse of Older People: a Training Manual for Detection and Prevention.* London: Jessica Kingsley Publishers.

Pritchard, J. (1996) *Working with Elder Abuse: a Training Manual for Home Care, Residential and Day Care Staff.* London: Jessica Kingsley Publishers.

Royal College of Nursing (1991) *Guidelines for Nurses: Abuse and Older People.* London: Royal College of Nursing.

Secretary of State for Health (1992) *Report of the Committee of Enquiry into Complaints About Ashworth Hospital.* Cm 2028–1. London: HMSO.

Social Services Inspectorate (1989) *Homes are for Living In.* London: HMSO.

Social Services Inspectorate/DoH (1992) *Confronting Elder Abuse.* London: HMSO.

Social Services Inspectorate/DoH (1993) *No Longer Afraid: The Safeguard of Older People in the Domestic Setting.* London: HMSO.

Social Services Inspectorate (1993) *Social Services Department Inspection Units: the First Eighteen Months.* London: Department of Health.

Social Services Inspectorate (1994) *Social Services Department Inspection Units Report of an Inspection of the Work of Inspection Units in 27 Local Authorities.* London: Department of Health.

Social Services Inspectorate (1995) *Social Services Department Inspection Units: Third Overview.* London: Department of Health.

Townsend, P. (1962) *The Last Refuge: a Survey of Residential Institutions and Homes for the Aged in England and Wales.* London: Routledge and Kegan Paul.

Wagner Committee (1988) *Residential Care: a Positive Choice.* London: HMSO.

Wardhaugh, J. and Wilding, P. (1993) 'Towards an explanation of the corruption of care.' *Critical Social Policy 13*, 1, 4–31.

CHAPTER 6

Elements of Risk and Supervision
Evaluating Outcome Decisions

Peter Burke

In this chapter I report on an empirical examination of work undertaken by two fieldwork teams and explain the methods used for data collection. The idea for the research resulted from my view that fieldwork practice in social work would vary according to the role and responsibilities accepted by the workers involved. This thought was sparked by an early study by Goldberg and Fruin (1976) which grouped referrals into broad categories, including requests for information, advice for services or for investigative work. However, in order to make an examination possible I initially identified categories of referrals reflecting a full range of user needs. The hallmark of such an approach considers social work as involving multiple activities – from practical service provision, such as providing aids to daily living, to complex risk assessments, which might include life-threatening situations. In all, the complexities of practice were reduced, following an examination of 312 referrals, to three response groupings: service delivery, advisory, and risk work. How this was achieved is explained below, and reflected by the referral groupings shown in Table 6.1. I also examine the supervisory input within these groupings to demonstrate variations in outcome achieved by different staff groupings.

Research which examines the relationship between referrals, allocation and case outcome, is compatible with current government policies (Department of Health *et al.* 1989) which particularly concern the need to monitor performance (p.42). However, because no coherent model of practice exists which allows for direct comparison between outcome decisions, it is difficult to evaluate outcomes in individual cases, and a system has to be devised which makes comparisons between outcome decisions possible. Social work includes a generalised repertoire of practitioner skills, and the application of those skills in different practice settings requires an attempt to separate the skills required and to evaluate the outcome decisions reached.

In this study the practice of social work was considered to be directly influenced by the case allocation system organised by the teams examined and by the nature of the cases themselves. The cases were monitored for up to one year to gather sufficient data for meaningful analysis, but to qualify for inclusion in the study an outcome decision had to be agreed between social worker and supervisor. It should be clear that an outcome decision was the professional judgement reached at the conclusion of work with the user, and was recorded on case notes to that effect. An example of the individual case record used by the supervisor is shown in Figure 6.1. Each of the thirteen social workers involved kept a record for all 312 allocated cases and produced the record, in a folder, for discussion during supervision with a senior colleague.

Identifying Response Characteristics

The individual case record includes agreed, albeit brief, comments on the social worker's involvement with the user. Concluding work with a user does not mean that further work is not necessary, only that at the stage of file closure intervention ceased and that this was agreed between the worker and supervisor. In such circumstances it would be expected that the user is informed of the decision.

It was clear that any examination of the 312 case details required some summary analysis to make sense of what was going on. This was achieved by examining each referral to determine common characteristics, initially looking at the information available on each one and then matching similar types of request. For example, requests for accommodation were divided between those for reception of a child into care and other accommodation needs such as a request for a place in local authority hostel or home for elderly people. Altogether twenty groupings were identified (see Table 6.1); common characteristics within the referrals enabled the initial responses to be classified as risk, advice or service requirements, a judgment finally based on case information provided by the worker involved.

All residential requests (including reception of a child into care and other types of residential resources such as hostel accommodation or day care) were annotated as service delivery work, whilst child abuse investigations were grouped with users referred because of depression as risk cases. Requests for

---

Individual Case Record

Name of Social Worker and Status   *Jo Smith Level 2 SW*

Date of Allocation   *22/2/89*
Date of Closure   *5/3/89*

Name of User (plus age)   *Richard Jones aged 8 yrs*

Reason for Referral
Richard is non-attentive at school,
always tired and listless, there are suspected
difficulties at home (referred by head teacher)

Supervisory notes (comment with date)
Home assessment visit: parents recently separated   *28/2/89*
Father living in lodgings, son distressed at break-up
Further visit – family re-united
Social work involvement: no further action required   *1/3/89*

Outcome at Case Closure (please tick the most appropriate box below)
1. *Resolved.*   ☐
2. *Partly resolved (some matters still outstanding,*
   viz: reallocation to another team/service).   ☐
3. *Not resolved or further review required.*   ☐

Figure 6.1: Example of Individual Case Record

---

various types of support were categorised as advisory work. Clearly, the classifications were not always straightforward because referrals were often not singular by nature; in the case of accommodation difficulties relating to a child absconder, for example, the referral might be classified as a risk case because of the risk to the child. My initial report (Burke 1990) examines the make-up of this three-way classification; subsequent accounts (Burke 1997a) took into account critiques of social work research and suggestions contained in the work of Goda and Smeeton (1993), and re-examined the basic need for supervision of cases which demonstrated risk characteristics.

Table 6.1: Referral information

Frequency	Referral information	Type of request Risk	Advice	Service
7	Child behavioural problem	X		
4	Divorcing parents/child access		X	
20	Reception into care (child)			X
10	Child abuse	X		
29	General family advice		X	
22	Financial difficulties		X	
19	Residential care (adult)			X
14	Day care			X
3	Hospital liaison required	X		
48	Registration as disabled person			X
41	Requests for aids and adaptations			X
6	Disabled car badge/buss pass			X
4	Medical problem (social worker requested)	X		
35	Assessment/review			X
5	Child in care/home on trial			X
19	User at risk through physical disability/circumstances	X		
13	Housing problems		X	
7	Depressed client	X		
2	Unemployment associated difficulties		X	
4	Financial difficulties			X
Total:	**312 cases**	**55**	**74**	**183**

The groupings of referrals were reconsidered following reference to the literature and the 'face value' characteristics. This process indicated that service delivery, advice giving, and risk problems were reasonable divisions for examining outcome decisions. The intention behind this examination process was to consider whether particular theoretical techniques of practice could be identified at the referral stage so, for example, that a 'risk' case might be identified with 'crisis intervention' reflecting an appropriate response characteristic, or other referrals with task-centred or behavioural work although the last of these seemed too narrow in scope to be identified as the team's theoretical perspective. In the context of this study, the individual social workers' theoretical orientation was non-specific or at least not apparent to the researcher.

The key characteristics of each referral was used to apply theory retrospectively to the work being done. This assumes social workers conceptualise about practice in their day-to-day work, albeit not necessarily recording their work in a way that lends itself to data analysis. Theory is considered here as derived from practice, and practice as dependent on the requests from users to whom social workers offer their services.

Practice Groupings and Theoretical Approaches

Since the early 1970s service delivery and crisis work have increasingly been part of social work practice and represent a polarisation of the practice skills required to deal with user problems (Goldberg, Gibbons and Sinclair 1985; Mattinson and Sinclair 1979). In this chapter 'service delivery' specifically refers to practical services and 'crisis responses' to users at personal risk of any kind. Naturally, a range of casework practices fits between these extremes, although the evidence from research on intake and neighbour-hood teams (Gostick and Scott 1982; Hadley and McGrath 1984) indicates that a two-level service of quick response crisis work and longer term work of a more routine nature is a practical necessity. Beresford and Croft (1986) examined the trend for certain local authorities to reduce secondment programmes on qualifying social work courses because of research evidence which identified quick response and task-based work as being more effective in meeting the needs of the majority of users (e.g. Goldberg and Warburton 1979) and explained how such a view would lead to deskilled practitioners in the social work profession. It is sometimes argued that most user situations need only a quick response, and that such a response not only provides a relatively straightforward resolution to the users' needs but often – as with crisis intervention in particular – addresses the most problematic situations and requires the highest level of professional skill. The need to examine the theoretical base of practice with problematic cases is imperative; con-sequently, in what follows, I examine the divide between crisis work, representing problematic cases, and service delivery work of a more routine nature.

Crisis Work

If one is to understand the need for a social work response when a user is experiencing some type of crisis, it is helpful to examine the theory of crisis intervention which, according to McGee (1984), originally developed from work linked to the notion of suicide prevention. Coulshed (1988) relates crisis theory to social work practice and refers to Caplan's (1964) four stages of crisis to locate the user's reaction to stress and the role required of the worker. The method, described by Rapoport (1970) as brief treatment, requires time-limited involvement and concerns situations where there is physical or emotional risk to the user; thus the social worker, therapist or volunteer responds at the point of crisis when the user most requires help and is most amenable to directed intervention. The objective of social work intervention is to relieve the user's stress and to facilitate a more adaptive response to future difficulties.

Risk is used here to represent an agency view: in this context it incorporates the need for crisis intervention when identified through the initial referral to the agency, and is applicable to all user groups as discussed above. However, an agency view of risk is qualitatively different to risk experienced by the user as a form of crisis; the two areas should be separated in practice.

Service Delivery

This is concerned with providing practical services and is conceptualised thus by Middleman and Goldberg (1973). Service delivery is more concerned with the service required than with the cause that resulted in the request for a particular service. This is attractive to social workers, according to Giller and Morris (1981), because it fits in with fixing criteria for resource provision where the precise circumstances or conditions under which a user qualifies for services are defined. The emotional aspects of need are not necessarily a precondition; field workers thus have a more structured approach to their work, and areas of work that have been accomplished are readily identifiable. The consequence of such action relates to Foster's (1983) view that social workers become professional gatekeepers to services required by their users. Accordingly, the services themselves become systematically rationed and overtly and explicitly dependent on agency resources.

A service delivery based response to social work intervention was criticised by Huxley, Korer and Tolly (1987) because they found that social workers also responded to the emotional needs of users when dealing with requests for services of a practical nature. This equates with the view that meeting service delivery needs cannot exclude the provision of support. The debate tends to suggest that service delivery and support co-exist as part of the ideology of social provision, a central tenet of community care.

The extreme positions of crisis intervention as a form of risk-taking and of service delivery overlap because 'risk' in terms of an urgent need for agency intervention, for example in responding to the needs of a child who has been abused, can be considered a form of 'service provision' by the agency. Practice differentiates between service delivery in which a service is provided on request, and risk in which the situation of the user generates concern and priority because of the need for intervention to protect the individual. Any analysis of referral data is readily clarified by the nature of the request made for social work involvement, but entails a little more detail than reflected in Table 6.1 and illustrates the 'hands-on' part of this research.

What is considered a risk situation can, in certain situations, also require a crisis response – risk being a broader based conceptualisation of a user's difficulties than crisis intervention. Crises intervention is more narrowly defined in relation to an individual's responsiveness to directive intervention; risk includes 'risk-taking' by the agency in making decisions about a course of action. Service might subsume risk, but I have chosen to differentiate between the two according to the request for social work intervention indicated on the referral. Such issues do not discredit the attempt to classify referral groupings; indeed, such an endeavour may help to identify more specific types of practice required when initially becoming involved with a service user.

The purpose of using categories is to create parameters for a research study. The evidence which is presented does no more than demonstrate a practical research application; the issues raised will help those interested in research to consider risk factors affecting social workers' intervention and the need for support systems for social workers undertaking difficult and complex work.

Results

An examination of the findings from this study show that the relationship between problem response categories (service, advice and risk cases) and outcome achieved varied under specific conditions: viz, high or low status worker and low or high frequency of supervision. Earlier findings from this research (Burke 1990) found an association between user categories and outcome decisions. This chapter explains the methods used to generate data, demonstrates how that data is relevant to social work practice and revisits its findings reported in Burke (1997a) concerning its need for supervising activity for social workers dealing with risk cases.

Discussion on the tables focuses on the trends identified therein. In Tables 6.2 and 6.3 an analysis of the problem groupings and outcome was made for qualified and unqualified social workers. In Tables 6.4 and 6.5, problem groupings and outcome are examined differentiating between low or high supervision rates. In the examination of supervisory activity, low supervision equates with three supervisory meetings or less. The value of three supervision sessions was selected after considering the mean value for supervision of 3.5 with a standard deviation of 3.3, the latter indicating that the data was skewed towards higher rates of supervision. Statistically evenly balanced tables would be preferable for analysis but, impressionistically, the value selected for supervision equated more with the day-to-day operation of a social work office. The issue of supervision remains debatable, and with hindsight I would have chosen a more statistically valid approach to the study. Consequently, I report findings as indicative of trends intending to raise debate rather than to offer irrefutable empirical evidence.

User problems, outcome and social worker qualification

If, as argued by Howe (1986), the nature of user problems and the status of the social worker involved are associated, then social workers with greater experience and/or level of qualification should be more assured in the outcome decisions they reach than less experienced colleagues.

It is worth noting that the results shown in Table 6.2 are statistically significant, indicating an association in the table between problem response categories and outcome for qualified social workers undertaking intervention work. Of the 163 cases overall, some 24 per cent were not resolved. The percentages of not resolved cases within the problem categories were: risk 28 per cent, advisory 35 per cent and service 16 per cent. It seems that advisory cases were the least likely to achieve case resolution, albeit that a partially resolved category exists which included 49 per cent service cases.

Table 6.2: User problems and outcome (qualified social workers)

Outcome	Problem response category			
	Risk n(%)	Advisory n(%)	Service n(%)	Total n(%)
Resolved	16 (44)	22 (48)	28 (35)	66(40)
Partially resolved	10 (28)	8 (17)	40 (49)	58(36)
Not resolved	10 (28)	16 (35)	13 (16)	39(24)
Total cases (=100%)	36	46	81	163

Chi square 15.27   4 df $p < 0.01$

Table 6.3: User problems and outcome (unqualified social workers)

Outcome	Problem response category			
	Risk n (%)	Advisory n (%)	Service n (%)	Total n (%)
Resolved	7 (37)	11 (39)	28 (27)	46(31)
Partially resolved	8 (42)	12 (43)	67 (66)	87(58)
Not resolved	4 (21)	5 (18)	7 (7)	16(11)
Total cases (=100%)	19	28	102	149

Chi square 8.83   4 df $p > 0.05$

In Table 6.3, the results were not statistically significant. It is notable that fewer cases were included in the not resolved category: 11 per cent of 149 cases compared with 24 per cent of 163 cases in Table 6.2. Examining the not resolved outcome for Table 6.3 shows that each of the problem response categories varied as follows: risk 21 per cent, advisory 18 per cent and service 11 per cent, compared with 28 per cent, 35 per cent and 16 per cent in Table 6.2. Table 6.3 had the highest percentage grouping for the two tables: 66 per cent of service cases were partially resolved to indicate some lack of certainty regarding its outcome decision reached in these cases.

In both Tables 6.2 and 6.3, service cases are mainly present in the partially resolved outcome category (36% qualified, 58% unqualified social workers), reflecting an apparent difference between the tables and suggesting the trend that unqualified social workers choose to follow a middle ground in determining case outcome. Unqualified social workers, nevertheless, had fewer not resolved cases (11% as opposed to qualified workers with 24%). The finding that unqualified social workers were less decisive in resolving cases is marginal, not statistically significant, and represents one possible interpretation given the limitations of the data. Any explanation of these findings must therefore be somewhat speculative. Perhaps, for example, unqualified workers were allocated cases which were more difficult to resolve, and chose a middle ground strategically – although clearly such an allocation would not square with a team culture in which cases perceived as difficult were allocated to experienced qualified workers. Alternatively, it is possible that qualified workers were more deliberate in their interventions with users, and consequently that outcome decisions were also clearer.

All cases were closed by the time the data were analysed so a partial outcome was not due to a decision not being taken. Accordingly, some unresolved issues or uncertainty concerning the user must have continued despite closure of the case. Such uncertainty may indicate a degree of tentativeness by unqualified social work staff in reaching firm closure decisions, and that no doubt they would have been guided by more senior and qualified colleagues; or indeed they may have been required to deal with cases more quickly in order to provide a 'service' to users who might otherwise have prolonged periods of waiting or, possibly, could have been denied any service whatsoever.

User problems and outcome: controlling for supervision

The research hypothesis was that the relationship between user problems and outcome would vary according to the frequency of supervision, with higher rates of supervision resulting in more successful outcome decisions than lower rates of supervision. Obviously, the reality would be unlikely to be so simple, since it might have been the complexity of the case, or the difficulties it caused, that led to higher supervision levels. So how do these counteracting dimensions balance out?

Tables 6.4 and 6.5 contrast user problems with outcome, controlling for lower and higher levels of supervision. Low levels of supervision signify three or less supervisory meetings per case and high levels of supervision four meetings or more; it was noted earlier that this distribution creates an imbalance in the tables which, with hindsight, might have been avoided by using the median value of 2 for supervision, achieving a more balanced distribution.

Table 6.4: User problems and outcome (low supervision)

| Outcome | Problem response category | | | |
	Risk n (%)	Advisory n (%)	Service n (%)	Total n (%)
Resolved	12 (37)	17 (46)	42 (31)	71 (35)
Partially resolved	13 (41)	9 (24)	84 (62)	106 (52)
Not resolved	7 (22)	11 (30)	10 (7)	28 (14)
Total cases (=100%)	32	37	136	205

Chi square 23.32   4 df $p < 0.001$

Table 6.5: User problems and outcome (high supervision)

| Outcome | Problem response category | | | |
	Risk n (%)	Advisory n (%)	Service n (%)	Total n (%)
Resolved	11 (48)	16 (43)	14 (30)	41 (38)
Partially resolved	5 (22)	11 (30)	23 (49)	39 (36)
Not resolved	7 (30)	10 (27)	10 (21)	27 (25)
Total cases (=100%)	23	37	47	107

Chi square 6.09   4 df $p > 0.05$

The results in Table 6.4 were statistically significant. Fourteen per cent of 205 cases that received low supervision as defined in this study were not resolved, indicative perhaps that such cases were less problematic than cases requiring more intensive involvement. The advisory group had the higher percentage of not resolved cases at 30 per cent.

In comparison, Table 6.5 shows that 25 per cent of cases (out of 107) were not resolved. It appears that high supervision is identified with a less satisfactory outcome overall. Within Table 6.5, the highest percentage of cases not resolved was 30 per cent for risk, compared with 27 per cent for advisory and 21 per cent for service cases. Interestingly, risk cases were numerically lower (23) than advisory (37) or service cases (47), a fact which is perhaps indicative of the special attention to risk cases in this sample of cases warranting higher rates of supervision and with the highest proportion of not resolved cases.

A reasonable interpretation of these findings might be that the decision to offer 'high supervision' is related to distinctive problem types – those where the input is designed to increase the likelihood of successful resolution and those where no such resolution is possible, but is constantly sought. In the latter situation then increased supervision might be directed less towards achieving a successful outcome with a particular type of risk case, and more towards damage limitation. Here the agency responsible might be constructed as 'at risk', and the need is to ensure it is reflected in a reasonable light, even though accepting professional responsibility for some error of judgement, as might be typified by services being withdrawn or indeed, not offered in the first place. The problem is a perennial one for welfare when the dilemma of over-reaction in child care, as illustrated by the Cleveland (HMSO 1988), is countered by under-reaction when children subject to child abuse remain at home (Department of Health 1982). This dilemma casts a shadow on preventive policies because of the uncertainty of their interpretations and outcome, an issue which is examined in greater detail elsewhere (Burke 1997b).

Conclusions

This chapter has emphasised the need to establish research parameters using the variables identified as risk, advice and service delivery which were utilised to monitor social work responses to users following case allocation. It was found that:

- The response categories were limited in scale.

- 'Risk' is used as an agency measure of concern. Risk work is clearly associated with agency risk where crisis work indicates a continuing need for worker involvement. The evidence of risk work, given its broad based 'agency' conceptualisation appears counter to the evidence from Beresford and Croft (1986) where 'crisis' was defined as 'quick response work'.

- Crisis and risk are ends of a spectrum of user need that requires further examination. Risk cases appear to represent the inherently complex cases which require more social work involvement and time commitment to reach a satisfactory outcome. However, combining 'risk cases' with 'crisis work' is perhaps not very helpful and the two should be separated.

- Service delivery work was predominantly undertaken by unqualified social workers but it indicates the need for a case management system to clarify decision making given the tasks associated with the service provider role.

- Some workers have difficulty in differentiating between the needs of different users.

- Social workers should improve skills appropriate to the needs of users, so developing and implementing theories from practice.

- Practitioners are in possession of data which could help the development of social work theory in practice.

It seems from this research that less experienced workers undertake more service type work, and this could be reinforced by a needs-led view of service. This happens when provision of service is the role of social workers and the danger exists that 'service' becomes equated with 'provision', not support. Consequently, an over emphasis on 'service provision' has the potential to devalue the role of practitioners offering casework skills.

The response categories work by linking the problem referred, not the ability of the worker to provide a particular kind of practice, to the outcome achieved. While the worker is professionally liable for offering a skilled service to users perceived as in need, it is equally clear that some workers would have difficulty in differentiating between the needs of different users. The basic requirement is to link individual workers' skills with service delivery, advice giving and risk work, and in specific circumstances this requires a supervisory input (i.e. with unqualified colleagues). Social workers could then follow a 'practice wisdom' approach to the task.

If we also consider that certain social workers currently have particular practice skills, it follows that these skills should be shared with unqualified colleagues in order to pass on more developed areas of expertise to others. The evidence from this study suggests that unqualified staff had some difficulty in reaching conclusive outcome decisions, and help should be offered by experienced staff who contribute to what otherwise might be one-to-one supervisory sessions. This might go some way towards determining an appropriate and decisive course of action. Certainly it should be the case that the most senior practitioners guide those junior to them towards the desired outcome, given the circumstances of each case.

If practitioners continue to assess users' need, then the response groupings begin to indicate the beginning and associated skills required.

This is important for understanding the theoretical basis of social work practice, for social workers should improve skills associated with the needs of users, so developing and implementing theories from practice. A consequence of this is that social workers might begin to link specific user problems with particular practice skills. The response categorisation of referrals, despite its simplified approach to determining outcome, is a step in the right direction and begins by identifying two basic parameters, risk and service delivery, as part of practice. This seems a necessary process if social workers are to meet the needs of users and respond effectively to crisis situations, however the latter are defined.

The scale of the research is modest, but even at this level confirms a number of current trends in social work practice and in particular the need for supervisory input. A more extensive study than that reported here might develop the research to incorporate a detailed exposition of the users served according to age, gender and ethnic origin. Clearly, though, this study begins to clarify methods of analysis and indicates the data available on every social worker's workload. Practitioners can help the development of social work theory in practice by considering their own practice in relation to that of their colleagues; all they need is a framework for examination, time to undertake a study, and then their practice will be that much better informed.

References

Beresford, P. and Croft, S. (1986) *Whose Welfare. Private Care or Public Service.* Brighton: Lewis Cohen Centre.

Burke, P. (1990) 'The fieldwork team response: an investigation into the relationship between client categories, referred problems and outcome.' *British Journal of Social Work 20*, 469–482.

Burke, P. (1997a) 'Risk and supervision: social work responses to referred user problems.' *British Journal of Social Work 27*, 115–129.

Burke, P. (1997b) 'Children with learning difficulties: primary prevention social work.' *Journal of Child Centred Practice 4*, 93–100.

Caplan, G. (1964) *Principles of Preventive Psychiatry.* London: Tavistock Publications.

Coulshed, V. (1988) *Social Work Practice.* Basingstoke: Macmillan.

Curnock, K. and Hardiker, P. (1979) *Towards Practice Theory: Skills and Methods in Social Assessments.* London: Routledge and Kegan Paul.

Department of Health (1982) *A Study of Inquiry Reports 1973–1981.* London: HMSO.

Department of Health, Department of Social Security, Welsh Office and Scottish Office (1989) *Caring for People: Community Care in the Next Decade and Beyond,* Cm 849. London: HMSO.

Foster, P. (1983) *Access to Welfare: an Introduction to Welfare Rationing.* Basingstoke: Macmillan.

Giller, H. and Morris, A. (1981) *Care and Discretion.* London: Burnett Books.

Goda, D. and Smeeton, N. (1993) 'Statistical considerations in social work research.' *British Journal of Social Work 23,* 277–81.

Goldberg, E.M. and Fruin, D.J. (1976) 'Towards accountability in social work: a case review system for social workers.' *British Journal of Social Work 9,* 3–22.

Goldberg, E.M. and Warburton, R.W. (1979) *Ends and Means in Social Work: the Development and Outcome of a Case Review System for Social Workers.* London: George Allen and Unwin, National Institute Social Service Library no. 35.

Goldberg, E.M., Gibbons, J. and Sinclair, I. (1985) *Problems, Tasks and Outcomes: the Evaluation of Task-Centred Casework in Three Settings.* London: George Allen and Unwin.

Gostick, C. and Scott, T. (1982) 'Local authority intake teams.' *British Journal of Social Work 12,* 395–421.

Hadley, R. and McGrath, M. (1984) *When Social Services are Local: the Normanton Experience.* London: George Allen and Unwin, National Institute Social Service Library no. 48.

Her Majesty's Stationery Office (1988) *Report of the Inquiry into Child Abuse in Cleveland 1987.* London: HMSO.

Howe, D. (1986) *Social Workers and their Practice in Welfare Bureaucracies.* Aldershot: Gower.

Howe, D. (1987) *An Introduction to Social Work Theory.* Aldershot: Wildwood House.

Huxley, P., Korer, J.R. and Tolley, S. (1987) 'The psychiatric "caseness" of clients referred to an urban social service department.' *British Journal of Social Work 17,* 507–20.

McGee, R.K. (1984) *Crisis Intervention in the Community.* Baltimore: University Park Press.

Mattinson, J. and Sinclair, I. (1979) *Mate and Stalemate.* Oxford: Basil Blackwell.

Middleman, R.R. and Goldberg, G. (1973) *Social Service Delivery: a Structured Approach to Social Work Practice.* New York: Columbia University Press.

Rapoport, L. (1970) 'Crisis intervention as a mode of brief treatment.' In R.W. Roberts and R.H. Nee (eds) *Theories of Social Casework.* Chicago: University of Chicago Press.

CHAPTER 7

Experience of Single-Case
Evaluation in a Small Agency

Angela Williams

As a small team of experienced social workers employed within an educational setting we have, over several years, looked for an effective and economical way of evaluating our work. During this time we have been prompted by a variety of incentives ranging from the interest and enthusiasm of students on practice learning placement to threats of financial cuts to the service. We recognise the need to examine the effectiveness of our contribution to the lives of school children, their families and teachers and to find ways of adapting and improving our practice in accordance with what we learn. We also need to demonstrate our usefulness to employers who come from a different professional background to our own and to those who have an investment in our continued existence as a service – mainly school staff and parents.

Background

The overall aim of the education social work service is:

> to provide a range of assessment, advisory and therapeutic services based on the application of knowledge and social work skills to vulnerable children (0–19 years), their families, carers and schools in Bradford. These services aim to broaden access to education for children whose potential skills and abilities are impaired by emotional, behavioural or psychological difficulties. (Butler and Hall 1995)

The origins of the service are within the former child guidance provision, and at present, distinct from a separate education welfare service.

Whilst we should have no difficulty in demonstrating the range of services we offer, the challenge of showing that we help to broaden children's access to education draws us into a far more complex and complicated procedure. There is a clear need to break down our contribution into more manageable objectives.

Although we play a part in supporting the statutory responsibilities of the Local Education Authority (LEA) we do not have any prescribed outcomes to our work other than to support the needs of vulnerable children in education. This has the advantage of leaving the way clear for us to explore and define our own measures to evaluate our work and the disadvantage of leaving us unsure that what is useful information for us is equally valid for others.

A team brainstorm of what questions we wanted answered by evaluation of our work produced the following list:

- Was the referral problem resolved?

- Is there a relationship between the number of sessions (offered to a family) and the perceived outcome by the family?

- How can we keep anchored to some basic questions, for example definition of the problem?

- What would success look like and how would you know you have achieved it?

- Is there a place for internal reviews for cases which have gone over a given period of time?

- Could we evaluate small parts of practice, for example the referral process?

The list reflects, to some extent, the sort of wide-ranging concerns with which we have struggled in attempts over recent years to evaluate what we do. These attempts include evaluation of effectiveness, equality of access to service provision and the efficiency of the work. Methods have been in the form of user interviews conducted by an external assessor for a review of the psychological service in 1990 (Bradford Metropolitan District Council 1991), internal monitoring of referrals 1990–91 and interviews of school headteachers by a social work student (Lines 1992). A code of practice for education social workers was drawn up in 1993 and used as a basis for a questionnaire to service users, conducted by another student (Waterman 1994). Whilst the feedback from these pieces of work has given us some valuable insights, we recognise the need for a more systematic method of evaluation which could easily be integrated with existing casework models.

Single-Case Evaluation

The theoretical background to Mansoor Kazi's work on single-case evaluation is described by him as follows:

> *Single-case evaluation* refers to the use of single-case designs by practitioners to evaluate client progress (Robinson, Bronson and Blythe 1988). *Single-case design* refers to a specific research methodology designed for systematic study of a single client or system. Continuous assessment over time is used as a basis for drawing inferences about intervention effects. (Kazi 1997, pp.419–420)

NASW's *Encyclopedia of Social Work* describes single-case design as:

> a research methodology that allows a…practitioner to track systematically his or her progress with a client or client unit. With increasingly rigorous applications of this methodology, practitioners can also gain knowledge about effective…interventions, although this is a less common goal. (Blythe 1995, p.2164)

A fundamental requirement of this methodology is the measurement of the subject's target problem – the object of the intervention or treatment – repeatedly over time. The practitioner is required to select an outcome measure that best reflects changes in the subject's condition, and then to apply the same measure over a period of time. In all cases, the resulting data will enable the tracking of systematic progress. In some cases the resulting data will also enable the tracking of systematic progress; it may also be possible to draw inferences as to whether the treatment programme was responsible for the observed changes in the subject's condition. However, such judgements can be made only if the outcome measure is used before, during, and after the treatment programme is implemented and when comparisons can be made between the treatment and no-treatment phases as in an experimental design (Bloom, Fischer and Orme 1995; Thyer 1993).

Some features of the method that appealed to members of our team were as follows:

1. *A systematic record or contract made with families about the purpose of our contact.* Whilst there would normally be full discussion about the reasons for our work together this would generally be done

verbally and in an informal way. A working agreement that relied upon clear definitions and targets appealed particularly to those with a working knowledge of solution-focused therapy.

2. *The concept of partnership implicit in the joint identification of targets with families.* As a non-statutory agency most of our work is entered into by families on a voluntary basis. Whilst acknowledging our power position as LEA workers, we aim to work in an open and collaborative way.

3. *The normalisation of the evaluation process.* In order to integrate on-going review of our work into everyday practice we recognised the need to make this part of the casework process. Whilst there was a some reservation expressed about how this would work in practice, it was agreed that it was appropriate to have this as an aim.

4. *An opportunity to analyse and improve our practice as a team and as individual workers.* We gain feedback about the casework methods we use and how we work in a variety of informal ways. Whilst different workers inevitably learn and develop new skills by different means, we hoped through single-case evaluation to collect data which will help us improve our practice.

5. *A possible opportunity to produce information about our work in a way that could be recognised and understood by non-social worker colleagues and which would enhance our credibility as a valuable resource within education.* This was seen as particularly appropriate for the casework part of our service. We readily gain recognition for the part we play in training, in dealing with crises and running projects and workshops where LEA colleagues and others benefit directly from our input. Therapeutic casework aligns us more closely with 'problems' for other workers and successful interventions can be perceived as 'just' bringing children into line with what is expected of a majority. Our involvement may go unnoticed to colleagues or is quickly forgotten.

Implementation of the Pilot – Feedback from Workers

As members of the social work team we approached the single-case evaluation model with different levels of interest and enthusiasm. There was no insistence from service managers that all new cases should be evaluated, just that everyone in the service should attempt to apply the model in a defined number of cases and to complete appropriate forms for submission at a later date. It was agreed that for a service system to be instigated in the long term, it would need to involve all team members. At the same time there was an expectation that if, at this stage, the method was thought to have a negative effect on the casework undertaken then it should be dropped. As a pilot there was plenty of scope for workers to use the model flexibly and to adapt it as they saw fit to their own working style. The two forms devised to record target problems and work plans are shown in Figures 7.1 and 7.2.

All therapeutic work is undertaken by pairs of workers who belong to one of two working groups. Working arrangements within the pairs vary depending on style and methodology and the requirements of the particular case. Workers provided feedback on twenty-eight cases to which they had set out to apply single-case evaluation. The composition of the pairs varied within the working group; altogether ten social workers and three social work students were involved in the trial run.

The feedback came in a variety of forms on completed evaluation sheets and with explanatory comments. The examples included here illustrate particular factors emerging from the pilot. Quotations are taken from workers' feedback. Some details about service users have been changed to protect their identity.

Engaging families in a joint working agreement

Nearly all the workers referred in their feedback to some aspect of this process and the impact of a requirement to establish at an early stage of the work both a baseline of behaviour(s) and agreed targets. Not all families could be involved in this type of evaluation as one worker comments:

> We had an idea that the family might be difficult for us to engage both from the referral information and a telephone call prior to the first appointment. We wanted to make sure we took care with this and thought that introducing the project and forms at this stage might hinder our engagement with the family. Looking back at the first two sessions we think that had we done this it may well have stopped the flow of conversation once we had started to hear their story.

Another referral was made by the social services department whilst the family was still involved in a court case about alleged physical abuse. The

Source of referral_____   Date of referral_____

Reason(s) for referral

_____

_____

_____

Location of Problem
School/home/peer group/other_____

Brief Description of What Needs Changing

Student's view   Date_____

_____

_____

Teacher's view   Date_____

_____

_____

Parent's view   Date_____

_____

_____

ESW's assessment   Date_____

_____

_____

_____

Figure 7.1: Target Problem

BRADFORD EDUCATION SOCIAL WORK SERVICE

Work plan for_____

What needs changing   Source (who says)

Date_____
Session and participants_____
Workers_____

Figure 7.2: Work Plan

parents cooperated with the social services department but resentfully. After filling out evaluation forms and giving 'before and after' sheets they did not come back. Although observation and some involvement in school continued it was not possible to re-engage the parents. They apparently felt the work should not have concentrated on them; in their view we should have been seeing the children.

Families come to us for a service with a certain set of expectations of what we are about and what they think or hope we will do. Many families refer themselves and tell us what they want; others are less clear and need time to explore possible ways of working. In the above cases the families were referred by workers from other agencies. Here the process of engagement is also influenced by the family's perception of the referrer's expectations of why they see a need for our involvement. We do not start our work with a completely clean slate and the process of reaching an agreed working arrangement and set of targets can take some time. The comments of one social worker illustrate this:

> I was reluctant to introduce the [evaluation] project in the early stages of the work as I thought there might be a clash of styles between the family's style and expectation of what we would do and how we would do it [the mother is on a counselling course] and the 'behavioural-chart filling in' style of the evaluation project. I felt uneasy about doing it. At session number five, however, we reviewed the work and introduced the evaluation project and filled in the section 'what needs changing – sources'.

Partnership

The relationship between ourselves as workers and those coming to us for help proved an important focus of feedback on the use of single-case evaluation. This was in part related to a shared style, as indicated above, in part to levels of openness in negotiating targets for the work and in part to the exploration of the balance of power relations between client, referrer and worker in establishing the focus of work and how these might be negotiated.

A worker's comments illustrate these steps towards partnership in a family where the mother was suffering from depression following the death of her baby and the school child had a number of behaviour problems:

> There was a dilemma for us about trying to use a chart. We wanted to cut down the paperwork for a family who are not particularly comfortable

with a written mode of communication. Another difficulty is that the problem concerned high frequency behaviour which happens at the most stressful time of the day. We failed to get a baseline and we did not get a measure other than a subjective retrospective feeling from parents and teachers.

Here the worker expresses concern that the requirement of the evaluation places a further burden on the family and has difficulty matching this with the process of re-empowering parents who are still reeling from the death of one of their children. The same worker refers in another case of a family with multiple difficulties to 'our continuing unease about use of forms with clients in relation to anti-oppressive practice'.

Identifying targets

The referred problem (or problems) provides a straightforward starting point to each piece of work. We take account of the fact that perceptions about what constitutes a difficulty vary according to different positions and early stages of work would always involve an exploration of this. The evaluation form for logging different views about what needs to change was generally accepted and more consistently completed by workers than the measurement charts (see Figure 7.1).

One worker was concerned that the evaluation format might encourage the identification of targets to be too firmly established at too early a stage:

Mother got in touch with the service concerning son's behaviour. At first interview it became fairly clear that the problem did not lie with her son but with other factors, some of which the parent had not talked about (but subsequently did). If we had filled forms in the 'problem' would have been identified as son's behaviour when in fact problems were largely parents' anxieties about future big changes and parenting issues. Future work did not involve the son.

Another example concerns a child referred by school staff for behavioural problems in school, involvement in bullying and low self-esteem. The engagement process was described by workers as 'difficult' but after several sessions they moved from hearing the family's complaints about school to an agreed target of reducing the incidence of the child's bed-wetting. This work was successful and after eight weeks he was dry every night. There was, however, no change in his behaviour at school.

Whilst this work focused on the parents' concerns it raises the question of the relationship between a formalised evaluation and who sets the targets. It also challenges us to define what constitutes 'success' and when and how it can be identified.

One worker describes a significant gap between what the parents in a family wanted changing and what the child wanted. This delayed the start of the evaluation process but kept the work closer in line with what the family were saying:

> Data collection was introduced at latter part of case involvement [session nine]. This timing felt right because the child and parent were more able to focus on what they could agree to work on. At previous sessions it has been important to listen to how difficult life has been [family illness, loss of earnings, crisis over whether or not mother seeking 'care' for her son]. At the beginning of involvement the father was not part of household as the parents had separated and by session three he had returned. Therefore, more time was spent discussing process of change and not targeting problems.

Many families are referred to us with multiple problems and workers often take the view that helping them to learn to identify their own way of overcoming one difficulty is a useful tool that can then be generalised to other areas of concern. In this respect the narrowing down to a manageable focus or desired outcome was experienced as helpful.

In some instances an important focus of the work might be to normalise the problem. With this student the worker resisted formalising what was presented as a difficulty and concentrated her attention on supporting the adults in accepting an understandable temporary disruption in the child's routine:

> There was one session with the parent following the death of S's father. The aim was to allow a discussion about children's response to bereavement, normalising a process. Short-term intervention followed to enable the adults around S to get on with their jobs. This avoided making a 'problem' of S's school attendance. No formal measure was used.

Working systemically

As may be detected in the way in which workers have described aspects of their work, we tend to approach referred problems systemically, taking account of the context within which problems are identified and the variety of ways in which the situation may be perceived. Some workers commented on a discrepancy between the 'linear' implications of a target-work-outcome model of evaluation and the 'circular' style of exploring a presenting problem. Not only was this seen as a clash of styles but it also cut across attempts to change ways of thinking about a situation and loosen the structure surrounding the difficulties. Workers were wary of using a method that might tighten up and therefore reinforce a problem at a time when further exploration of factors supporting it seemed more appropriate.

There seemed to be a general agreement that there was a time for clarity of purpose in the work but also a time for allowing a complex picture in order to reach a more informed set of targets. In setting a context for change rather than channelling energy into early formalised decisions about what needed to happen this worker helped the parent reach her own revised decision about how to proceed:

> This parent is seeking a letter from us to her husband in prison so that he can take seriously the change in their child's behaviour since his father went into prison. To have sat down and worked out a written plan of change in behaviour would have detracted from mother's flow of 'her' story of what had happened to her family and the changes they have encountered. By session two there were dramatic, positive changes in child's behaviour and his mother has managed to talk to her husband.

Single-case evaluation could not have been sensitive to all that needed changing for this family. This became clearer when the parent went away and thought it out for herself and came to her own objectives. How useful would it have been for us overtly to guide and coach this process?

Measurement

Some of the measurement charts within the single-case evaluation model were already known and used by workers in the service. Before and after charts, mood and attitude ratings and frequency scales had all been used to help get a clear description of behaviour and to give meaning to statements. One worker commented:

> I do not think the evaluation process influenced the kind of questions I would have asked anyway. Rating scales were used in-between other questions to look for preferences (for example, who is closest friend).

Multiple choice questions also helped the process of developing a conversation around the subject area.

To use these scales as an external demonstration of progress was, however, a new procedure for workers. Questions hitherto used to elicit more detailed information became part of a standardised procedure from which 'objective' information could be gathered.

In some instances the process of measuring contributes to a change in perceptions and behaviour. Parents may be asked to examine and record problem times to help them take a more objective view of processes at work around the problem.

Measurement scales, 'before and after', were filled in for a while by the parents but after a while the child was said to have 'been brilliant' and in third session a benevolent circle seemed to have got going.

In other situations it seemed less obvious how to integrate the measures as an appropriate feature of the work. One worker asks: 'How do we measure anything other than behaviour in a concrete but non-intrusive way?'

Formalised measures imply access to information we do not always have, for example, baseline measurements and clearly defined beginnings and endings to the work. To have completed the evaluation form-filling meticulously would have undoubtedly involved a lot of guessing and/or chasing up people to obtain more detail. We need to decide what additional data collection is legitimate to justify the time this takes and the relative gain for us in doing it. One worker suggested that a qualitative appreciation of all aspects of the work was a more useful tool for our learning and development but recognised that this was harder to record systematically and less useful as a clear indicator of our effectiveness. This also supported a concern that there may be a difference between information which is useful for our learning and that which could be useful for external purposes.

The timing of a final evaluation also came under scrutiny from workers, as did the implications of the experimental aspect of the evaluation model. For example, if the problem re-emerged following closure of our involvement how far can this be seen as an indication of the success of our intervention? This question is raised, in the following case, by the worker:

This boy was referred because he would not go to school – he was screaming and kicking if taken there. At the third session we filled in the evaluation 'work plan sheets' [Figure 7.2] which effectively focused the work on a gradual entry into school. I wrote a detailed plan and did some careful negotiation with the school. The boy's mother seemed pleased that we were concentrating on the practical problem rather than delving into the past, although she did have some ideas about the boy having been affected by his father [now divorced] constantly letting him down.

The boy went back to school after quite a long holiday break and I wrote a closure summary. Two weeks later the boy had a stomach upset and re-fused to go back to school. The mother felt unable to cope and de-manded that his father take him. With hindsight it seems that the concentration on the practical business of helping the boy back into school was at the expense of pursuing some of the more systemic hy-potheses about family functioning; had we hedged our bets and done both I believe it would have made it less likely that the boy's mother would have despaired when the boy refused to go to school again.

Highlighting this example as an effective piece of work at the point of closure only gives part of the whole picture and the observation that a positive link could be established between our involvement and the return to school was not sufficient to satisfy the worker.

What about us?

Before drawing together the threads from feedback given by social workers and attempting to look forward to next stages in devising an evaluation system that works for us, it is important to consider the human aspect of involvement with the project.

Several workers referred to the effect that introducing a new dimension to the work (single-case evaluation) had upon their practice. Well-established work patterns and routines had to be re-appraised and, in the rush of new information and concentrated attention to detail, evaluation sometimes got forgotten:

> We did not use a form or put it on paper with them. This could have been useful for referring back with them. We did not specify measures which could also have been useful.

> I think what stopped me taking the next step [forms, measures] was not being in the habit.

> I could have used it in this case if I had been more disciplined.

> Filling in forms with families – our own inexperience can cause problems: 'These two do not know what they are doing'...

The pilot period was relatively short (five months) and from concerns being raised about various aspects of the evaluation process we clearly needed to review and revise where we were going at this stage. A longer period would, however, have given us all time to adjust and adapt in a way that possibly would have given a greater sense of confidence in and control over the more positive aspects of the process.

Some Basic Questions

There is a general agreement within the team that it has been useful for us to have had the opportunity to pilot single-case evaluation. There are clearly aspects of the process we want to incorporate into a system of our own. It has also given a focus for our thinking about how we make other parts of the process more congruent with our working style and method.

To take this forward we first need to re-consider certain basic questions:

1. *For whom are we doing the evaluation?* This question re-emerged halfway through the pilot and it may be that we did not consider its full implications sufficiently well at the outset. The pressure to evaluate comes, as stated, from both internal and external sources. Single-case evaluation can help us as workers to consider carefully the desired outcomes of our work and even, possibly, some ideas about the impact of our work in helping families to reach those goals. For us to learn more about the effectiveness of what we do we need also to look closely at the processes involved in our work. A survey of workers' comments would suggest that the process of engaging families in joint work and of working out an appropriate partnership are key areas we need to consider beyond the restrictions of single-case evaluation.

   If the evaluation is intended to demonstrate to others, external to the service, the benefits of our work then a closer examination of what we do within the case work relationship would possibly be less relevant. We might need to look more closely at more experimental aspects of evaluation which could demonstrate the effectiveness of our contribution. We are at a very early stage of thinking about this as a team and would need to look at a whole range of ethical, financial and resource implications before deciding to pursue this further.

We have two particular problems with a focus that seeks to isolate the impact of our work upon the desired outcome. We would generally want to work with families in a way that helped them find their own solutions rather than depending upon us to be around to support the changes made. Also in a climate of more integrated service approaches to helping families we would often expect change to be the result of combined efforts and contributions from a variety of sources, not just our own.

2. *If we are doing the evaluation for us, where do we focus our energy?* Areas emerging from the original brainstorm on what questions we want answered by evaluating our work are only partly covered by single-case evaluation, which helps us focus on goals and outcomes. We have, in the past, made tentative moves to find out about what those on the receiving end of our services think about what we do and how we behave towards them. A more systematic development of this process could be another option. Recent interest from some team members in developing therapeutic consultations could provide a useful starting point in considering our responses to families in light of their model of expectations about us, what we can or will do to help them and how we are likely to do this (see Street, Downey and Brazier 1991). Equally we could put more time into monitoring access to the service through data which can readily be made available to us through our current database. Clearly we cannot justify time in developing all these aspects of evaluating what we do and we need to make some choices.

3. *If we decide to stick with a single-case system of evaluation, how do we incorporate the positivist aspect of the process within a heuristic, humanistic activity? How do we marry science with art?* A systemic approach to social casework understanding and process implies a complex appraisal of inter-connected variables. Any attempt to isolate and track one element of the system could skew the overall understanding of what is happening and over-emphasise this element (often an unacceptable behaviour) as the most significant factor in the process.

We have identified benefits of simplicity, clarity and discipline within the single-case model but are wary of possible over-simplification of complex problems and closing down options when maybe we should be opening up new perspectives. Positivism pays less attention to abstract, speculative principles which can be important in our work but we also need to incorporate a more empirical dimension to the process of measuring what could be described as an art or craft within a scientific framework. There could be possible ways forward with this through using information technology to build up a bank of key phrases or associations, giving scope for a more holistic appraisal of factors contributing to the process of change. This would, however, take time and energy. There may be implications, too, for examining the use of personal construct theory to incorporate subjective and symbolic principles within a formal process of categorisation. Again, this would require a concerted effort to devise and implement.

Some Conclusions

Whatever the responses to these questions there are certain principles we may extract from the experience of piloting single-case evaluation.

- It is useful to have an integrated system of evaluation congruent with work method and style which is applied by all workers to all cases.

- A systematic and comprehensive recording of information which can be used for evaluating our work is essential.

- Working in pairs gives scope for separating work responsibilities in relation to evaluation. Whilst no specific reference was made by workers in the feedback to the significance of co-working as a factor to be considered in the evaluation process, it may nonetheless be helpful. At present workers may use this working model to gain 'inside' and 'outside' perspectives on what forces are at play within the dynamics of a family or school situation. These perspectives could be used in separating circular (inside) and linear (outside) aspects of the work and allow scope for a linear analysis of progress or development without interrupting the circularity of the method used.

- Reflecting on our own practice produces valuable information and should be logged for use as part of an evaluation process.

- Any method of evaluating what we do is likely to have elements of objectivity and subjectivity. We should be as honest as we can be about the degrees of each that can be ascribed to information produced.

- We need to consider more closely what we mean by partnership with families and the implications of this for shared objectives and relationships with those who refer families to us.

- We need to be clear about the purposes of the evaluation and how the resulting information will be used.

- It is valuable to have external appraisal of the work we do. We should consider using existing and new systems to develop this perspective.

- There are resource implications for evaluation. What time and money can we justify spending on the process?

The experience of piloting single-case evaluation has contributed a number of pointers and ideas about what we develop as an evaluation system for our service in the future. We are clear that what we want from a system of evaluation is information that we can use to improve our practice, both by examining successful outcomes to the work and by exploring factors involved in the process of the work with families and schools that help to make a difference. Through re-appraising existing procedures and forms and identifying when and how evaluation can be incorporated into our work processes we are now working on a relatively simple (and hopefully useful) method of gathering information from casework that will identify both views on outcomes and feedback on the effectiveness of the working relationship. The experimental aspect of single-case evaluation has proved more problematic. Whilst we would like to know what our part in the work has contributed to the identified success of work outcomes, we recognise that this may be too difficult to isolate and to hold up as certain evidence of the effectiveness of what we do.

References

Bloom, M., Fischer J. and Orme, J. (1995) *Evaluating Practice: Guidelines for the Accountable Professional.* Boston: Allyn and Bacon.

Blythe, B.J. (1995) 'Single-system design.' In R.L. Edwards (ed) *Encyclopedia of Social Work 3*. Silver Spring, Maryland: National Association of Social Workers.

Bradford Metropolitan District Council (1991) *Review of Bradford Psychological Service.* Bradford: BMDC.

Butler, J. and Hall, G. (1995) *Bradford Education Social Work Service Plan 1995/96.* Bradford Metropolitan District Council (unpublished).

Kazi, M.A.F. (1997) 'Single-case evaluation in British social services.' In E. Chelimsky and W.R. Shadish (eds) *Evaluation for the 21st Century: A Handbook.* Thousand Oaks: Sage.

Kazi, M.A.F. and Wilson, J.T. (1996) 'Applying single-case evaluation methodology in a British social work agency.' *Research on Social Work Practice 6*, 1, 5–26.

Lines, A. (1992) *Schools' Referral Patterns to Education Social Work.* Bradford Metropolitan District Council (unpublished, student assignment).

Robinson, E.A.R., Bronson, D.E. and Blythe, B.J. (1988) 'An analysis of the implementation of single-case evaluation by practitioners.' *Social Service Review 62*, 285–301.

Street, E., Downey, J. and Brazier, A. (1991) 'The development of therapeutic consultation in child-focused family work.' *Journal of Family Therapy 13*, 311–333.

Thyer, B.A. (1993) 'Single-system research designs.' In R.M. Grinnell Jr. (ed) *Social Work Research and Evaluation.* Itasca, Ill: F.E. Peacock.

Waterman, C. (1994) *Gathering and Evaluation Feedback from Service Users.* Bradford Metropolitan District Council (unpublished).

Acknowledgements

Everyone in Bradford Education Social Work Service contributed in some way to the piloting of the single-case evaluation model described in this chapter. The team at the time consisted of Jane Butler and Gabrielle Hall (job share Principal Education Social Worker), Riffut Aziz, Patsy Barrow, Helen Cooper, Pam Cutts, Janice Ellingworth, Stephen Mason, Ann Overton, Kate Stewart, Colin Waterman and myself. Three Diploma Social Work students on placement also took part in the pilot. They were Nick Bartholomew, Tony Chandsoor and Julie O'Kane. These social workers worked hard to apply the single-case evaluation to their casework practice and provided written and verbal feedback and discussion about their experience.

Nick Bartholomew helped to examine the main points from the feedback. Gabrielle Hall and Stephen Mason attended the conference on Evaluation of Social Work Practice, held at Huddersfield University in September 1995, when Stephen presented this feedback from the team's experiences.

Denise Midgley typed the original paper, working to a tight schedule.

Service users (children and families) have naturally played an important part in working with us to implement the pilot study and have provided useful feedback in a variety of ways, helping us to develop our practice.

CHAPTER 8

An Evaluation of Social Work Practice in Relation to Poverty Issues
Do Social Workers' Attitudes and Actions Correspond?

Monica Dowling

Introduction

This chapter aims to enlarge understanding about social workers' attitudes to poverty and the relationship between these, their working environment and their actual behaviour. A further aim is to identify field observation with social workers as an effective method of evaluating practice. The fieldwork data presented is based on a thirteen-month participant observation study of two social work teams – 'Silverton' and 'City' – in different local authorities. The evaluation of social work practice cannot rely on researching attitudes of social workers to their work but must also observe social workers at work and be ready to account for similarities and differences in attitudes to the work setting and behaviour in the work setting.

Key Research on Poverty and Social Work

One way of knowing about social work practice is to research the views and opinions of social work practitioners concerning, for example, the relationship between poverty and social work. This research perspective assumes social workers' attitudes are constant and that they have a direct link with social workers' behaviour and consequently social work practice.

Parsloe and Stevenson's (1978) research with social services teams and Becker's (1987) research on social workers' attitudes to poverty tend to describe social workers' opinions as individual, preformed and static. As a result of conducting fifty in-depth interviews and a survey of 451 social workers, Becker suggests that a 'positive' attitude to poverty is associated with social workers who are young (25–40), with a degree and social work qualification, who have experience of claiming benefit, who decided to become social workers early in their lives or while unemployed, who lived in small cities in their childhoods and now live in relatively deprived areas, who have some prior experience of social work and who are relatively new to practice. However such individual attitudes may be affected by the attitudes and actions of others in the workplace, the policies of the organisation in which they work and the wider social policy environment. Becker (1987, p.549) points out that further research on the relationship between social work and poverty is necessary.

> Until social workers, their managers and agencies understand how poverty impacts upon clients and how attitudes, structures and contradictions affect the nature and delivery of social work services, then it is unlikely that the poor will receive a service that is appropriate to their needs.

Without follow-up studies it is not clear whether social workers' attitudes to poverty remain the same, nor whether attitudes are congruent with social workers' practice. Reeser and Epstein (1987) compared the findings of surveys of the National Association of Social Workers in 1968 and 1984 and found that social workers in the 1960s viewed social work as a profession involved in broad social change and the elimination of poverty, whereas the majority of social workers in the 1984 survey were supportive of the social class system. However, any change in attitudes may be symptomatic of a wider social mood and may not reflect social workers' behaviour in the workplace. Craig and Coxall's (1989) bibliography of investigations into the Social Fund from 1985–1989 lists 227 investigations, of which forty-four deal with the relationship between social workers and the Social Fund. However these research titles indicate that this aspect of social work with poor people is understood in terms of policy issues and attitudes of social workers to the Social Fund rather than evidence of actions of social workers in relation to the Social Fund. Researchers such as Atherton *et al.* (1993) offer a dependable scale that shows reliability and validity in measuring social workers' attitudes to poverty but still the problem of whether attitudes and actions correspond continues to be a key question in evaluating practice.

The research on attitudes to poverty is loosely entitled 'snapshot', in that this research approach fixes the data in terms of a particular time and place.

The literature on poverty and social work tends to favour this approach rather than the alternative one of researching attitudes and actions through field observation.

Psychological theories on attitudes and actions connect with the 'snapshot' approach because the former have definitions of attitudes that imply they are fixed and constant. However social psychologists do move on to suggest how attitudes are translated into actions (see Figure 8.1) and propose that factors such as perceived control, confidence, resources and opportunities will create important differences in terms of whether attitudes correspond with actions (Ajzen and Madden 1986; Schifter and Ajzen 1985).

Other researchers have a different perspective on how we come to know about social work practice. They have not been solely concerned with understanding social work responses to poverty and have developed a methodology and a theoretical framework based on the idea that social workers' knowledge and ideologies cannot be measured in objective ways but are based on subjective interactions with others which vary from time to time and place to place (Satyamurti 1981; Smith 1980; Pithouse 1988). A theoretical framework that highlights the difficulties of defining set attitudes and actions in relation to poverty is that of the social constructionists (Dean and Fleck-Henderson 1992; Potter and Edwards 1992). They are concerned with how accounts and actions construct reality and use participant observation data to produce accounts of motivation in naturally occurring situations – in this case social work practice. However, their theoretical framework differs from psychological concepts because they would not assume a fixed or objective reality where 'real' attitudes exist. In relation to the fieldwork a perspective which examines behaviour and includes attitudes and actions can provide insight into why social workers' attitudes and actions are not always consistent. Social constructionists would argue that social workers would account for their social work practice differently on different occasions depending on the purpose of the discussion and to whom they were talking and that knowledge is created by the individual's interaction with the environment. For example Dean and Fleck-Henderson (1992) suggest the constructivist perspective can inform the teaching of social work practice and theory by addressing how the client attributes meaning, how the professional attributes meaning both practically and theoretically and whether there is a collaborative process of problem construction and resolution.

Social Work and Poverty – A Participant Observation Approach

By using methodologies that explore both the more objective 'snapshot' approach (group discussion and interviews), and also the subjective 'interactive' approach (thirteen months' participant observation), this research has been able to demonstrate an understanding of the value and use of both epistemological frameworks. By using theoretical constructs that understand attitudes and actions as being fixed concepts (the theory of planned behaviour – see Figure 8.1) and that attitudes and actions are both behaviours and can be appreciated best from a more fluid interactive base (social constructionists theory), the study has developed a knowledge and understanding of social workers' attitudes and actions in relation to poverty

Figure 8.1: A Social/Psychological View of the Relationship between Attitudes and Actions – Social Workers' Attitudes and Actions towards Poor Social Service Users

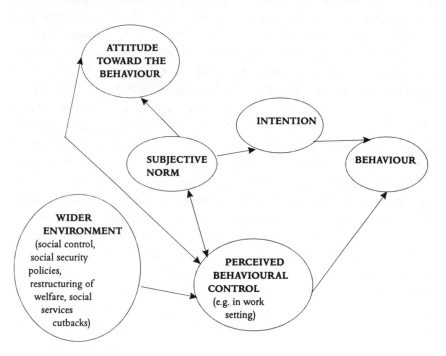

Source: Theory of planned behaviour, adapted from Ajzen and Madden 1986, p.456.

that integrates and develops previous findings on the relationship between poverty and social work.

Methodology

A number of methods were used within the two social work teams to explore social workers' attitudes and actions in relation to poverty issues. Twelve in-depth interviews were conducted with divisional officers, social workers, social work assistants, welfare rights officers and welfare rights assistants and a feedback group discussion on poverty issues was tape recorded with each social work team. Eighteen interviews took place with social service users with financial problems in their own homes. An analysis of twelve months referral data concerning those at the Silverton office who had asked for help with financial difficulties was also included. However, the primary method in understanding social workers' attitudes and actions to poverty related issues was participant observation. Negotiations took place with the two social service departments and later with individuals in the social work teams to accompany social workers and social work assistants on visits as well as observing them in the duty room, attending staff meetings and training days and working with individuals in the office.

At an initial meeting with the two social work teams who agreed to participate in the research, they stressed that the research must not interfere with their daily work. One team had complained to the research officer present that survey research for the Social Fund had involved extra paperwork without the opportunity to comment fully on the issues. Consequently the introductory meeting explained in a three-page paper the main aims, background, progress so far, methodology, benefits of the research for the practitioners and possible final outcomes. All individuals and the social services departments discussed in the research were assured of anonymity. Interviews were conducted and *ad hoc* questions were asked during the observation period when it was convenient for the individual concerned. At the end of the period of field observation both teams were given a three-page feedback paper which was considered with the researcher at team meetings. Recommendations from the papers are discussed later on in the chapter.

All individuals involved in the fieldwork understood that the research brief was concerned with investigating the relationship between attitudes and actions in relation to poverty issues. In the Silverton team, as I observed their practice for three days a week for nine months, the research question appeared to have very little effect on their day-to-day work. I became an accepted member of the team to the extent that the team leader offered me a job at the end of the observation period. The City team, although welcoming, were more aware of research issues and occasionally appeared guarded in their language and behaviour in relation to the research topic. However the length of the second observation period of two days a week for five months meant that the observer and observed were generally relaxed with each other.

As someone whose background and experience as a social worker are complementary with my research interest, my role as a fieldwork observer fits in with Bulmer's (1982) classification of the overt 'insider' who is a 'socialised' stranger. It seems likely that I was accepted and trusted by social services staff in a shorter space of time than it may have taken other researchers because of my understanding of the tasks and processes involved in being a social worker. This would also be true of practitioner researchers. Studies such as Bulmer's have shown that the overt observational approach provides data equal in richness to that yielded by the covert approach and gives access to a wider range of data over which it is possible to exercise a greater degree of control. Bastin (1985) suggests observation is a method that is greatly under-utilised as a contribution to policy planning and is particularly applicable where changes (such as the Social Fund) are likely to have a direct influence on peoples' lives.

There are a number of important considerations that researchers need to take account of before embarking on a participant observation study. First, recipients – both social workers and social service users – need to be assured that the research will be of benefit to them. This could involve producing a report and organising a discussion of the key findings of the research with staff and social service users or discussing with social service users the benefits of social work teams knowing more about users' opinions of the services provided. Second, all individuals need to know that what they say and what they do cannot easily be identified by colleagues or social workers. This may involve not only changing names and locations but combining two fieldwork examples for example, so that an individual's history or an incident is not recognisable. Practitioner researchers would be advised to select social work teams from another authority from the one in which they work, in order to preserve confidentiality and anonymity.

Participant observation has the advantage of being interactive and longitudinal rather than 'snapshot' so there is the opportunity to reinforce particular findings and conclusions. For example feedback periods at the end of the observation period were where policy initiatives were suggested by the researcher but were actively discussed and criticised by the participants rather than them being merely 'objects' of the research. The fieldwork methodology also 'fitted' the research question. I was interested in establishing how social workers' attitudes to poverty could be understood in relation to their actions. Very few other methods allow the researcher to record and observe attitudes and also observe actions. Without a familiarity with the subjects of the study and the environment over time, it would be impossible to assess whether such attitudes and actions were contrived for the researcher.

The study of two social work teams demonstrated practice that was generally more complex and contradictory in relation to poverty issues than previous studies such as Becker's (1987) study of attitudes to poverty or Pithouse's (1988) observation study of childcare teams. This may be because few studies of social work practice have observed social workers at work with social service users. Researchers who wish to understand the working of social work face similar barriers in terms of evaluating professional practice as social science researchers who are researching other professional groups or elites. Pithouse (1988), not a qualified social worker, did not observe social workers on visits or on the duty desk. Practitioner researchers are more likely to be able to negotiate a fully participant observation.

Most of us, if interviewed, are likely to give an account of our work which might not completely reflect the reality. Participant observation can thus offer a valuable method with which to understand how attitudes and actions interact. It appears relatively unacknowledged as a research methodology that can lead to action research and the development of policy initiatives (Burgess 1988).

The Fieldwork Findings

Section 17 (formerly Section 1) of the Children Act 1989 allows social workers to give cash help to parents to prevent their children coming into or continuing to be in care. Food, food vouchers and primarily direct cash help was the main form of financial help that social workers or team leaders had the power to authorise. Even though they were only allowed to give small amounts of cash, there was high demand for Section 17 money. Social workers in both teams disliked taking turns at duty – covering all the public enquiries that came in on a particular day or half day. Social workers' attitudes to Section 17 money in both teams were also generally negative. They felt uncomfortable about being in the position of judging who should and who should not get cash help.

Keith was a qualified social worker in the City Team. Keith's attitudes and actions to people with financial problems during the five-month observation period appeared positive. He had invited me to accompany him on a visit to a solicitor with a female client of his with learning disabilities. She had been wrongly advised that she could buy her council flat and had paid a small deposit. He was concerned that she was being exploited and had arranged a reduced-fee legal aid visit with her to sort out the problem. A month later I was observing his time on the duty desk. His attitude and actions to clients of his that he considered 'deserving' was in contrast to his attitudes and actions to individuals who came to claim Section 17 monies from the duty desk. They appeared consistent in each case but would vary according to how he perceived the client. Some colleagues and other staff in the workplace supported the notion that giving out money was not the job of social workers, should be sorted out by the Department of Social Security (DSS) and was an inconvenience to social work and administrative staff. Some staff also made the distinction between 'deserving' (mostly people who did not come to social services at all) and 'undeserving' (those people who knew about Section 17 money and were able to weave a credible 'hard luck' story). In terms of the Ajzen and Madden (1986) model, Keith also perceived behavioural control from his work setting concerning how much he could give to individuals on the duty desk. Restrictive social security policies contributed to pressure on social work staff such that the City team had been obliged to write to all social service users in their area telling them that they would not be able to claim extra resources from social services after the Social Security Act 1989. Furthermore the City social services department was being faced with additional cutbacks.

A young-looking grandmother came in to see Keith on the duty desk. Mrs Grant was looking after her two grandchildren aged three and five years. Her daughter was in prison and she was living on £42 a week income support. She had come to social services because the probation service, who were helping her with furniture after her daughter's flat had been burgled, had sent her. The welfare rights officer had suggested Mrs Grant come to the social services department when he could not get her child benefit sorted out with the DSS. She had not had any child benefit for six weeks since her daughter had gone to prison. She explained: 'I went to borrow money from a neighbour and she said to come here... It's really the bus fares I can't manage.'

Her daughter lived some distance from her, so it was two buses each way to the local school. What did the social worker do? First he questioned her about her story and said social services did not have any money. He then said abruptly without explanation, 'Well, we could take the children into care'.

She chatted to me while he went to check with the receptionist about her request for a letter concerning toys from a charity.

Mrs Grant:	I was really dreading coming here.
Interviewer:	Is it as bad as you thought?
Mrs Grant:	Don't know – what he said was.
Interviewer:	You mean about going into care?
Mrs Grant:	Yes.

Keith later admitted that the statement about the children going into care was said 'partly as a deterrent to stop people keep coming back for money'.

I had assumed he was thinking he could apply for the local authority to take responsibility for the children on paper and then apply to the fostering panel for the grandmother to become the foster mother. However, he had asked no further questions of Mrs Grant regarding taking the children into care, for example how long her daughter was likely to be in prison. Mrs Grant received £5 from Section 17 monies, though I suspect Keith would have preferred to give her nothing but felt constrained by my presence. Although Mrs Grant might not come back to social services as she seemed genuinely frightened, she could quite easily tell friends and neighbours that she had received £5, so the deterrent effect of threatening to take the children into care would be diminished.

Later that day Keith told me he had only got £15 left to spend on duty cases. The team leader had told him that the limit was £30 per day as the social services budget was overspent after the first six months of the year. Another social worker had spent £10 not knowing about the £30 limit, and Mrs Grant had £5. We discussed a woman with twins who had rung him up to say the DSS had not sent her milk tokens. Keith was worried she was going to come in and ask for money.

Keith had management pressure to keep within a financial budget and the administrative officer acted as the department's gatekeeper. He did not want to be a substitute for a DSS officer and his actions concerning maintaining the income of an individual when the DSS had failed to pay Mrs Grant child benefit put him in this category. He also wanted to be seen as a 'good' social worker and the perceived behavioural control and norms (see Figure 8.1) from the social services department appeared to be concerned with managing a caseload effectively and keeping within the departmental budget. Keith discussed another social work team who, in making a protest about financial deprivation in their area, had given out Section 17 monies to individual families on demand resulting in a large overspend on the Section 17 budget. This was not seen as 'good' social work practice by managers in City social services department. Keith's intention was to dissuade people coming to the duty desk for money. Despite his positive attitudes and actions for clients in financial need on his caseload, Keith's comments on a number of occasions were cynical about people coming to social services for money. He seemed to see the process as some sort of game with them 'trying it on' and him 'turning them off'. This sort of process implies different attitudes and actions for the different players in the game and has different outcomes according to social constructionist theory for Keith, Mrs Grant, the administrative officer and others. No one account of the process is the 'true' account.

> The psychologist's (or sociologist's) privileged position of being able to define, over the heads of participants, the true nature of events has proved a powerful one in experimental studies, but it is a position that can also be illusory (there is no single, definitive version of everyday events), and risks losing sight of what is real for participants themselves. It focuses attention on objective truth and error, and underestimates the constructive, occasioned and rhetorically designed nature of how events are ordinarily described (Potter and Edwards 1992, p.5).

From a social constructionist perspective both attitudes and actions are forms of behaviour and cannot easily be separated into discrete units. Individuals construct their behaviour which includes attitudes in order to accomplish social actions. Using this cognitive model (Potter and Edwards 1992) the field observations confirmed that Keith had no overall 'attitude' to poverty or poor people. His attitudes and practice varied depending on the situation and his assessment of individual need in relation to what he saw as the role of a social worker.

Conflicting attitudes and actions to giving out Section 17 monies are illustrated in the fieldwork by the example of the Silverton team leader and the social work staff in that team. Silverton social workers sometimes lent or gave their own money to social service users in financial difficulties because the team leader was only prepared to sanction Section 17 monies for ongoing casework. Again the team leader's attitudes and actions were consistent in that those individuals who were referred by professionals and were seen on a regular basis were defined as more 'deserving' than those who referred themselves to social services for financial help even though they often had other needs too.

It is unlikely that the part of a social worker's role which is concerned with aiding those in financial difficulties will disappear. Government legislation and policy seems to indicate the 'cash' role may well become a greater part of the social work task in the future in a number of different ways: the social worker as community care purchaser rather than provider, the social worker advising on or allocating community care grants, and the social worker having to make direct cash payments because of low benefit entitlement or simply insufficient resources.

However, this study did also show that positive attitudes and actions could achieve positive results when welfare rights issues were tackled in conjunction with a welfare rights officer. Often social work assistants whose attitudes in interview were that practical benefits were extremely important in helping people in need were motivated to work closely with welfare rights officers. One social work assistant with help from a social worker and welfare rights officer had set up a weekly benefits clinic at a day centre for the elderly. Another with support from the welfare rights officer managed to claim a lump sum from the Department of Social Security for a wrongly assessed benefit claim for a lone parent with learning disabilities. The mother, her young son and elderly mother were able to pay for a holiday at Butlins with the proceeds.

Is There a Way Forward?

How can social workers and others – professionals and claimants/clients be better prepared for working with the problems of poverty? First, if the link between cash and care is to be effective, it must be based on some commonly accepted minimum income for all (Leaper, 1988; George and Howards 1991). Second, an ombudsman, such as those set up in some local authorities as a result of the community care legislation, who could safeguard social service users' rights regarding cash and care decisions would probably be more relevant than the tribunal system for social security issues. Social services departments which are now, more than in the past, subject to pressures regarding income maintenance should be equally willing to have their decisions regarding poverty issues subject to scrutiny. Third, training on poverty awareness and welfare benefits for social services staff would reinforce how important the issue of practical and financial help is for social service users and carers.

The most common finding from the fieldwork was that in the two social work teams observed, overworked and understaffed social workers tended to be unaware of the effects of their decisions regarding income maintenance issues. Poverty was such a common part of the everyday work of a social services office that it tended to be overlooked, ignored and treated superficially. Many of the social workers in the two teams saw work on the duty desk as less important, less 'deserving' of their time than statutory child care work and their caseloads.

From interviews with social service users, it became clear that going to a social service waiting room and asking for help was very important and was the only way that users could ask directly for help rather than being referred by professionals. Hill, Tolan and Smith (1984) note that the majority of social workers only became involved in financial problems because social service users brought the problems to them and not because social workers felt them to be an important part of their work. As Beresford and Croft (1993, p.50) comment in relation to community care, 'they [users] want services which respond to their needs, which consult with them, in which they have a say and sometimes which they run themselves'. Stewart and Stewart (1991) have also shown that financial debt is often linked to significant and traumatic life events. Early social work intervention on a practical level might prevent more intensive work at a later stage.

In terms of the theory of planned behaviour (Figure 8.1), it could be argued that social workers' attitudes towards poverty were positive but that subjective norms of colleagues, team leaders and higher management tended to recognise, for example, excellence in statutory child care work rather than the relief of poverty as an indication of a 'good' social worker. As Stewart and Stewart (1988, p.28) note: 'Priority in local authority social work is given to statutory work, particularly involving child care, and beyond that it is a matter of reacting to bombardment.'

The conflict between attitudes and actions in the Silverton team was concerned with having positive attitudes to aiding those in poverty and negative attitudes to dealing with welfare rights in some cases and in other cases to income maintenance. Actions in relation to users were concerned with giving out money, clothes or food vouchers but not working with users to claim what they were entitled to. Conflict in the City team was more likely to be concerned with positive attitudes towards welfare rights, but being able to do very little in practice. Perceived behavioural control from management, which usually involved statutory cases, was stronger than the pressure for help from users with financial problems.

From a social constructionist perspective, social workers' accounts which define users as 'undeserving' may include all users who are not in a casework relationship with a social worker, because this version of events would construct social work as social workers may wish to perform it. Alternative accounts of social work constructed by social service users or carers, managers, the DSS, the government or social work academics might have a different purpose.

The Feedback Sessions from the Fieldwork

Social workers in both teams participated in feedback sessions on the research and had opportunities to comment on a paper documenting disjunctions between their behaviour and general attitudes or the relationship between their behaviour and external influences. The feedback paper for each team identified a number of ways in which poverty issues could be dealt with more effectively. Although I had a good relationship with most of the social workers in both teams, there was some cynicism in the group discussions concerning the research findings. They had not chosen the research topic and although they were interested in the results, they did not expect the recommendations to alleviate the stressfulness of their present work situation.

The Silverton team was based in a rural area with high unemployment and social work staff were generally well-known and local. Their feedback paper reported that an analysis of referrals over the last year had shown approximately 25 per cent of referrals as financial and designated 'No Further Action' and that the majority of social work cases observed during the nine months with the team involved financial deprivation. A duty officer who had extra training in welfare rights and whose sole responsibility was to help people who have financial enquiries was therefore recommended. The team felt this was a role no one would wish to take on as this type of work would be too 'boring'. A limited caseload of people who had long-term financial problems and who were to be allocated to a social worker, could make it more interesting. A further recommendation was that a training and support day once a month where poverty-related issues were discussed, perhaps with members of the welfare rights team, was organised. This would not necessarily be a welfare rights information giving session but a workshop/surgery where social workers could present cases connected with poverty that are proving problematic and hear advice or information from whoever was there. It could also provide a useful forum for discussing more general issues like the Social Fund or imminent changes in social security benefits. This had a positive reception from the Silverton team who were generally keen to gain more information and wished to be supported in their work. However the team leader was not convinced that more meetings would be useful.

The City team also had a generally long-serving staff group but were based in a poor inner city area. A once-a-month team meeting was suggested to tackle poverty issues with or without welfare rights workers. Individual cases could be presented, thus sharing advice and support in a more formal way. Newcomers and students could learn more about the contacts and networks that existed and the information exchanged could increase everyone's knowledge of the area (the team operated on a patch basis), its clients and its resources. In this team, the team leader was keen to develop this recommendation but individual team members were less positive because they appeared to feel such meetings would add to their feelings of being overwhelmed with their work. Their feedback paper was entitled *A Team under Siege*.

I could only make, not enforce, the recommendations in the two feedback papers. The team leaders in both teams and divisional officers who had approved the research would need to implement the research findings if they thought they were useful for the social work teams.

Conclusion

Observation of social workers appeared to show that perceived practice in relation to poverty issues was more unsatisfactory than other studies of poverty and social work would suggest. This is an important finding which was not anticipated at the start of the research. There were examples of good, sensitive practice with individual social service users in financial need in both teams but more examples of neutral practice where the users' financial problems were ignored or not taken seriously.

It seems likely that the reader should be wary of studies which research attitudes and behaviour of social work practice but do not include field observation or theoretical models that explain whether attitudes and actions correspond. Social constructionist's theory and social psychological theories on the relationship between attitudes and actions are not complementary but rather in epistemological opposition to each other – the roots of the former being sociological and the latter psychological. The position of this research is that attitudes and actions of social workers in relation to poverty issues were sometimes affected by subjective norms, prior beliefs and management pressure as the social psychological theoretical approach and the 'snapshot' methodological approach suggest. On other occasions, social workers responded 'on the hoof' to individual circumstances in ways that would fit better with a social constructionist theoretical position and a participant observation methodology. It is suggested that social constructionist theory and social psychological theory can develop our understanding of why social workers behave as they do in relation to poverty issues, and that the purpose of using two alternative theoretical frameworks concerning attitudes and actions is so that the reader can understand how each of the models 'fits' the fieldwork findings in different ways and in different places.

Social work practice cannot be evaluated by merely examining only attitudes or actions of practitioners. Further evaluative research needs to demonstrate the use of a variety of different methodological tools and, equally importantly, needs to develop a range of theoretical constructs from which social work practice can be viewed.

References

Ajzen, I. and Madden, T. (1986), 'Prediction of goal-directed behaviour attitudes, intentions and perceived behavioural control.' *Journal of Experimental Social Psychology* 32, 453–474.

Atherton, C., Gemmel, R., Haagenstad, S., Holt, D., Jensen L., O'Haran D. and Rehner T. (1993) 'Measuring attitudes towards poverty: a new scale.' *Social Work Research and Abstracts 29*, 4, 28–30.

Bastin, R. (1985) 'Participant observation in social analysis.' In R. Walker (ed) *Applied Qualitative Research*. Aldershot: Gower.

Becker, S. (1987) 'Social workers' attitudes to poverty and the poor.' PhD Thesis, University of Nottingham.

Beresford, P. and Croft, S. (1993) *Community Care and Citizenship in Community Care – A Reader.* Buckingham: Open University Press.

Bulmer, M. (1982) 'When is disguise justified? Alternatives to covert participant observation.' In R. Burgess (ed)*Qualitative Sociology.* London: Human Science Press.

Burgess, R. (1988) *Studies in Qualitative Methodology.* Middlesex: JAI Press.

Children Act 1989. London: HMSO.

Craig, G. and Coxall, J. (1989) *Monitoring the Social Fund. A Bibliography 1985–9.* Bradford: University of Bradford.

Dean, R. and Fleck-Henderson, A. (1992) 'Teaching clinical theory and practice through a constructivist lens.' *Journal of Teaching in Social Work 6,* 1, 3–20.

George, V. and Howards, I. (1991) *Poverty Amidst Affluence.* Aldershot: Edward Elgar.

Hill, M., Tolan, F. assisted by Smith, R. (1984) *Impact of Changes in the Supplementary Benefits System upon Local Authority Social Services Departments.* School of Advances Urban Studies, University of Bristol (unpublished).

Leaper, B. (1988) 'Cash and care in a European perspective.' In S. Becker and S. MacPherson (eds) *Public Issues, Private Pain.* London: Insight Books.

Parsloe, P. and Stevenson, O. (1978) *Social Services Teams: The Practitioner's View.* London: HMSO.

Pithouse, A. (1988) *Social Work: The Social Organisation of an Invisible Trade.* London: Sage.

Potter, J. and Edwards, D. (1992) *Discursive Psychology.* London: Sage.

Reeser, L. and Epstein, I. (1987) 'Social workers' attitudes toward poverty and social action: 1968–1984.' *Social Service Review 61,* 4, 610–22.

Satyamurti, C. (1981) *Occupational Survival. The Case of the Local Authority Social Worker.* Oxford: Blackwell.

Schifter, D. and Ajzen, I. (1985) 'Intention, perceived control and weight loss: an application of the Theory of Planned Behaviour.' *Journal of Personality and Social Psychology 49,* pp.843–851.

Smith, G. (1980) *Social Need.* London: Routledge and Kegan Paul.

Stewart, G. and Stewart, J. (1988) *The Beginning of the End? Welfare Rights Workers' Experience of the Amended Single Payment Regulations.* Middlesborough: Cleveland County Welfare Rights Service for WROG.

Stewart, G. and Stewart, J. (1991) *Relieving Poverty: Use of the Social Fund by Social Work Clients and Other Agencies.* London: Association of Metropolitan Authorities.

Part Two

Evaluating Social Work

Some Ways Forward

CHAPTER 9

Analysing the Content of Social Work
Applying the Lessons from Qualitative Research

Susan White

Introduction

The last decade has delivered many important developments in the evaluation of social work interventions. The drive to demonstrate efficacy and efficiency has been fuelled by ascending managerialism and consumerism (Newman and Clarke 1994; Pollitt 1990) within public services, but social work practitioners have also wanted to evaluate and improve their practice. Positive though many of these developments are, 'evaluation studies' are currently dominated by the empiricist paradigm. That is, they tend to rely upon the development of measurable criteria against which interventions are retrospectively judged. In turn, the generation of such criteria depends upon certain presuppositions, which, in themselves, remain unresearched. Hence, a concentration on *outcome* can render the social work *process* immune from analysis. It can obscure as well as illuminate.

In one sense, my own position builds upon a well-established 'single-case' design (see, *inter alios*, Kazi, this volume; Sheldon 1983, 1986) in social work evaluation studies, because I, too, believe that social workers and managers *must* build evaluation and self-monitoring into their work. However, my recipe for analysing the 'content' of social work is a synthesis of practitioner/evaluator approaches, Holland's (1990, 1991, 1993) work on metatheory and reflexivity in social work, and more recent discourse analytic approaches to professional encounters (e.g. Stancombe and White 1997) which will be referred to below. As such it signals a clear departure from the dominant empiricist tradition.

In many ways, the ideas in this piece are the product of the particular circumstances in which I found myself during the mid-1990s. The gestation period for the original version of this paper (White 1995) coincided with a time in which I had entered academia, whilst also remaining employed as a manager of a 'children and families' team in a local authority social services department. This experience cast into sharp relief the competing conceptual demands imposed by these two 'worlds', but also illuminated some striking similarities between the analytic processes of theory generation and the ways in which the sense-making activity in social work assessment *ought* to be conducted. My disciplinary background in sociology and a methodological commitment to ethnography in my doctoral research pushed me to develop the analogy further. I had a sense of being pulled back and forth – from the position of experienced practitioner to that of naive researcher. In the process, I experienced the unveiling of many of my own practice preconceptions as I endeavoured to render explicit the tacit assumptions upon which 'thinking as usual' (Atkinson 1995) depends. I believe that this was a wholly positive thing for my practice, and this belief led me to consider how research may help to nurture critical self-reflection in others.

Arcane debates have long been taking place within interpretive sociology, and also amongst social work academics, concerning the nature of knowledge, how it may best be acquired and how disputes between competing versions of 'reality' should be settled. Should we aim to be rigorous scientists or intuitive artists? Should we strive for objectivity or embrace subjectivity and emotional connectedness? These debates are not confined to academic circles. They rage, in different guise, throughout social work practice. Paradoxically, it has been possible for social workers to use both objectivism and subjectivism to justify their knowledge claims. Recourse to formal 'scientific' knowledge and categorisations can grant legitimacy to accounts that contradict lay opinion; yet practitioners often invoke the subjective concept of 'empathy' in order to signal their superior understanding of a situation and thus to warrant their own interpretation.

It has become important for these (meta) theoretical questions to be made accessible to practitioners and managers. It would be naive to suppose that a consensus about 'good practice' could thus be achieved and, indeed, this would not be desirable: for consensus can stifle debate and close down new possibilities. However, the tacit assumptions underpinning the interpretive processes of assessment must be made more explicit if we are to be able to capture and appraise the 'content' of social work.

My formula to this end draws upon what Brewer (1994) has called 'the ethnographic critique of ethnography'. Brewer is referring to debates within social science about the validity, reliability and practical utility of ethnography. I have discussed these issues elsewhere (White 1997a) and I shall begin this chapter by revisiting some of the salient points of this argument. The theoretical aspects of the arguments are discussed further in this earlier work, but here I shall summarise my position by locating the information gathering and analysis associated with assessment as interpretive and essentially ethnographic activities. I shall discuss the ways in which philosophers and social scientists have sought to understand the processes involved in 'sense-making', and shall identify some evaluative criteria which may be used in supervision and in social work education to further our understanding of, and allow us to make judgements about, the 'content' of social work.

However, in this paper, I should like to push the discussion a little further, and to talk about the transformative and critical potential of *research* activity which eschews *prescription*, in favour of detailed analytic *descriptions* of the activities and language used by social workers in their everyday encounters. Thus, alongside the discussion of practice, I shall consider the implications of my arguments for social work *research* agendas, drawing, for example, upon current methodological debates within 'psychotherapy process research' (e.g. Seigfried 1995).

Comparing Assessment and Ethnography

What is ethnography?

First, it is essential to draw the distinction between different research traditions and the forms of understanding they generate. The discussion below is heavily condensed and simplified. I leave the thornier dimensions of debates about 'reality' (ontology) unstated, and gloss over some of the nuances of particular epistemological (issues concerning the nature of knowledge) positions. In so doing, I run the risk of reproducing the myth that qualitative and quantitative methods are mutually exclusive or in competition. This is not my intention; quantitative data must be *interpreted* and the more recent approaches accept that enquiry of *any* kind cannot be stripped of presuppositions or be conceptually neutral (Sayer 1992). Similarly, qualitative research should pay attention to the *frequency* with which a particular phenomenon occurs (Hammersley 1992; Silverman 1986, 1993). My primary purpose here, however, is to consider the particularly interpretive nature of ethnography and of social work assessment and their shared reliance upon familiarity and the 'insider' view, and it upon these issues that I have focused the discussion.

Qualitative research and ethnographic methodology have been in the ascent within sociology since the late 1960s. This shift was initially spawned from the critique of 'positivism' of which objectivity is the cherished bedrock, with researcher and researched seen as separate and distinct. Positivism is concerned with the testing of hypotheses, with *observable* phenomena, and the production of generalisable 'laws'. Clearly this methodology has continued relevance in the natural sciences and has considerable utility within social sciences. However, it has been criticised on a number of counts, and centrally because of the assumption that the researcher can remain 'outside' of the phenomenon under investigation. Positivism has also been largely unconcerned with lay accounts, treating them as corrigible or irrelevant (Blaikie 1993). This has left the processes by which individuals understand the world and the *meanings* they ascribe to it unexplored. In the context of social work, this neglect has rendered invisible the meanings service-users ascribe to events, but it has also obscured some of the meanings and models of causation which *social workers* routinely (and habitually) attribute to events.

Interpretive social science, on the other hand, has been centrally concerned with the construction of *meanings* and with the *generation* of theory *from* data. Explanation thus ideally flows from *description* rather than being presupposed in the form of a hypothesis. This process is often referred to as 'analytic induction'. The interpretive approach, then, emphasises authenticity rather than objectivity, and is deeply sceptical about linear models of causation.

Assessment as an interpretive activity

The term 'assessment' is now applied to a diverse range of activities and is necessarily influenced by particular social policy initiatives, by the pro formas produced by the Department of Health (e.g. DoH 1988), and so forth. However, following Lloyd and Taylor (1995), I believe that, except in their most trivial form, even prescriptive assessment schedules require certain analytic skills to be employed in their interpretation. In undertaking this activity, many social workers would (cl)aim to possess the external and detached ('professional') qualities revered by positivism. However, the notion of empathic understanding seems contradictory to this position. It involves some notion of immersion in the lived experience of the service user and thus the boundaries between subject and object become blurred. The criterion of 'detachment' is thus rendered problematic, leaving us with the question 'how should the validity of a worker's account be assessed?'

Ethnographic research, too, is characterised by the researcher's 'deep familiarity' (Lofland 1995) with the objects of study. Indeed, 'familiarity' is routinely invoked by researchers to authenticate their knowledge claims (Atkinson 1990). Thus, the status as 'witness' is a crucial aspect of both social work assessment and ethnographic research.

This shared characteristic is also identified by Sheppard (1995), who argues that social work assessment has much in common with the technique of 'analytic induction' characteristic of qualitiative methodologies. Sheppard goes on to suggest that this technique (treated by him as synonymous with 'retroduction', see below) may be used as a heuristic device to help us to understand and evaluate the process of assessment. Sheppard's analysis is useful, but he leaves certain problematic areas unexplored, and he tends to reinforce the dominant practice ideologies which can lead to workers 'jumping to conclusions' – a practice he is seeking to remedy. Before expanding on these criticisms, however, I must consider some philosophical questions.

Capturing 'Reality'?

Social work has not traditionally concerned itself with philosophy, and a similar inattention has been noted amongst ethnographers. However, Hammersley warns:

> There is no escape from philosophical assumptions for researchers [social workers]. Whether we like it or not, and whether we are aware of them or not, we cannot avoid such assumptions. And, sometimes, the assumptions that we make lead us into error. (1992, p.43)

At the heart of these assumptions is the belief that the products of research (or assessment) should directly correspond to a fixed and unproblematic external reality. This assumption may be contrasted with the interpretivist view of lay understandings and the associated commitment to uncovering the *meanings* which social actors routinely use to understand their world. This latter premise leads inevitably to the view that 'reality' is mediated by human consciousness.

Parallels may be drawn here with social work's commitment to 'anti-oppressive' practice. It has attempted to achieve critical distance from ethnocentric or patriarchal (Western scientific) interpretations, whilst simultaneously asserting the validity of its own professional interpretations. 'Oppressive' viewpoints are accepted as social products, but our own professional interpretations are 'true'. However if we were to treat *all* our knowledge claims as contingent upon a particular set of pre-suppositions we would potentially enter an abyss in which the progressive nature of knowledge acquisition may be questioned. The critics of such 'relativism' assert that if everything were 'socially constructed' we would enter a Peter Pan world of infinite possibilities, where we could fly or be eternally young if only we believed it strongly enough. Clearly, under such a regime patently cruel practices (or even murder or infanticide) could be treated as acceptable so long as the account of the perpetrator was internally consistent. Such nihilism is incompatible with the purpose of social work.

It will now be clear that, far from being highly esoteric and irrelevant, these controversies have been affecting social work for some time. Hammersley suggests that there is a way out of the realism vs. relativism conundrum and urges researchers to 'adopt a more subtle view of realism' (Hammersley 1992, p.50). This version of 'realism' acknowledges the existence of an independent reality but accepts that research (or assessment) can never faithfully reproduce it. Representation must always be partial and fallibilistic, which allows for the coexistence of competing but equally valid claims about the same phenomenon. So, whilst it is not sufficient for social workers to claim that they 'know' certain things because they witnessed them (or because they have a handy theory which seems to fit), neither can a worker's assessment be easily invalidated by, for example, a parent's claim to know their child best. Both of these claims would be making 'rhetorical appeals to naive realism and they are not sustainable because of the weakness of that philosophical position' (Hammersley 1992, p.52). Rather, such claims should be treated as evidence, with the central concern becoming the reflexive monitoring of the underlying *assumptions* and the *actions* taken as a result of them. Holland (1993) makes a similar point in relation to social work practice, suggesting that the knowledge and skills social workers need for practice should be built upon an awareness of the consequences of seeing the world through a particular set of theoretical lenses.

This does not mean that competing knowledge claims will always be 'equally valid'. This is patently nonsense, and even those most fervently

accused of anarchic relativism would eschew such a notion. Richard Rorty
has been so accused and notes:

> 'Relativism' is the view that every belief on a certain topic, or perhaps
> about *any* topic, is as good as every other. No one holds this view... The
> philosophers who get *called* relativists are those who say that the grounds
> for choosing between opinions are less algorithmic than had been
> thought. (Rorty 1980, pp.727–28)

Rorty's point is that it is often inappropriate to rely on 'algorithmic' means to
justify knowledge claims (that is those which are generated by some
procedure which purports to be sure and certain and which thereby
guarantees their validity). This shuts down debate and hence makes error
more rather than less likely. I explore the consequences for social work of this
kind of complacent certainty below.

What's wrong with ethnography?

The acceptance that ethnographic accounts may be only one of a number of
equally valid interpretations of a particular phenomenon raises implications
for evaluation. For social workers the link between data (observation and
dialogue) and subsequent 'problem' construction cannot be side-stepped,
since the ideas so generated have powerful material consequences for service
users, and so-called 'naive realist' accounts are often demanded by the courts,
who will frequently reject more 'hedged' testimony (Bourdieu 1986;
Teubner 1989). I return to this issue briefly later in this chapter, but can we
learn something from parallel debates within interpretive sociology?

To summarise some very complex debates, there appear to me to be three
primary criticisms of some ethnographic works, which equally may be
applied to social work assessment. First, whilst an account may satisfy basic
criteria of plausibility and may be supported by evidence which suggests a
particular causal relationship, it will remain problematic if the researcher does
not consider *other* competing explanations (or *disconfirming* evidence).
Second, the *frequency* of occurrence of a particular phenomenon is often
ignored. As a result ethnographies (and assessments) are potentially
indistinguishable from anecdote and prejudice. Third, ethnographers are
accused of failing to make explicit the theoretical preferences and personal
values which saturate the interpretations of their findings.

It is tempting for social workers to adopt a complacent 'we know all this
already' attitude to these criticisms. Are we not old hands at 'empowerment'

and 'anti-oppression'? The psychodynamic legacy of our profession, with its attendant concepts of transference and countertransference, has made self-awareness a pre-requisite and elevated introspection to centre stage. We are surely streets ahead of the ethnographers. Unfortunately this is often not the case, for we frequently fail to recognize the potential for our theories to become dogma and naively treat them as truth. In order to develop this point I must return to Sheppard's arguments.

What's wrong with assessment?

The major potential deficiencies and pitfalls of assessment are identified by Sheppard (1995, p.278–9) as follows:

> Poor practice is marked by a lack of clarity in hypothesis formulation. The search for disconfirming evidence is made difficult by the difficulty in identifying what it is that is being disconfirmed... Sensitivity to disconfirming evidence has two dimensions. First, it is possible for a practitioner to proceed in a manner which seeks to confirm initial impressions or preconceived ideas... The second relates to evidence, although collected during assessment, which, because it contradicts explicit or implicit hypotheses, is ignored... These instances represent the professional equivalent of 'jumping to conclusions'.

This is clearly the case, and Sheppard's analysis has much to commend it. However, he, too, treats some of the dominant theoretical models in use in social work as unproblematic, and appears to subscribe to a naive realist epistemology. For instance he implies that if a sufficiently rigorous approach is adopted it should be possible to scientifically differentiate between the better and the worst interpretations of a given presenting problem. Sheppard does not consider the possibility of competing accounts of equal validity, and, moreover, he inadvertently displays his own theoretical preferences as follows:

> A 14-year-old may be referred by his...parents because he is disobedient and close to being 'out of control'... The parents may themselves present this as a personality issue: this is an awkward life stage and a nasty egocentric boy. As a loose initial hypothesis (presenting problem) this can be examined by seeking evidence. Initial interviews with him may show him to be more sensitive than presented by the parents... We then may search for alternatives, examining family dynamics. We may

discover that his mother has been increasingly 'snappy' over the past year, has...shown no interest in what he is doing and communicated this lack of interest dismissively and with verbal aggression. Both parents have been arguing. Such a line of investigation contains an implicit hypothesis that the parent–child relationship is poor...the father and mother have been arguing frequently, and this relates to poor performance of her traditional (maternal) role... We may then hypothesise that the woman is depressed because she feels trapped within the limits of her traditional role expectations. Although the boy's problems cannot be ignored, the central problem is in fact the mother's depression, arising from her individual experience of oppression. (Sheppard 1995 p.276)

Sheppard has a particular interest in maternal depression (1994a and b), and his preference for this as a (linear) causal explanation is apparent. Moreover, my own work (White 1997b) shows that social workers show a clear preference for 'stories' which hold parents responsible for problems experienced by children, which I term a 'parent as culpable for problems in the child' discourse. Thus, far from demonstrating a rigorous scepticism, Sheppard simply reproduces a 'preferred', but tacit professional presupposition. This kind of error can easily occur in practice if the meanings service users give to situations are simply treated as obstacles to be overcome.

Settling on one version of 'reality' or causation is necessarily governed by choice. This choice is not completely arbitrary, but neither is it objective and neutral. What is required is a particular form of reflexivity through which one can recognise one's own location within a paradigm (discourse, professional ideology). Bourdieu calls this 'epistemic reflexivity' and contrasts it with 'textual reflexivity' (see Bourdieu and Wacquant 1992), by which he refers to the trend for researchers to bare their soul in the writing of their ethnographies, treating the reader to an autobiography of the research experience. This kind of reflexivity is familiar within social work, but it is not enough. The choice of hypothesis is not unfettered but 'occurs in the context of ontological, conceptual and theoretical assumptions' (Blaikie 1993, p.168), held by the researcher (practitioner). It is only be fostering epistemic reflexivity that we can render explicit the tacit assumptions which underpin 'business as usual'.

The particular hypothesis a worker presents to their manager, to a court or to another third party, is more likely to be treated as credible if it conforms to dominant professional background expectancies (cf. Hak 1992). These will shift over time and can become dominant to a point where they appear to be incontrovertible and uncontroversial truths. Parton (1991), Howe (1992) and Thorpe (1994) have variously charted the dominance of child protection within social work discourse. I have argued elsewhere (White 1996) that the ascendancy of attachment theory in child care practice and its incorporation into assessment tools has led to certain 'preferred' formulations. The assessment pro formas, with their scientific gloss, appear to offer algorithmic certainty. These theories and tools may 'fit' with the particular (but necessarily partial) representation the worker is giving of the case, but they have the potential to *generate* that particular viewpoint in the first place. There is thus an intrinsic circularity embedded in the research strategy advocated by Sheppard. Evaluation is about more than falsification and scepticism, it is about *meanings* and *consequences*. We need to take note of Hall's adage:

> The only theory worth having is that which you have to fight off, not that which you speak with profound fluency. (Hall 1992, p.280)

Beyond retroduction?

The problems with the 'retroductive' approach, outlined above, have also been hotly debated within sociology and philosophy resulting in what has been called the 'Abductive' research strategy. This is 'the process used to produce social scientific accounts of social life by drawing on the concepts and meanings used by social actors' (Blaikie 1993, p.176). This approach is exemplified by ethnomethodology (see, for example, Garfinkel 1967) and by grounded theory (Glaser and Strauss 1968). This may appear to open the door to 'anything goes', however there are so many competing professional or scientific interpretations of the same phenomenon (for example, models of causation of mental health problems) that there is scant evidence that the imposition of formal 'scientific' categories results in a less anarchic practice terrain. The practitioner is still left with contingent choices about which way to approach a particular problem.

Implications for Practice and Research

I have already argued that the dominance of the empiricist paradigm has led to a neglect of the *meanings* ascribed to events by service users *and* by social workers themselves. In this concluding section, I should like to examine the implications of the ideas I have outlined above, first, for practice and second, for research.

Practice: evaluative criteria for assessment?

So, what should be done to ensure that the interpretive process of assessment is as rigorous and as *useful* as possible? My first point is that assessments should be judged against the measures of reliability and validity appropriate to the interpretivist paradigm (see Hammersley 1990, 1992; Hammersley and Atkinson 1995; Silverman 1993). Sheppard describes many of these – explicit awareness of theoretical influences, the generation of possible competing explanations and the rigorous search for disconfirming evidence. I have also argued that assessments should give an indication of the *frequency* with which a particular event occurs. This is particularly important where inferences are being drawn on the basis of observed behaviour, such as parental 'emotional unavailability', for example. Simple counting may serve to expose situations in which observations are being selectively reported.

Second, assessments should, as far as possible, 'fit' with lay explanations. There is little value in redefining a parent's request for day care as covert rejection and offering attachment work instead. Sometimes parents are denied access to resources which may help them to feel (and hence to care and cope) better and offered interventions designed to reinforce normative standards of behaviour instead (White 1996). Of course, it is sometimes necessary to try to change the stories families offer about their lives, such as when individuals within families are being seriously hurt or abused. This fact should not deter the worker from beginning the assessment process with what the service users say they need and justifying deviation from it. This approach involves a healthy scepticism on the part of the worker about tidy linear causal models. The fact that we have found a neat fit does not make a particular view the 'best' (most helpful and efficacious) option. For, as Smail notes in the context of psychodynamic explanatory frameworks, 'what psychotherapy has the perspicacity to understand it has not the power to put right' (Smail 1996, p.4).

Third, it is essential that social work moves away from a naive realist epistemology and accepts that it is futile to try to achieve a simple correspondence between 'reality' and an assessment of it. In the field of human relations reality is rarely so static. Rather than seeing the existence of multiple explanations as negative, uncertainty can be embraced, for it carries more hope for change than deterministic and linear explanations.

If we accept that there are a number of ways in which a given situation may be interpreted and that, by using the criteria above, we have eliminated the possibility of wild inaccuracy, how may we go about 'searching for a better story' (Pocock 1995)? The more helpful stories will shift from case to case and therefore this process cannot be reduced to mechanistic technique. For example, as Pocock suggests, it is a step forward to redefine a child's challenging behaviour as a consequence of her anger at her parents' separation, rather than as intrinsic badness. In another case, however, it may be better to suggest that a baby's excessive crying is the consequence of infantile colic rather than reinforce a mother's view that the child's distress is the result of her own inability to give enough love (see White 1997a for a more detailed discussion of practice implications).

However, as I suggested earlier, social workers have to communicate with other professionals in other arenas, some of whom (notably those in the courts) demand *certainty*, not equivocation. They must also make practical judgements about 'risk'. This means that a wholesale shift to 'subtle realism' is not possible. However, the demands that the law and child welfare science places upon social workers to present (and also to perceive) certain arguments as incontrovertible truths, should not deter practitioners from trying to work differently. By trying new ways of helping, which will often be simpler and less theoretically driven, they may avoid some of the more antagonistic encounters with service users which increasingly characterise work with children and families (Jones and Novak 1993). This is not an argument in favour of the intellectual 'gutting' (Jones 1993) which has accompanied recent changes in the organisation and delivery of services and training. In order to be able to 'fight off' their more theoreticist notions, social workers must be able to navigate through the paradigm map, otherwise a few rather deterministic theories become, to paraphrase Hall's adage, 'spoken with [horrifying] fluency'.

Social workers and their managers must be able to engage at a 'meta' level with social and psychological theory, and with the discourses and ideologies that inevitably saturate their practice, and they must do this without assuming that their constructions are always superior to the 'common sense' and practical reasoning of service users. They must also be brave in legal and quasi-legal arenas and, where necessary and possible, 'own' their equivocation. If they are uncertain about their arguments they must be prepared sometimes to 'show their working' (Antaki 1994). This does not indicate sloppiness, but analytic rigour. It demands a rediscovery of conversation, debate, dissent and controversy.

Research: the problematics of applied sociology

Turning now to the implications for research. The rising consumerism and accountability in contemporary welfare encourages research which purports to be exploring linear, causal, process–outcome issues. However, I suggest that social work has much to learn from 'psychotherapy process research', which, in seeking to identify the 'active ingredients' of therapy, was, until recently, exclusively dominated by empiricist methodologies. However, some problems have been identified with the traditional paradigm which may be summarised as follows:

> ...research questions proposed from within the parameters delimited by the canons of scientific research tend to be disconnected from psycho-therapy and indeed transform it into something else. For not only are the questions we bring to therapy theory laden, but our theories construct the phenomena they are designed to explain...the theory driven distinc-tions we draw determine the questions we ask, the nature of our findings, and thus the picture we draw on the basis of our results. (Kaye 1995, p.38)

In response to such criticisms, Seigfried (1994, 1995) advocates a theoretical turn to ordinary language. Similarly, Kaye (1995) argues that underlying meaning is embedded in the language used in therapy, and that 'discourse analysis' may be an appropriate means to get access to tacit or covert meanings. He construes such research as 'productive rather than repro-ductive' and 'creative rather than representational' (p.52).

Evaluation studies, too, are currently overwhelmingly dominated by a concern with the identification of process–outcome variables. Clearly, such studies have their place. It is, for example, essential that 'outcomes' in residential child care are examined, and it is equally necessary for practitioners to think through whether their interventions are working, and for them to be given meaningful tools to use in that evaluative process. Some interventions (e.g. behavioural approaches) are quite amenable to this kind of evaluation and I do not wish to invalidate such activities. However, there has been a conspicuous neglect by researchers of social workers' talk and written accounts as topics for investigation in their own right, and as sources of information about routine and *habitual* ways of sense-making about cases (Bull and Shaw 1992). The preferences of funding bodies and local authorities for research which has obvious 'policy relevance', means that work which has a general rather than specific importance for practice is squeezed out.

Hence social work is replete with social scientific artefacts of various kinds and this has led to massive swings and fashions in practice orthodoxies, which Minty (1995) dubs professional 'slogans'. This militates against the development of a reflexive approach by practitioners, who are told to embrace the latest idea as *the* newer, purer, quicker, cleaner, less oppressive way to practice. In short, they embrace another hideously pure certainty which shuts down dialogue. This is an unintended consequence of the 'enlightenment' (Bryant 1991) or 'state-counsellor' (Silverman and Gubrium 1989) model of applied social science, which relies on the assumption that social science can make things better by providing information, and that such change is linear and progressive.

Of course, piecemeal change can take place in this way, but there is scant evidence that it leads to wholesale, cost free, positive change. Law notes:

> ...when local conclusions are, for a moment, reached, those conclusions will be transferable only with effort, difficulty, care and caution from where they were created. For what reduces cruelty in one place may simply increase it in another. (Law 1994, p.193)

Hence, I suggest that, alongside important developments in evaluation research, there is room for approaches which seek to understand and explore (and hence to render visible and conscious) ways of conducting business as usual. For example, in the context of family therapy, John Stancombe and myself (Stancombe and White 1997) have recently undertaken a detailed analysis of talk taking place between a therapist and a family, exposing the artful ways in which blamings are accomplished by participants in the cut and thrust of the session. We illustrate how certain tacit and normative assumptions about the right and proper way for mothers, fathers and children to behave are invoked by participants for rhetorical effect. Our intention is not to provide a prescriptive guide on 'how to do therapy without blaming anyone', or to pass judgement on whether blamings affect outcome. Rather, it is to explore the way in which certain statements 'work' in the session, and serve to accomplish a particular version of events. That is, we are concerned with the performative and constitutive potential of language. Such work inevitably enhances practitioners awareness of such processes and it must, in some way, (materially) affect their practice. We have, then, taken our lead from Foucault (1981) and Silverman (1986; 1997), with the view,

Although the researcher cannot tell practitioners how they should be-have, understanding the intended and unintended consequences of act-ions can provide the basis for fruitful dialogue. (Silverman 1997, p.223)

This view of research as facilitative and dialogical puts the practitioner (evaluator) in the driving seat. It places the problem of 'how to practise' firmly with 'the subject who acts' (Foucault 1981, p.13), and expands the research agenda by legitimating approaches which eschew prescription and linear models of causation. Assessment and research rely on the same interpretive processes, and, in the current climate of intellectual 'gutting', we need to nurture the analytic and reflexive practitioner-evaluator. In this piece, I hope that I have opened up some conceptual space towards that end.

References

Antaki, C. (1994) 'Common sense reasoning: arriving at conclusions or travelling towards them?' In J. Seigfried (ed) *The Status of Commonsense in Psychology.* Norwood, New Jersey: Ablex.

Atkinson, P. (1990) *The Ethnographic Imagination: Textual Constructions of Reality.* London: Routledge.

Atkinson, P. (1995) *Medical Talk and Medical Work.* London: Sage.

Audit Commission (1994) *Seen and Not Heard: Co-Ordinating Community Child Health and Social Services to Children in Need: Detailed Evidence.* London: HMSO.

Blaikie, N. (1993) *Approaches to Social Enquiry.* Cambridge: Polity Press.

Bourdieu, P. (1986) 'The force of law: towards a sociology of the juridical field.' *Hastings Law Journal 38*, 814–853.

Bourdieu, P. and Wacquant, L.J.D. (1992) *An Invitation to Reflexive Sociology.* Cambridge: Polity Press.

Brewer, J. (1994) 'The ethnographic critique of ethnography: sectarianism in the RUC.' *Sociology 28*, 1, 231–244.

Bryant, C.G.A. (1991) 'The dialogical model of applied sociology.' In C.G.A. Bryant and D. Jary (eds) *Giddens' Theory of Structuration: A Critical Appreciation.* London: Routledge.

Bull, R. and Shaw, I. (1992) 'Constructing causal accounts in social work.' *Sociology 26*, 4, 635–49.

Department of Health (1988) *Protecting Children: A Guide for Social Workers Undertaking a Comprehensive Assessment.* London: HMSO.

Foucault, M. (1981) 'Questions of method.' *Ideology and Consciousness 8*, 13–14.

Garfinkel, H. (1967) *Studies in Ethnomethodology.* Englewood Cliffs NJ: Prentice Hall.

Glaser, B.G. and Strauss, A.L. (1968) *The Discovery of Grounded Theory.* London: Weidenfeld and Nicholson.

Hak, T. (1992) 'Psychiatric records as transformations of other texts.' In G. Watson and R.M. Seiler (eds) (1992) *The Text in Context: Contributions to Ethnomethodology.* California: Sage.

Hall, S. (1992) 'Cultural studies and its theoretical legacies.' In L. Grossberg, C. Nelso and P. Treichler (eds) *Cultural Studies.* London: Routledge.

Hammersley, M. (1990) *Reading Ethnographic Research.* Harlow: Longman.

Hammersley (1992) *What's Wrong with Ethnography.* London: Routledge.

Hammersley, M. and Atkinson, P. (1995) *Ethnography Principles in Practice.* London: Routledge.

Holland, R. (1990) 'The paradigm plague: prevention cure and inoculation.' *Human Relations 43,* 23–48.

Holland, R. (1991) 'Reflexive practice and usable theory in family work.' *Issues in Social Work Education 11,* 44–61.

Holland, R. (1993) 'A metatheoretical adventure.' In L. Harrison (ed) *Substance Misuse, Designing Social Work Training.* London: CCETSW.

Howe, D. (1992) 'Child abuse and the bureaucratisation of social work.' *Sociological Review 40,* 3, 491–508.

Jones, C. (1993) 'Distortion and Demonisation: the right and anti-racist social work education.' *Social Work Education 12,* 3, 9–16.

Jones, C. and Novak, T. (1993) 'Social work today.' *British Journal of Social Work 23,* 195–212.

Kaye, J. (1995) 'Postfoundationalism and the language of psychotherapy research.' In J. Seigfried (ed) *Therapeutic Discourse and Everyday Discourse as Behaviour Change: Towards a Micro-analysis in Psychotherapy Process Research.* Norwood, NJ: Ablex.

Law, J. (1994) *Organizing Modernity.* Oxford: Blackwell.

Lloyd, M. and Taylor, C. (1995) 'From Hollis to the orange book: developing a holistic model of social work assessment in the 1990s.' *British Journal of Social Work 29,* 6, 691–710.

Lofland, J. (1995) 'Analytic ethnography: features, failings and futures.' *Journal of Contemporary Ethnography 24,* 1, 30–67.

Minty, M. (1995) 'Social work's five deadly sins.' *Social Work and Social Sciences Review 6,* 1, 48–63.

Newman, J. and Clarke, J. (1994) 'Going about our business? The managerialization of public services.' In J. Clarke, A. Cochrane and E. McLaughlin (eds) *Managing Social Policy.* London: Sage.

Parton, N. (1991) *Governing the Family: Child Care, Child Protection and the State.* Basingstoke: Macmillan.

Pocock, D. (1995) 'Searching for a better story: harnessing modern and postmodern positions in family therapy.' *Journal of Family Therapy 17,* 149–173.

Pollitt, C. (1990) *Managerialism and the Public Services.* Oxford: Basil Blackwell.

Rorty, R. (1980) 'Pragmatism, relativism and irrationalism.' *Proceedings and Addresses of the American Philosophical Association 53,* 719–38.

Sayer, A. (1992) *Method in Social Science: A Realist Approach.* London: Routledge.

Seigfried, J. (ed) (1994) *The Status of Commonsense in Psychology.* Norwood, New Jersey: Ablex.

Seigfried, J. (ed) (1995) *Therapeutic Discourse and Everyday Discourse as Behaviour Change: Towards a Micro-analysis in Psychotherapy Process Research.* Norwood, New Jersey: Ablex.

Sheldon, B. (1983) 'The use of single case designs in the evaluation of social work.' *British Journal of Social Work 13,* 477–500.

Sheldon, B. (1986) 'Social work effectiveness: review and implications.' *British Journal of Social Work 16,* 223–42.

Sheppard, M. (1994a) 'Maternal depression, child care and the social work role.' *British Journal of Social Work 24,* 1, 33–51.

Sheppard, M. (1994b) 'Child care, social support and maternal depression: a review and application of findings.' *British Journal of Social Work 24,* 3, 287–310.

Sheppard, M. (1995) 'Social work, social science and practice wisdom.' *British Journal of Social Work 25,* 3, 265–294.

Silverman, D. (1986) *Qualitative Methodology and Sociology.* Aldershot: Gower.

Silverman, D. (1993) *Interpreting Qualitative Data: Methods for Analysing Talk, Text and Interaction.* London: Sage.

Silverman, D. (1997) *Discourses of Counselling: HIV Counselling as Social Interaction.* London: Sage.

Silverman, D. and Gubrium, J.F. (1989) 'Introduction.' In D. Silverman and J.F. Gubrium (eds) *The Politics of Field Research: Sociology Beyond the Enlightenment.* London: Sage.

Smail, D. (1996) 'Environmental cause and therapeutic cure: the impotence of insight.' *Psychotherapy Section Newsletter 19,* 4–16, British Psychological Society.

Stancombe, J. and White, S. (1997) 'Notes on the tenacity of therapeutic presuppositions in process research: examining the artfulness of blamings in family therapy.' *Journal of Family Therapy 19,* 21–41.

Teubner, G. (1989) 'How the law thinks: towards a constructivist epistemology of law.' *Law and Society Review 23,* 5, 727–56.

Thorpe, D. (1994) *Evaluating Child Protection.* Buckingham: Open University Press.

White, S. (1995) 'Capturing the Content of Social Work: Applying the Lessons from Qualitative Research.' Paper presented at Evaluation of Social Work Conference, University of Huddersfield, September.

White, S. (1996) 'Regulating mental health and motherhood in contemporary welfare services: anxious attachments or attachment anxieties?' *Critical Social Policy 16,* 1, 67–94.

White, S. (1997a) 'Beyond retroduction? Hermeneutics, reflexivity and social work practice.' *British Journal of Social Work, 27,* pp.739–753.

White, S. (1997b) 'Performing Social Work: An Ethnographic Study of Talk and Text in a Metropolitan Social Services Department.' Unpublished PhD thesis, University of Salford.

CHAPTER 10

Promoting Evaluation Research on Social Work Practice

Bruce A. Thyer

Governmental funding and public support for social services is weakening. In the United States, Canada and Great Britain, increases in public welfare funding are not keeping up with increased need, and in some cases funding is being reduced or simply eliminated. Even in the Scandinavian countries, the exemplars of the welfare state, we can see an erosion of public social services. To some extent, in the United States and in some other countries, social workers who have elected the career track of providing mental health/ psychotherapy services are sheltered from the weakening social welfare infrastructure, but even in the private sector, managed care corporations, insurance companies, and state and federal funding sources are reducing the amounts they reimburse for services provided by mental health professionals, including social workers.

There are a number of obvious reasons why this is happening. One is that an increasing proportion of the federal budget goes towards payments on the national debt. This has generated a sceptical examination of many traditional services provided by the state. Not just social services, but virtually all governmental operations – defence, agriculture, arts and so forth – are being affected by budget reductions. Welfare and other human services are taking their share of these cuts. What can we as a profession do to ensure that our discipline does not bear a disproportionate share of the burden in the government's efforts to reduce the national debt? What can we do to ensure that the social care, health and mental health services provided by social workers (who in the US are the largest providers of psychotherapy services in the public sector) are seen as valuable contributions to the functioning of society? To some extent, I believe that the answer is for us as a discipline to undertake a much more extensive effort at empirically demonstrating that what we do provides concrete and effective results – to demonstrate that the clients seen by social workers are significantly and clinically benefited following receipt of our services.

There are a number of ways to try and demonstrate empirically that what we do is beneficial. One approach is to undertake government-funded, large-scale, multi-site, controlled clinical trials. These have the potential benefit of strong methodological rigour, but at the expense of being unable to generalise the results to routine social work services not provided within the context of such carefully supervised experiments. Also, experience has shown that even the best such controlled clinical trials often have sufficient flaws to preclude unambiguous conclusions (Cnaan 1991).

Another approach is to undertake a large-scale critical analysis of recently published literature, hopefully being able to come up with a positive conclusion about the efficacy of social work services. Examples include such recent reviews as MacDonald, Sheldon and Gillespie (1992), published in the *British Journal of Social Work*, Videka-Sherman's (1988) meta-analysis of outcome studies on social work mental health services, and Gorey's (1996) more up-to-date meta-analysis. These too can be extremely valuable additions to the generalised knowledge base of social work practice and of its efficacy, but what they cannot provide is justification for the continuation of funding for a *given* social work agency, service or programme.

There is yet a third approach to demonstrating the value of social work services, and that is for practitioners themselves to undertake small-scale, agency-based evaluations of the outcomes of their own practice. While such local efforts may not yield knowledge which is automatically generalisable to other agencies or practitioners, they do lend themselves very nicely to providing the answers to the most fundamental questions facing our field, namely *Do my clients get better?* or *Do our centre's clients improve?* Expertise in such small-scale evaluation research can be taught to social workers and subsequently applied by them in their practice. In the United States, most Masters programmes teach two required research courses, the first being a general 'survey' of the entire field of research, and the second focusing on evaluation research. Many Masters (MSW) and Bachelors (BSW) programmes require their students to conduct simple evaluations of the outcomes of their own or their internship agency's services.

The revised Code of Ethics recently adopted by the US National Association of Social Workers includes the following statements:

Social workers should monitor and evaluate policies, the implementation of programs, and practice interventions. Social workers should promote and facilitate evaluation and research to contribute to the development of knowledge. Social workers should...fully use evaluation and research evidence in their professional practice. (NASW 1996, p.20)

Similar sentiments can be found in the Code of Ethics of the British Association of Social Workers and the educational standards promulgated by the British Central Council for Education and Training in Social Work (see Cheetham *et al.* 1992, p.5).

The combination of professional training, ethical standards and increasing demands from governmental and private payers for concrete evidence that clients are benefiting are all militating in the direction of social workers becoming more involved in the evaluative research enterprise. One follow-up study of ninety-eight recently trained US MSWs found that over one-third had conducted such studies since graduation (within the past six years) (Yegidis 1993). Interestingly, when clients are asked about the acceptability of using simple evaluation procedures to help assess the outcomes of practice, a large majority of them find such techniques to be very acceptable (Campbell 1988).

These developments are compatible with the vision expressed by American social worker (and former student at the London School of Economics) Edith Abbot over sixty-five years ago:

The faculty and students of a professional school of social work should be together engaged in using the great method of experimental research which we are just beginning to discover in our professional educational programme, and which should be as closely knit into the work of a good school of social welfare as research has been embodied in the programme of a good medical school. (Abbott 1931, p.55)

This seems to be happening. At present there are at least eight Canadian and thirty-seven US social work research centres, mostly located within schools of social work (Nutter and Hudson 1997), as well as a number in Great Britain, such as those at the universities of Stirling and Huddersfield (Cheetham 1994; Kazi 1996).

In returning to the title of this paper, I would like to discuss practical ways in which social workers can evaluate the outcomes of their own practice, and that of their programmes, and in doing so generate knowledge which can be truly useful to them, to agency administrators, to public officials, and ultimately to the recipients of social services.

What is Evaluation Research?

Evaluation research can address many important practice issues beyond those of empirically assessing client or programme outcomes. Needs assessments, formative and process evaluations, quality assurance studies and cost effectiveness studies are but a few examples of evaluative research which does not focus primarily on service outcomes. Royse and Thyer (1996) provide a thorough review of these other approaches, and of the various qualitative and quantitative methodologies which can be used therein. The scope of the present chapter has a more modest focus, however, providing encouragement to practitioners to evaluate empirically the outcomes of their work.

Evaluation research on the outcomes of social work services can be undertaken with individual cases, and it can be done with grouped data from large numbers of clients. There is really only one prerequisite to conduct outcomes-based evaluation research, and that is to have available some reliable and valid indicator of the client's state of affairs. If this is available, and the client's state of affairs can be empirically evaluated at one or more points in time, sometimes before but certainly after social work treatment, then one can undertake simple evaluation studies. There are a number of recent books which provide useful summaries of available rapid assessment instruments, suitable for evaluation research purposes, including information on their reliability, validity and scoring. Agencies interested in undertaking evaluation research are well advised to purchase some of these resources (e.g. Bowling 1997; Fischer and Corcoran 1994; Royse and Thyer 1996).

Outcomes research conducted at the agency or programmatic level does not usually require sophisticated experimental designs, because the questions being asked are not sophisticated. You only need complex designs to answer complex questions. Keep your questions simple, and simple designs are sufficient to provide useful answers.

Take for example the simple question 'Do my clients get better?'. This can be answered with elementary single-case designs such as the 'B' or 'A-B' designs, or perhaps by the simple uncontrolled group designs like the 'post-test only' (or 'X-O') or the 'pre-test–post-test' or 'O-X-O' designs (Royse and Thyer 1996). Both types of simple designs can provide answers to simple questions. One need not employ a more complex design than is necessary to provide a satisfactory answer. And I suspect that most social workers (and their agency directors) would be absolutely delighted to have empirical data answering the question 'Do our clients improve following social work intervention?' in the affirmative.

More complex questions require more involved designs. For example, the question 'Did the social work programme *cause* the clients to improve?' necessitates much greater methodological rigour. One must use a design which controls for various threats to internal validity, rival explanations which could explain client improvement, other than social work services. For example, some problems often remit considerably with the passage of time; or clients may tend to come in during a crisis and, in the fullness of time, their problems tend to resolve regardless of professional involvement; or some extra-therapy events may occur which promotes client improvement. To account for rival explanations such as the mere passage of time, regression to the mean, or concurrent history, various methodologies of experimental control are usually necessary. In single-system designs, this may involve taking baseline data before beginning intervention, deliberately discontinuing treatment, or using baselines of differing lengths. With group designs, some form of no-treatment control may be necessary, ideally one constituted by randomly assigning clients to treatment versus no-treatment or, less ideally, comparing treated clients with an unrelated group which did not receive treatment.

You can readily see that the methodological demands of answering the causal question ('Did social work *cause* the clients to improve?') are exponentially greater than those of answering the more simple evaluative question 'Did my clients get better?'. A major impediment to social workers attempting evaluation research is professional training which conveys the message that only more complex and sophisticated research is worth doing. Let me reiterate: answering the simpler question first is a highly worthwhile endeavor. Attempt to answer more complex questions only after satisfactory answers have been obtained for the simpler ones.

Almost fifty years ago this perspective was aptly stated by John Morgan:

> A continuous succession of fruitful small research enterprises – putting all our weight behind inspiration wherever we find it – will do more good for our cause than overelaboration in planning and frustration in performance. (Morgan 1949, p.153)

The balance of this paper will describe some evaluation research projects which exemplify the small-scale, low-demand strategy I am advocating.

Many of these examples were conducted in collaboration with MSW and PhD students and with agency staff. These projects were conducted in a variety of social work settings, with most being public sector agencies. All these projects have been published in respectable journals in the human services or have been submitted for publication to such outlets. As will be evident, these studies are by no means perfect. Many possess serious flaws, according to the standards of conventional social science research, yet all, I submit, produced useful knowledge for the practitioners involved and ultimately to the clients that they served.

Evaluating a Homeless Shelter's Case Management Services

For many client problems of concern to social workers, it is not possible to obtain some form of pre-test or baseline information. This sometimes makes it difficult to interpret post-test outcome data. However, this need not necessarily be a fatal flaw. For some problems, the absence of formal pre-test data is unnecessary. Take for example, evaluating the outcomes of an agency specialising in adoptive and foster care placements. For these social workers, the most salient outcome measure would be the *numbers* of children placed in adoptive of foster homes and the durability of such placements. Formal pre-test measurements are unnecessary. Another example concerns services to homeless persons.

In my home town of Athens, Georgia (USA), we have a forty-bed homeless shelter, which had an MSW student, Mr George Glisson, serving as associate director. Together Mr Glisson and I planned an evaluation of the homeless shelter services, which went beyond providing a warm place to sleep and several meals to some fairly intensive case management work intended to help the shelter's guests find safe, affordable and long-term housing. Mr Glisson examined all guest records for a four-month period in 1991 and located a total of 100 (out of 124) guests who were not transient individuals. Rather these were persons with a history of living in Athens, and who had been rendered homeless through some circumstance such as a fire in their home, domestic violence or unemployment. Mr Glisson made intensive efforts to track down these individuals some nine to eleven months after they left the homeless shelter and he achieved a remarkable degree of success, locating 71 out of 100 former guests. Of these 71 persons, 41 (58%) were in long-term, safe and relatively affordable housing. What is unusual about this simple outcome study is that we have found *no* similar studies in the homeless literature. Very few, if any, prior studies have examined the success of homeless shelter programmes in helping homeless persons locate satisfactory homes. In terms of research design, this study could be said to be an 'X-O', or post-test-only, design. It is not conventionally seen as a very rigorous design, methodologically, but please note that it was very suitable in helping to answer the question 'Did the guests receiving case management services intended to help them find stable homes residing in suitable housing at follow-up?' The answer is that a surprisingly (to us) large number of them were in such favourable circumstances. Considering that there appeared to be no prior similar studies, we believed this to be a useful contribution to the programme evaluation literature on helping homeless persons. This is an important consideration when evaluating the scientific merits of a proposed research design – namely, are there better studies available in the literature already? If not, then even extremely simply designs represent a potential advance in knowledge. More details of this study can be found in Glisson and Thyer (1996).

Evaluating a Community Service Programme for Criminal Offenders

Dr Gill McIvor conducted an evaluation of a community service (CS) programme for non-violent criminal offenders in Scotland. In lieu of large fines or prison sentences, these offenders were sentenced to provide various forms of CS, ranging from 40 to 240 hours of unpaid work to be completed within one year. What are the effects of CS as a sentencing option? Dr McIvor studied a number of outcomes (McIvor 1992). While one important element in such an evaluation are the subsequent offences possibly committed by those receiving the CS sentence, another element is to assess the possible benefits to the community. Dr McIvor carried out the first study of these benefits. Five hundred and sixty-five beneficiaries (typically older citizens) of CS labour were surveyed to assess the type of services provided by the offenders and the recipients' satisfaction with the quality of the work. Substantial majorities reported that the services they received (for example, painting, gardening, other manual labour, shopping, etc.) were performed competently, and 96 per cent would be willing to use CS workers again. Almost all got along well with the offenders and found the work to be of good quality.

This is a marvellous example of using the simple X-O design to conduct a preliminary evaluation study of a large-scale programme. The independent variable was the CS sentencing option, and although no one would contend that the Scottish approach could be precisely replicated elsewhere, this study illustrates that programme evaluation can indeed be useful, even if the independent variable is not scientifically described. The outcome measure was the survey instrument designed by Dr McIvor, assessing the idiosyncratic aspects of this service. Although its reliability and validity are unknown, the relatively unambiguous nature of the issues being assessed suggest some confidence in the results. Dr McIvor has published a number of articles on the Scottish experience with CS programmes, some of which have used relatively simple research methods for programme evaluation (McIvor 1993).

Now we will look at a few examples from the other end of the practice spectrum.

Evaluating the Treatment of Obsessive Compulsive Disorder

Mr Joseph Himle is a clinical social worker with the Department of Psychiatry at the University of Michigan. He was treating a man meeting the criteria for Obsessive Compulsive Disorder who presented primarily with obsessions, not overt rituals. Following the rather limited empirical literature on treating the purely obsessional patient, Mr Himle used exposure therapy techniques. The client agreed to listen to a tape recording of the major obsessional ideation, to read a similar vignette and to write his obsessions aloud, doing each of these exercises about ten times per day. He was instructed to record the maximum amount of subjective distress he experienced during each such homework exercise (on a scale of 0–100). Within thirty days the anxiety evoked by forcefully confronting (as opposed to suppressing) his obsessional ideation declined from ratings in the 70s and 80s (very high) to zero. Concomitant with this decline in anxiety evoked by the homework exercises, the client reported a dramatic decrease in the frequency of spontaneous obsessions and related distress. At two-year follow-up he reported being almost entirely free of obsessional thoughts, despite his twenty-year history of such intrusive ideations. This self-evaluation can also be construed as a 'B' design, and the graphically depicted data clearly demonstrated the client's rapid improvements. Further details can be found in Himle and Thyer (1989).

Evaluating Public Policy

In my home state of Georgia, the legislature passed a mandatory automobile safety belt use law in 1988. As a master's degree research project, one of my students, Mrs Margaret Robertson, examined the state-provided statistics on injuries and fatalities for each month for the year before and the year after the passage of the new law. She was attempting to answer empirically the questions 'Do fatalities and serious injuries decline following the implementation of this new public policy?' Unfortunately, the answer appeared to be no, in both instances. The graphically depicted data certainly did not suggest any appreciable declines, and inferential statistics corroborated this conclusion. The portrayal of these data are in accord with an 'A-B' single system research design, wherein the units of analyses (or outcome measures) were the state-gathered statistics, and the intervention was the new law. This simple study was also published in a peer-reviewed journal (Thyer and Robertson 1993).

Evaluating Inpatient Psychiatric Treatment for Children and Adolescents

Two of my MSW students, Robin Robinson and Jan Powers, were completing their social work internships at a private, for profit psychiatric hospital in Georgia. Mrs Robinson was working on an inpatient unit serving children, and Mrs Powers on a ward serving adolescents. As their MSW research project, each opted to undertake a simple programme evaluation. The most common diagnosis given on each unit was that of depression, therefore both students located several pencil and paper measures of depression which were appropriate to each age group. They arranged for each newly admitted child or adolescent client with a diagnosis of major depression or dysthymia to be administered these simple but reliable and valid scales and for them to be given again just prior to the patient's discharge.

Now, my students ended up with much smaller sample sizes than they had anticipated. Fewer admissions occurred than expected, and sometimes hospital staff were not consistent in notifying them of new admissions or of imminent discharges. Mrs Robinson ended up with a group of seven child patients with pre- and post-test data; Mrs Powers with complete data for fifteen adolescents. Despite the small samples, statistically significant improvements were found on two (Global Assessment of Functioning and the Hopelessness Scale for Children) of the three outcome measures for the children, and on all three measures used with the teenagers (Beck Depression Inventory, Index of Self-Esteem, Generalised Contentment Scale). Thus, a preliminary answer to the question 'Do depressed children treated at our hospital improve? was obtained (see Robinson et al. 1990 for more details).

How confident can we be in this conclusion? It depends. To the extent that our outcome measures are valid, we can be fairly certain that this positive conclusion holds for the patients we assessed. How representative were those we measured, versus all patients? Probably fairly representative, inasmuch as we assessed consecutive admissions for a couple of months, missing only a few because of communication failures. Does this imply that the hospital does a good job for non-depressed children and youth? No, the results have no bearing on outcomes for, say, conduct disorder, adjustment disorder, or other common youthful diagnoses. I do submit to you that a hospital which conducts some form of reliable and valid assessment of patient symptomatology upon admission and again at discharge, will likely have a more accurate picture of what happens to their patients than one which does not do such assessments. When the empirical data are combined with staff clinical observations and other qualitative indicators, a social worker has firmer grounds for asserting that patients benefit from treatment than a social worker lacking such corroborative data. It is also possible that funding sources will be more likely to support such programmes with empirical support, relative to those lacking it.

Can we assert from such simple O-X-O studies that it was the hospital treatment which produced improvements? No, we usually cannot. It is possible that the patients benefited from simply being removed from a depressing home, from a change in diet, or relief from a stressful school situation. We also lack knowledge about what elements of the hospital programme were critical in producing any improvements. Was it the medication regimen? Was it milieu therapy, group therapy, individual psychotherapy, recreation? We cannot say. But this is all right, keeping in mind that our original question was 'did patients improve?' We answered our question. We did not, nor did we try, to answer more ambitious questions such as 'did patients get better because of our programme?', or 'what are the critical ingredients to our programme?' I recommend that most social worker practitioners do not even try to conduct such studies. They require a degree of experimental control, rigour, time and resources most of us do not possess. Considering that our colleagues in psychiatry, psychology, nursing, education and related fields often do not have evidence that their clients improve, much less proof that it was their disciplinary services which gave rise to such changes, we need not be embarrassed.

Another Example of Evaluating Treatment of People with Obsessive Compulsive Disorders (OCD)

You may recall Mr Joe Himle's earlier work, described above, using a 'B' single-system design with an individual client suffering from obsessive thoughts. Mr Himle continued his efforts in the self-evaluation of his own practice, by reporting on the first-ever outcome study of the effectiveness of group therapy techniques for clients with this condition. Drawing upon the earlier work of British psychiatrist Dr Isaac Marks, Mr Himle conducted a series of small group therapy sessions for clients with OCD. At the beginning of each group, clients completed the Yale-Brown Obsessive Compulsive Inventory, and the Beck Depression Inventory. These standardised, reliable and valid measures were repeated at the conclusion of the group therapy programme, and again at three months follow-up. A total of thirty-six patients seen in three different groups completed the programme, with strikingly positive results for both OCD symptoms and depression.

This time Mr Himle made use of the more sophisticated pre-test–post-test group research (O-X-O) design and some simple inferential statistics to help answer empirically the question 'do clients seen in our group therapy programme benefit?' In the case of OCD, it is well known that the disorder rarely remits with the passage of time, and is not significantly improved due to placebo influences. Thus a no-treatment or a placebo control would have been an unnecessary imposition on both the clients and on Mr Himle. Note that this study was conducted as a regular part of Mr Himle's practice. He did not have any grant funding, he did not have a doctoral degree, he did not have any release time to conduct research, but he did make the effort to write this project up and to get it published in the top-ranked journal *Behaviour Research and Therapy* (Krone, Himle and Nesse 1991). This was a truly original contribution to the empirical knowledge base of psychosocial treatments for a severe psychiatric condition. As a full-time practicing social worker, Mr. Himle continues his work in this area, and is preparing a study comparing short-term versus long-term group therapy in the treatment of OCD, this time with a sample of over one hundred clients.

Evaluating a Letter-Writing Campaign to Promote Voting Among Low-Income Black Voters: a True Experiment

In the United States, we sometimes have very low voter turn-out in elections. This can be seen as a problem for the field of social welfare inasmuch as lower income and lower educated citizens tend to vote less often than the well-to-do. Thus poor and discriminated groups exert a smaller influence at the polls than their absolute numbers would suggest. Various strategies have been employed to encourage poor citizens to vote, and one of my MSW students, Kelly Canady, evaluated a letter-writing campaign using a randomised post-test-only experimental group design.

In the town of Dublin, Georgia, Mr Canady obtained a list of all registered voters in the poorest section of town. Census data indicated that this area has a large number of public housing projects in it, with a Black population of over 90 per cent. A randomly selected sample of 400 voters, out of a total of over 5000, were randomly divided to one of four groups. Group 1 received a letter mailed by Mr Canady a few days before the presidential election of 1988. The bipartisan letter was signed by the local chairs of the Republican and Democratic parties, and was a friendly reminder of the importance of voting, the significance of the issues, and urged them to be sure and cast their ballot.

The 100 or so voters assigned to Group 2 received two such letters, one a week before the election and a second a few days before it. Those assigned to Group 3 received three such letters, two one week before the election and a third a few days before; while those assigned to Group 4 did not get any letter reminding them to vote.

Thus Mr Canady had a relatively sophisticated research design, using both random selection and random assignment. His intervention was the letter, administered in various 'doses', and the outcome measure was the public record of whether or not each of our 400 subjects had voted, obtained several weeks after the election (not how they voted, but if they voted). We anticipated that those receiving the letter would have voted in greater numbers than those who did not get the letter, and that those receiving more than one letter would be even more likely to vote. Regrettably our statistical analysis failed to show that the letter had any effect at all. All four groups were equally unlikely to have voted (Canady and Thyer 1990).

However, science does not promise us answers that we will find agreeable. If you conduct evaluation research, be prepared for unpleasant outcomes remembering that such results can serve as the stimulus for productive change. They need not paralyse us.

Conclusion

In this chapter I have reviewed a number of examples of simple programme evaluation efforts conducted by social work practitioners. These cases exemplify our field's commitment to developing empirical data to demonstrate whether or not our clients are well served by our interventions. Sometimes the answer is a gratifying 'Yes!': clients are better off after receiving social work treatment. Sometimes the answer is a disappointing 'No!': our efforts were not followed by a positive outcome. Such is the price we pay for presuming to evaluate. I do believe that it is better to know that something is not effective, than to not know that fact. Such negative appraisals can serve as a stimulus to review, revise and re-evaluate our work, rather than allowing inadvertently ineffective services to be continued.

The above examples were not intended to test any theory. Many involved analysing data through visually inspecting graphically presented information, not by calculating complex statistical tests. The evaluation designs were at the low end of the hierarchy of internally valid research strategies. Little use was made of control groups, of randomly selected clients, or of random assignment to treatment conditions. The independent variable, the social work intervention programme, was often not well defined. And the findings were likely of limited generalisability (i.e., external validity). By the conventional standards of social science research, these studies can be seen as miserably deficient. Keep in mind however, that one standard by which evaluation research is judge is a different one, namely, 'did you get adequate evidence to answer *your* question?' In most cases, the above examples did answer the question posed. Moreover, if the findings obtained in original programme evaluations are replicated in other settings by other social workers our confidence can grow that a particular treatment is an effective one for many clients.

Social workers who provide empirical data to demonstrate that their clients have benefited following receipt of our profession's services will be in a greatly strengthened position to withstand budget cuts. Conducting evaluation studies and publicising the positive results can be seen as an important element of our professional practice. Such efforts represent a true integration of the science and art of social work. The skills involved are well within the scope of most trained members of our profession. Most of us would like to acquire empirical data to supplement our clinical judgements. My purpose in this chapter is to illustrate that relatively simple outcome evaluations using group and single-system research designs are a practical approach to demonstrating empirically what we do.

Almost eighty years ago, Winston Churchill wrote to Lloyd George on the day after Christmas in 1918:

> I hope that you will gather together all forces of strength and influence in the country and lead them along the paths of science and organisation to the rescue of the weak and the poor. (Addison 1993, p.198)

This remains sound advice for today's politicians. Social workers respond with another Churchill request, made in 1941 under somewhat differing circumstances: 'give us the tools and we will finish the job' (Hume 1994, p.89).

References

Abbott, E. (1931) *Social Welfare and Professional Education*. Chicago, IL: University of Chicago Press.

Addison, P. (1993) *Churchill on the Home Front: 1900–1955*. London: Pimlico.

Bowling, A. (1997) *Measuring Health: A Review of Quality of Life Measuring Scales*. Buckingham: Open University Press.

Campbell, J.A. (1988) 'Client acceptance of single-system evaluation procedures.' *Social Work Research and Abstracts 24*, 2, 21–22.

Canady, K. and Thyer, B.A. (1990) 'Promoting voting behavior among low-income Black voters: an experimental investigation.' *Journal of Sociology and Social Welfare 17*, 4, 109–116.

Cheetham, J. (1994) 'The social work research centre at the University of Stirling: a profile.' *Research on Social Work Practice 4*, 89–110.

Cheetham, J., Fuller, R., McIvor, G. and Petch, A. (1992) *Evaluating Social Work Effectiveness*. Buckingham: Open University Press.

Cnaan, R.A. (1991) 'Applying clinical trials in social work practice.' *Research on Social Work Practice 1*, 139–161.

Fischer, J. and Corcoran, K. (1994) *Measures for Clinical Practice*. New York: Free Press.

Glisson, G. and Thyer, B.A. (1996) *A Program Evaluation of the Effectiveness of Homeless Shelter Services*. Manuscript submitted for publication.

Gorey, K. (1996) 'Effectiveness of social work intervention research: Internal versus external evaluations.' *Social Work Research 20*, 119–128.

Himle, J. and Thyer, B.A. (1989) 'Clinical social work and obsessive compulsive disorder: a single-subject investigation.' *Behavior Modification 13*, 459–470.

Hume, J.C. (1994) *The Wit and Wisdom of Winston Churchill*. New York: HarperCollins.

Kazi, M.A.F. (1996) 'The centre for evaluation studies at the University of Huddersfield: a profile.' *Research on Social Work Practice 6*, 104–116.

Krone, K.P., Himle, J.A. and Nesse, R.M. (1991) 'A standardized behavioral group treatment for obsessive-compulsive disorder: preliminary outcomes.' *Behaviour Research and Therapy 29*, 627–631.

MacDonald, G., Sheldon, B. and Gillespie, J. (1992) 'Contemporary studies of the effectiveness of social work.' *British Journal of Social Work 22*, 615–643.

McIvor, G. (1992) *Sentenced to Serve*. Aldershot: Avebury.

McIvor, G. (1993) 'Community service by offenders: how much does the community benefit?' *Research on Social Work Practice 4*, 385–403.

Morgan, J.S. (1949) 'Research in social work: a frame of reference.' *Social Work Journal 30*, 148–154.

National Association of Social Workers (1996) 'Code of ethics.' *NASW News 41*, 10, 17–20.

Nutter, R.W. and Hudson, J. (1997) 'A survey of social work research centers.' *Research on Social Work Practice 7*, 239–262.

Robinson, R.M., Powers, J.M., Cleveland, P.H. and Thyer, B.A. (1990) 'Inpatient psychiatric treatment for depressed children and adolescents: preliminary evaluations.' *The Psychiatric Hospital 21*, 107–112.

Royse, D.P. and Thyer, B.A. (1996) *Program Evaluation: An Introduction (2nd edition)*. Chicago, IL: Nelson Hall.

Thyer, B.A. and Robertson, M. (1993) 'An initial evaluation of the Georgia safety belt use law: a nul MUL?' *Environment and Behavior 25*, 506–513.

Videka-Sherman, L. (1988) 'Meta-analysis of research on social work practice in mental health.' *Social Work 33*, 325–338.

Yegidis, B. (1993) 'The influence of the graduate student research project on practice research.' *Research on Social Work Practice 3*, 83–90.

CHAPTER 11

Putting Single-Case Evaluation into Practice

Mansoor Kazi

Introduction

Single-case evaluation – the use of single-case designs in evaluating practice – is part of the empirical practice movement, a critique of which also appears in Shaw's chapter elsewhere in this book (Chapter 12). This chapter draws on the experience of practitioners to argue that single-case evaluation can be integrated into the daily practice of social workers, and that the criticisms do not take into account the recent developments in the requirements of single-case evaluation, as well as the recent emergence of a method-ological-pluralist approach to research and evaluation.

It was in the 1980s that the empirical practice movement began to develop, claiming to provide practising social workers with the means to evaluate their own practice. Back in 1981, Joel Fischer referred to the development of single-case evaluation as the 'social work revolution'. He argued, 'a research technology that can be built into practice and can serve a number of functions that will enhance practice is now available to social workers. In and of itself, this development may be the highlight of – and certainly is a key to – the revolution in practice' (Fischer 1981, p.201). However, by the end of the decade it became clear that this 'revolution' had directly affected only a small part of social work.

There were two main reasons for this lack of enthusiasm. First, the earlier definitions tended to emphasise experimental designs which would not only track client progress, but also attempt to provide a causal link between client progress and the social work intervention used. Such designs involved a systematic introduction and withdrawal of interventions to test their effects (Sheldon 1988; Thyer 1993) and were seen by many social workers as unsuitable to the needs of their practice. Second, based on this earlier emphasis, the introduction of single-case designs in social work research came under fierce opposition as part of the epistemological debate between those who favoured the positivist approach (which included single-case designs) and those who favoured the naturalistic or qualitative approach. For example, it was argued that this type of evaluative research was incompatible with most social work practice, and that the use of measures in single-case designs was reductionist and incapable of representing the reality of most social phenomena.

This author's work to promote the use of single-case evaluation by social work practitioners in a variety of settings has been reported elsewhere (Kazi 1996, 1997; Kazi and Wilson 1997). This apparent willingness of social work practitioners to use single-case evaluation is due to three main developments: changes in the requirements of the methodology which enable an improved response to the needs of practice; the emergence of a synthesis in the quantitative versus qualitative debate and the development of a pragmatic approach to mixing methods; and the building of a partnership between academic researchers and social workers to evaluate practice.

Changes in Requirements

The *Encyclopaedia of Social Work* describes single-case design as 'a research methodology that allows a social work practitioner to track systematically his or her progress with a client or client unit. With increasingly rigorous applications of this methodology, practitioners can also gain knowledge about effective social work interventions, although this is a less common goal' (Blythe 1995, p.2164). Therefore, the emphasis is on continuous assessment over time to track client progress, and not on attempting to determine a causal link between such progress and the social work intervention. The basic hypothesis addressed is that a social work programme will lead to client progress – and not necessarily that the programme would cause the changes to happen. Therefore, alternative explanations cannot be ruled out – for example, some other changes in the client's family situation or environment may have actually caused the improvements. Nevertheless, systematic tracking of client progress would enable both the practitioner and the client to evaluate, on a regular basis, whether the desired objectives of the social work intervention were being achieved or not.

With this limited purpose in mind, the only fundamental requirement of this methodology is the measurement of the subject's target problem (i.e. the object of the intervention) repeatedly over time, using an appropriate indicator of progress which is made as reliable as possible. The practitioner is required to select an outcome measure that best reflects changes in the subject's condition, and then to apply the same measure repeatedly over a period of time. The initiation and withdrawal of social work interventions is determined by the needs of practice. In all cases, the resulting data will enable the systematic tracking of client progress in the period when repeated measurement takes place.

A recent project in a probation service (Kazi and Hayles 1996) illustrates this shift in requirements of rigour. The authors worked with all twelve students (and their seven practice teachers) on final placements with West Yorkshire Probation Service in 1996 to encourage them to use single-case evaluation to demonstrate the effectiveness of probation orders with adult offenders that they were supervising as part of their practice. This evaluation project was commissioned by the agency and began in response to the internal and external pressures on probation services to be more accountable to society and to demonstrate the effectiveness of their work. According to McGuire and Priestley (1995 p.24):

> There is a responsibility…for the creation of a culture of empirical evaluation: for an atmosphere in which programme design, delivery and evaluation are seen as natural accompaniments to each other, and for the habit of evaluation to become firmly embedded in the thinking of managers and practitioners alike.

Part of this process is the growing need for students on qualifying courses (i.e., trainee probation officers) to provide evidence of their ability to evaluate the effectiveness of their work (CCETSW 1989). It was felt that the students on final placements would benefit from an evaluation project to enable them to evaluate their practice; and that, at the same time, the experiences generated could provide a catalyst for developing the use of evaluation procedures within the agency as a whole.

Single-case evaluation procedures included the use of recording systems to identify objectives, the intervention programmes and monitoring of client progress. The practitioners were encouraged to use published measures of high reliability (standardised measures in Fischer and Corcoran 1994), and also to create their own measures appropriate to the needs of their clients. The practice teachers participated in this process together with the consultant, to help practitioners create such measuring tools and to help them to select appropriate measures to meet the needs of each particular client. The measures created included a variety of rating scales, client self-report diaries, and specific measures for monitoring drug and alcohol use, attitudes and risk factors associated with criminal behaviour.

Single-case evaluation procedures (i.e. repeated measurement) were combined with other classificatory outcome indicators to enable a judgement to be made regarding the extent of progress achieved. These classificatory indicators were:

1. Whether tangible changes were made such as obtaining appropriate employment or housing, including steps towards these goals such as joining a job club or approaching housing associations;

2. Whether the client was arrested for further offences in the period of supervision;

3. Whether the client was breached for failing to comply with the requirements of the probation or licence supervision process.

The outcome was that all twelve trainee probation officers with the agency at the time used single-case evaluation procedures to evaluate the effectiveness of their supervision of probation orders with seventy-one adult offenders (Kazi and Hayles 1996). The following is a case example from this project.

CASE EXAMPLE 1

Male offender D was convicted of drink-driving and causing criminal damage and sentenced to twelve months' probation order with a condition to attend a local drink-drive programme. He was also disqualified from driving for two years and ordered to pay £105.75 compensation and £75 court costs. In the first supervision session, the trainee probation officer and D agreed the following objectives of the probation order (in addition to the requirements of regular supervision and avoiding behaviour likely to lead to further offences):

1. Explore consequences of alcohol on offending.

2. Consider consequences on others.

3. Pursue mediation and reparation.

4. Take on board issues of bereavement, health, self-esteem and personal finances.

The student described the method of intervention during supervision as 'task-centred work within a cognitive/behavioural framework'. The outcome measures selected included attendance, a drink diary and a standardised measure for self-esteem.

1. ATTENDANCE

D regularly attended at the drink-drive programme for the specified eight weeks. He also regularly attended supervision sessions at the probation office as required.

2. DRINK DIARY

D regularly completed a drink diary which identified the amount of money he spent daily on alcohol consumption. The data was then charted as the amount spent per week over eleven weeks. Figure 11.1 indicates that the amount spent was very high in the first week; but from then onwards, considerable progress was made in lowering the amount spent to under £10. The reliability of this measure was entirely dependent upon D's honesty; but the trend of improvement was also confirmed by independent reports from staff at the drink-drive programme.

3. STANDARDISED MEASURES FROM FISCHER AND CORCORAN (1994)

The measure used was Hudson's Index of Self-Esteem (ISE), a 25-item scale designed to measure the 'degree, severity or magnitude of a problem the client has with self-esteem' (p.283). It's reported reliability is high, and it has two cutting scores: scores below 30 (+or-5) indicate absence of a clinically significant problem, and scores above 70 'nearly always indicate that clients are experiencing severe stress with a clear possibility that some type of violence could be considered or used to deal with problems' (p.283). The ISE was administered on three occasions, as follows:

Date	Score
3/2/96	131
13/2/96	73
2/4/96	58

The first score indicated a severe problem of self-esteem, which considerably improved at each subsequent occasion. The differences in score indicate that, although self-esteem still remained a problem for D, significant progress was made in this period.

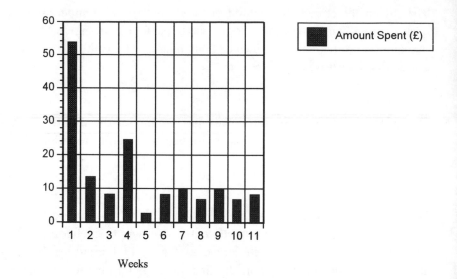

Figure 11.1: Drink Diary: Amount Spent on Alcohol Consumption per Week

The single-case evaluation procedures used in D's case provide evidence of considerable progress. D reported regularly and complied with the condition attached to the probation order. The ISE scores indicate a significant increase in self-esteem in this period. The drink diary indicates significant progress was also made with this target problem. These measures were corroborated by other observations, namely that D paid the compensation and court costs, remained in employment, and improved the quality of leisure time spent with his wife (e.g. playing bingo and swimming) – and he was not charged with further offences in this period. The single-case designs used enabled systematic tracking of client progress, using measures which became part of daily practice. In the event, it could be concluded that D made a great deal of progress in the supervision period, but it cannot be established that these improvements were caused by the probation order, or were the result of other factors in the client's circumstances. It could be argued that the above data does not demonstrate the impact of the client's feelings and the effect of his environment – but the probation service's recording system required some assessments of these other factors, and although the single-case designs in themselves could not address these questions, they supplemented the essentially qualitative agency records with some objective data reflecting D's achievements.

Pragmatic Approach to Mixing Methods

The second development helping in the wider use of single-case evaluation is the synthesis now emerging from the epistemological debate which recognises that the various evaluative research approaches all have a role to play and can be combined in a methodological-pluralist framework (Cheetham *et al.* 1992), and which values a range of research methods originating from both the positivist and naturalistic approaches. This pragmatic approach recognises that each research method or approach has its limitations, and that one should begin with the evaluation questions and then select a method (or a combination of methods) which can be applied appropriately to address the relevant questions. From this perspective, all methods originating from both schools of thought are valued, and none is ruled out purely on the basis of ideological preferences. Within this perspective, for example, single-case evaluation would not be seen as a panacea, but as one of the methods available to evaluate social work practice. Its limitations would be recognised and other methods would be used to address the questions that this methodology is unable to address. This perspective has helped in the growing acceptance that single-case evaluation can be used alongside other methods.

CASE EXAMPLE 2: OAKES VILLA REHABILITATION UNIT'S CLIENT NO. 65

The second example is a case from Oakes Villa, an adult rehabilitation project in Huddersfield. The purpose of the project was to help older people who were living independently prior to an acute condition (e.g. a stroke) to regain their independence. The staff agreed to incorporate single-case evaluation procedures into their daily practice as part of a multi-method strategy to evaluate the project. The outcome measure used at the Oakes Villa unit is a 7-point rating scale (at first, the measure was a 6-point rating scale as reported in Kazi (1997)) created by the staff themselves in consultation with the author. It is essentially a rating scale ranging from 1 to 7 as follows:

7 – independent

6 – independent with equipment

5 – independent with supervision

4 – receiving enabling assistance, i.e. setting the scene

3 – receiving slight assistance, i.e. finishing off with partial help

2 – receiving moderate assistance, i.e. quite a bit of help to do the task

1 – totally dependant, i.e. requiring someone else to undertake the task.

The project's staff enhanced the scale's reliability by providing specific examples to anchor each point of the scale, by agreeing the definitions as precisely as possible within the group as a whole, and by measuring on the scale as a group activity. Each variable (i.e. specified client activity) is assessed daily against the scale, and then expressed as a weekly percentage:

$$\% = \frac{\text{Total of actual scores in the week}}{\text{Maximum possible in the week}} \times 10$$

The measure was used with all 106 clients who were admitted to the rehabilitation unit between January 1995 and March 1997 inclusive (the evaluation period agreed with the stakeholders – see Kazi and Firth (1997) for a more complete report). One of these clients was client no. 65 (male, aged 69), referred from a local hospital. He had suffered a stroke and had been very ill in hospital for about four months before staying for seven weeks at Oakes Villa. In order to be rehabilitated back to his own home, he was expected to make progress with a number of specified activities of daily living (see Figure 11.2).

Figure 11.2 is an example of a single-case design that enables a systematic tracking of client progress. The staff used this measure daily, although it is presented here as a weekly percentage. The specified activities were agreed with the client from the outset, and the client was informed of each daily assessment in order to set realistic targets for improvement. The chart shows that the client's ability to perform these activities ranged from 14 per cent to 35 per cent in the first week, but progressed steadily until it reached 100 per cent against six out of the eight variables. He did not achieve 100 per cent independence with medication and mobility, but still reached 86 per cent and 71 per cent respectively. At the end of seven weeks, client 65 was rehabilitated back to his own home, and a six-month follow-up assessment visit indicated that he continued to maintain the levels of independence achieved.

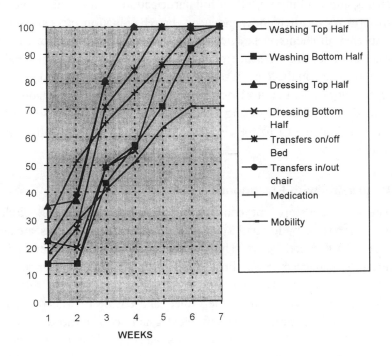

Figure 11.2: Progress of Activities of Daily Living (Client 65)

In the evaluation of Oakes Villa Rehabilitation Service, the data from single-case evaluation was combined with other research methods. The staff's perception of the rehabilitation process was obtained through naturalistic group interviews, a postal survey was done of service users to obtain their perception, and a further survey of the referring social workers was carried out, to obtain a more complete evaluation of the unit. All of these other methods provided further evidence of the unit's effectiveness. The outcome indicators used showed that out of the 106 clients included in the evaluation, eighty-nine (or 73%) were rehabilitated in their own homes, and out of these, fifty-eight were still independent six months after discharge. Twenty-nine out of forty-one clients indicated that Oakes Villa was very helpful in helping them to return home. Nine out of ten referring social workers indicated that their clients had made considerable progress at Oakes Villa. The interviews with staff indicated a commitment to partnership with clients, and working with their full participation in an enabling role to help them to regain their independence. The rehabilitation process valued and respected all clients in practice. What was the contribution of single-case evaluation to this evidence of effectiveness? The individual single-case designs based on the 7-point rating scale illustrated above demonstrated that eighty-eight clients out of one hundred and six (or 83%) made progress towards independence during their stay at the unit, including some of those who did not return to their own homes, but went on to other forms of residential care.

Partnership with Practitioners

The third development contributing to the wider use of single-case evaluation is the building of a partnership between academic researchers and social work practitioners. The starting point is an agreement with the agency's managers, responding to the need to evaluate practice through procedures that can be incorporated into practice. It helps if the agency's managers also participate in the project and ensure that adequate time is provided to help motivate the staff. Next, a number of sessions are held with the staff to introduce them to the requirements of single-case evaluation, illustrated with examples from social work settings where it has been used, including both standardised measures (Fischer and Corcoran 1994) and other measures created by social workers.

The next stage is to ask practitioners to discuss particular cases from their recent or current practice. They should be enabled to go from global to specific descriptions of target problems and to determine what outcome measures might be appropriate. In this process of assessment, they should be encouraged to work in a collaborative way with the service user. It should be emphasised that practice considerations are paramount and that evaluative research serves practice. Together with the service managers, the researcher should provide on-going consultancy and support and, in addition, arrange several further meetings with the whole staff group. The practitioners who have used the method should be encouraged to take centre stage and share their experience with others who are still at the planning stage. Recording systems should be developed or amended to facilitate the process of evaluation. The measurement of outcomes should be made integral to case recording systems, and formats of potential measures should be included so that they are readily at hand. Arrangements should be made in advance regarding the forwarding of data to the manager and/or the researcher for the purposes of aggregation and inclusion into a research report, to be done by the researcher together with the agency and presented to the practising social workers. In this way, a partnership is built between the academic researchers and social work practitioners – a partnership that develops as practice unfolds. Such a partnership can help any agency that wants to develop evidence-based practice.

Some Methodological Considerations

The recent changes in the methodology of single-case evaluation, the emerging synthesis in the quantitative versus qualitative debate, and the developing partnership between academic researchers and social workers have created the conditions where social workers in a number of settings are more willing to use this methodology to evaluate their practice. As part of a pragmatic, methodological-pluralist strategy, single-case evaluation is one in a wide range of methods from both positivist and naturalistic approaches. The limitations of each method are recognised, but in the context of addressing relevant evaluation questions. Despite such developments, there is still a tendency to criticise and to rule out particular methods mainly because of ideological preferences. For example, in this book Shaw (Chapter 12) notes four problems with the empirical practice movement. Let us consider each of these in turn, in the light of experience from the use of single-case designs by social workers.

First, it is argued that it may not be possible to apply this approach to all or even most of social work. Practice speaks louder than such arguments from those who do not intend to use single-case evaluation. This author has worked with social workers and allied professions in education, probation, residential, adult rehabilitation and child protection settings where empirical practice has been applied by large numbers of social workers. However, a limitation of single-case evaluation is that it can be applied only in circumstances where repeated assessments can be made; therefore it is not suitable in 'one-off' sessions of work with clients.

Second, it is argued that the demands of measurement are incompatible with the realities and meaning of practice. The charge of reductionism is relevant, for example, in the earlier illustration of the probation case where single-case designs provided evidence of progress but could not determine which factors in the clients' circumstances led to the progress achieved. A limitation of single-case evaluation is that it cannot address such wider questions; other methods can be used for this purpose. However, single-case evaluation should not be criticised for not helping in areas it is not designed to help – it is simply a verification procedure to determine if the client is making progress as desired.

Third, it is argued that ethical issues have been given too little attention. The use of single-case evaluation alongside other methods in the evaluation of Oakes Villa demonstrates that empirical practice is not incompatible with the values of social work – it simply provides additional information to both the worker and client about the progress made to achieve the client's goals and provides evidence of effectiveness of the social work intervention. The emphasis on measurement in both the probation and adult rehabilitation projects did not lead to a dependence on 'technical expertise' or 'performance culture' that Shaw refers to – on the contrary, it complemented existing practice in such a way that partnership between worker and client was strengthened, with the client participating in the process of evaluation – one of the preconditions for anti-discriminatory, anti-oppressive practice.

Finally, the intrusion of research design was not as great as feared by Shaw in his fourth point – the procedures were readily integrated into practice in both of the contexts illustrated in this chapter, and practice unfolded as it would have done naturally. The 'marginal effect' on the services concerned was a focus on the objectives of the probation order or the adult rehabilitation process – a focus which was welcomed by both the social workers and the clients.

Single-case evaluation cannot answer all the evaluation questions of social work practice, but it is useful as a means of systematic tracking of client progress. Therefore, it is not the only way to evaluate practice – it is one of a wide range of methodologies available, including both qualitative and quantitative approaches. Single-case evaluation is one method that can be incorporated into social work practice to provide on-going evidence of effectiveness – it can be used as part of a pragmatic, methodological-pluralist framework to address the complex evaluation questions that are relevant to the needs of social work practice.

References

Blythe, B.J. (1995) 'Single-system design.' In R.L. Edwards *et al.* (eds) *Encyclopaedia of Social Work*, 19th. edition, vol. 3. Silver Spring, Maryland: National Association of Social Workers, pp.2164–2168.

CCETSW (1989) *Requirements and Regulations for the Diploma in Social Work*, Paper no. 30. London: CCETSW.

Cheetham, J., Fuller, R., McIvor, G. and Petch, A. (1992) *Evaluating Social Work Effectiveness*. Buckingham: Open University Press.

Fischer, J. (1981) 'The social work revolution.' *Social Work 26*, 199–207.

Fischer, J. and Corcoran, K. (1994) *Measures for Clinical Practice: A Source Book*, vols. 1 and 2. New York: The Free Press.

Kazi, M.A.F. (1996) 'The Centre for Evaluation Studies at the University of Huddersfield: a profile.' *Research on Social Work Practice 6*, 104–116.

Kazi, M.A.F. (1997) 'Single-case evaluation in British social services.' In E. Chelimsky and W.R. Shadish (eds) *Evaluation for the 21st Century: A Resource Book*. Thousand Oaks, California: Sage Publications, pp.419–466.

Kazi, M.A.F. and Firth, K. (1997) *Evaluation of Oakes Villa Rehabilitation Unit*. Huddersfield: University of Huddersfield, The Centre for Evaluation Studies.

Kazi, M.A.F. and Hayles, M. (1996) *Single-Case Evaluation in a Probation Service*. Huddersfield: University of Huddersfield, The Centre for Evaluation Studies.

Kazi, M.A.F. and Wilson, J. (1996) 'Applying single-case evaluation in social work.' *British Journal of Social Work 26*, 699–717.

McGuire, J. and Priestley, P. (1995) 'Reviewing "what works": past, present and future.' In J. McGuire (ed) *What Works: Reducing Reoffending*. Chichester: Wiley, pp.3–34.

Sheldon, B. (1988) 'Single case evaluation methods: review and prospects.' In J. Lishman (ed) *Evaluation*. London: Jessica Kingsley, pp.40–57.

Thyer, B.A. (1993) 'Single-system research designs.' In R.M. Grinnell Jr. (ed) *Social Work Research and Evaluation*. Itasca, Ill: F.E. Peacock, pp.94–117.

CHAPTER 12

Practising Evaluation

Ian Shaw

Social work is not easy. Morally it demands judgement and action. It obliges a recurring inquiry and effort to pin down intractable evidence. Evaluating within direct practice requires the same moral calculus as any other aspect of practice, and presses upon social worker and service user questions of how we may best know whether we have good grounds and evidence, what conclusions can probably be drawn, and what plausibly justified action should be taken for, by and with the service user. Commitment to judgement, ascertaining evidence, and risking action do not – perhaps cannot – take place in an ordered sequence. This chapter reflects on these questions. I briefly review debates regarding how social workers ought to gain evidence, and move from there to consider the implications for these debates of some recent research in which practitioners tried to make sense of their day-to-day endeavours to evaluate their work. The chapter concludes with a manifesto for how evaluation can develop as a direct practice competence.

Evidence for Practice

Evaluation involves 'both *the generation of evidence* about an activity, a policy, a programme or a project, and *the process of making judgements about its value*' (Everitt and Hardiker 1996, p.4). Risking oversimplification, social workers have advocated one or other of three broad answers to questions of the nature of evidence in social work, and the general methodologies that should be adopted to gain that evidence.

Empirical Practice

The approach represented by the 'empirical practice movement' (cf. Reid 1994; Seigal 1984) generally emphasises planned, rational, outcome-targeted methodologies. There has been a revival of confidence in the ability of social workers and practitioners working with offenders to deliver effective interventions. This is sometimes, although by no means always, associated with an advocacy of positivism, as when Thyer concludes that:

> Our clients deserve the best services our profession can provide, and for the determination of social work effectiveness there is no substitute for controlled experimental research, guided by the philosophy of science known as logical positivism and the tenets of the hypothetico-deductive process. (Thyer 1989, p.320)

Advocates of empirical practice urge a 'move away from vague, unvalidated and haphazardly derived knowledge traditionally used in social work toward more systematic, rational and empirically-oriented development and use of knowledge for practice' (Fischer 1993, p.19). Articulated most clearly through the advocacy of single-system designs, and the 'What Works?' literature and programmes in the field of probation work (e.g. Andrews and Bonta 1995; Bloom 1993; Grinnell 1993; McGuire 1995), the protagonists of empirical practice view 'research and practice as virtually the same phenomena in the clear and consistent way one views client problems, formulates hypotheses, collects information, and resolves problems' (Fischer 1993, p.21; Blythe, Tripodi and Briar 1995). Fischer is sufficiently optimistic to prophecy the end of ideology, and to predict that 'by the year 2000, empirically-based practice – the new social work – may be the norm, or well on the way to becoming so' (p.55).

Most practitioners and writers working from this perspective emphasise the following practice implications of their position:

- focus on the behaviour that needs targeting
- keep clear and usually behaviourally linked problem definitions
- state and agree clear and measurable objectives
- include cognitive and behavioural intervention methods
- ensure that the planned intervention is delivered with technical 'integrity' so that the planned service is actually delivered
- maintain a strongly change-focused intervention.

The movement for empirical practice has important strengths. It offers precision in measuring process and progress, and educates the practitioner to expect and respond to feedback on performance. It gives practitioners more control over evaluation of their own work, and may reduce inappropriate management pressure for evidence of accountability. It may help to generate a culture of critical curiosity, and, in a period where social workers are in danger of being reduced to technicians, some forms of empirical practice help reinforce the belief that social workers possess special human service expertise.

There remain, nonetheless, several important questions which are problematic for advocates of empirical practice. First, it is not clear that empirical practice methods can be applied to all or even most of social work practice. Complex problems, unpredictable, crisis or infrequently occurring behaviours, and the large numbers of single-contact social work interventions all pose problems for the measurement of empirically oriented practice which have been partially recognised but as yet are unresolved (cf. Robinson, Benson and Blythe 1988).

Second, the charge has sometimes been levelled that empirical practice models place demands of measurement on social workers and service users which, though consistent with behavioural interventions, are incompatible with the realities and meaning of practice. This charge of reductionism is acknowledged by some researchers within the empirical practice movement (e.g. Penka and Kirk 1991; Rotheray 1993), and careful work has been carried out in recent years to counter this criticism by applying single-system designs to other areas of work such as non-behavioural practice, multiple interventions, the evaluation of practice wisdom and narrative family therapy (Besa 1994; Jensen 1994; Nelson 1993; Reid 1993).

Third, ethical issues have been given too little attention. Bloom, who must be exempted from this criticism, has suggested the outlines of a code of ethics for evaluators in practice, in which he attempts to add the evaluative dimension to the basic Hippocratic ethics of medicine. Hence, 'providing help' becomes 'providing demonstrable help', and 'doing no harm' becomes 'demonstrating that we do no harm' (Bloom and Orme 1993). He has also consistently criticised on ethical grounds those single-system designs that require the alternating withdrawal and reinstatement of intervention (Bloom and Block 1977). Other ethical concerns have been given less attention. Empirical practitioners can too easily reject a view of the client as socially constrained, and instead overemphasise human responsibility. When applied to probation practice this marks 'the renaissance of the ideology of the calculating, culpable, and hence rational offender' (Pitts 1992, p.145). Meyer is right to warn enthusiasts for empirical practice against forgetting the constraints of the wider social system (Meyer 1984). Furthermore, the general neglect of issues of anti-discriminatory practice by those working in this tradition is worrying. For example, issues of sexism in research typically are treated as technical problems of 'bias' which can be mitigated if not eliminated by stronger adherence to rigorous evaluative designs (e.g. by McHugh, Koeske and Frieze 1986 and Thyer 1989). In addition, despite the emphasis on service users being involved in providing evaluation data, empirical practice is at root a non-participatory form of evaluating in practice. There is a welcome emphasis on securing agreement on which problems will be addressed. However, genuine participatory evaluation is put at risk by the stress on measurement in single-system designs, which leads to a dependence on technical expertise beyond the scope of many service users, and also by the ease with which empirical practice fits in to an ethos of management control and the performance culture (cf. Lewis 1988).

Finally, in an influential paper on research and service in single-system evaluation, Thomas rejected convincingly and in detail the hope that the union of science and practice could be achieved through such methods. His general argument was that the intrusion of service requirements on research design and the intrusion of research considerations on service, combine to suggest that 'it may be a misuse of single case experimentation to employ it for purposes of service evaluation' (Thomas 1978, p.29). Although this threat of disruption of service may in some cases be marginal, it 'cannot be passed off as inconsequential or marginal. These threats pose special problems of ethics that require appropriate protections' (p.28). In response to this criticism there has been less emphasis in recent work on the potential of empirical practice to provide experimental evidence of effectiveness.

Reflective and Empowering Evaluation

A very different approach to the methodology of evaluation is represented by a diverse cluster of writers whose work emphasises the central part played by choice, intention and human decision making. Much of this work adheres to a qualitative methodology. Some writers in this field argue forcefully that qualitative methodologies represent a distinctive paradigm, and that the differences between qualitative and quantitative approaches are fundamental and probably not bridgeable. Others adopt qualitative approaches on more instrumental grounds and are ready to accept some of the thinking within the empirical practice movement. There are divergences within this approach to evaluation. Some lay the main stress on the generation of reflective practice (e.g. England 1986; Gould and Taylor 1996; Hess 1995; Schon 1983,

1992), while others emphasise the goal of empowerment (e.g. Everitt and Hardiker 1996; Everitt *et al.* 1992; Fetterman, Kafterian and Wandersman 1996; Humphries and Truman 1994). Within this approach there has also been a recent move away from pure constructionist interpretations of meaning, and an emphasis on what is often described as a realist approach to research (cf. Sayer 1992).

Qualitative methodologies hold great promise for evaluating in practice, in ways I sketch in the final part of this chapter. They are strong at those very points where the empirical practice movement is weak. However, there are a number of problematic and troublesome issues. Blythe is right to lay down the challenge that social workers committed to qualitative and humanist methodologies should 'begin detailing just how they can actually be applied in practice' (Blythe 1992, p.268). Practitioners often find the practice consequences of qualitative work difficult to synthesise, and even distantly 'academic'. There has also been limited attention to ascertaining whether qualitative evaluating makes for better practice than other methodologies, although Everitt and Hardiker (1996) have suggested helpful ways in which evaluation should be assessed against an explicit commitment to good practice. Qualitative evaluators have as yet done little to suggest how direct practice will be different.

An unfortunate feature of work in these areas is that advocates of empirical practice and humanist positions often seem to be talking past each other. There is an acutely unhelpful tendency in the empirical practice literature to blame practitioners, agencies and academics working in qualitative methodology traditions for the failure of empirical practice hitherto to gain more than a toehold on agency cultures. Sheldon and MacDonald (1989–90) criticise social workers in a heavy-handed way for their failure to draw on the practice consequences of effectiveness research. First, 'we are the herbalists of the helping professions. We feel we just know from personal experience which approaches work and which do not'. Second, early evaluations reported in the 1960s and 1970s were disastrous in their consequences: 'The classic recipes of a generation of textbook-writers appeared, when tried out in the kitchen, to produce either unappetising stodge or, on occasion, the social work equivalent of food poisoning'. Finally, social workers do not read much or keep up with new thinking, and employers do not encourage 'such distractions from the day-to-day work of doing good' (pp.211, 212). Probation officers, for example, have been criticised for their failure to implement effective practice, and described as 'a professional or personal preference-led service, strongly influenced by ideological positions' (MacDonald 1994, p.419–20). Academic advocates of qualitative methods have been dismissed out of hand as 'intellectual Luddites' (Thyer 1995). In-house problems tend to be ducked as when Hudson dismissively claims that the philosophical problems of positivism alleged by critics are 'far more trivial than some would have us believe' (Hudson 1988, pp.60, 63).

The responses of advocates of qualitative method are equally likely to miss the mark. The references to positivism in social work are almost always negative and often angry, as when the broadside is fired that 'Positivists not only see their work as uncontaminated: they see themselves as pure and safe in their objectivity, an elite who have managed to transcend the constraints of subjectivity' (Everitt et al. 1992, p.6).

The propensity of some social work writers to use 'positivism', along with its companions 'empiricism', 'scientism' and 'objectivism', as global swearwords and slogans is unhelpful. In this connection Hammersley has criticised the tendency to talk of positivism as a 'paradigm', because it implies that all the characteristics of positivism come as a package, and also that there are no internal differences. 'It obscures both potential and actual diversity in orientation, and can lead us into making simplistic methodological decisions' (Hammersley 1995, p.3). Paradigm talk of the kind criticised by Hammersley is evident, for example, in the text by Everitt et al. While the authors helpfully seek to promote research-minded social work practice, they claim that one of the problems of 'the positivist paradigm' (sic) is that 'the research endeavour is mystified; esoteric skills and techniques serve the interests of the powerful'. They reach the conclusion that 'the essential values of positivism, objectivity, neutrality and determinism are…at variance with the value base, and the purposeful and humble activities of social work practice' (Everitt et al. 1992, pp.35, 55, 61).

Generalisations of this kind do not do justice to the challenge posed for social work by the epistemology and methodology of people working in the positivist tradition. Perhaps more significantly, they risk producing an insufficiently self-critical approach to the profession and practice of evaluating, and to ensuring an authentic relationship between action and understanding in social work.

Disciplined Eclecticism

Perhaps tired by the 'paradigm wars' described above, and influenced by more pragmatic approaches to evaluation through writers such as Michael Patton, and serious methodological efforts to develop a *rapprochement* between qualitative and quantitative approaches to evaluation (e.g. Bryman 1988; Shadish, Cook and Leviton, 1991), some social workers have resorted to a disciplined pluralism. Difficult though it may be to encapsulate the essence of this broad position it is probably the front runner in evaluation practice, and is represented by this book and also by the field-leading role occupied by the Social Work Research Unit at Stirling University (see Cheetham, Fuller, Petch and McIvor 1992).

The growing attention to practitioner research (for example, Broad and Fletcher 1993; Epstein, 1995; Fuller and Petch, 1995), clinically relevant methods of evaluation (for example, Nelson 1993; Tripodi and Epstein 1980), and a renewed concentration on strategies for research utilisation and dissemination (for example, Epstein and Grasso 1992; the establishment of a Department of Health utilisation and dissemination unit at Exeter University), all premise a 'live and let live' response to epistemological dispute, and a pragmatism governed by a readiness to go for good practice without too much navel-gazing regarding methodological credentials.

Evaluating in Practice – an Alternative Profession and Practice

If it is correct to argue that social workers and evaluators of various persuasions have made too limited progress in making evaluating part of the warp and woof of practice, are there any promising leads that will rescue us? I think there are. It is possible to sketch the lineaments of a profession and practice of evaluating that will simultaneously challenge social workers to a critical, reflective and enabling practice, while taking into account the significance of practitioners' existing evaluating practices. In the remainder of this chapter the main anchorage points for such a strategy are identified, and brief illustrations given of how these anchor points 'work'. The 'anchor' metaphor sounds more assured than I intend. Altheide and Johnson's phrase about 'floating stepping stones' may express better the combination of firmness yet shift that will mark evaluating in practice (Altheide and Johnson 1994). There are four such 'stepping stones'.

First, evaluating by practitioners of the kind outlined later in the chapter cannot be dismissed as the 'confused impressions of the mob' (Durkheim, quoted in Hughes 1980), in the way that tends to mark the main position statements of the empirical practice movement. A plausible strategy must start from the tacit knowing of social workers, and from a much enriched understanding of how experienced and reflective practitioners evaluate in their day to day work. I try to illustrate the value of this approach in the following section of the chapter.

Second, evaluating in practice will find its dynamic in *reflexive* evaluating. Practitioners will 'turn back on the action and on the knowing which is implicit in the action' (Schon 1983, p.50). Marked by a 'disciplined subjectivity' (Erikson 1959), such practice will be based on description carried out in such a way that it renders access to and evaluation of its strengths and weaknesses feasible (England 1986). Social workers have very belatedly begun to explore the relevance of the work on reflective practice undertaken by Schon (for example, Hess and Mullen 1995; Gould and Taylor 1996; Schon 1992). The comparable work of Heron (Heron 1996) and Reason (Reason 1988, 1994a, 1994b) has yet to receive similar critical attention by social workers.

Third, by taking the stance of the 'outsider on the inside' (Collins 1986), evaluating in practice will rest on falsifiable evidence; falsifying, in that social workers will be constantly trying to 'force favourite assumptions to become probable inferences' (Erikson 1959, p.94). Social scientists have too easily assumed that the work of Karl Popper is 'positivist', and have hence disregarded it. They have wrongly assumed, if they have considered the question at all, that falsification entails testing fallible theories with infallible facts. They are prone to neglect or to misread Popper's opposition to relativism and his thoroughgoing objectivism, as entailing a determinist worldview. Nothing could be further from Popper's position. His wholehearted anti-determinist stance was built on a belief that indeterminacy is an objective characteristic of the cosmos, and not just a product of our ignorance (Popper 1979). For Popper, we are not constrained, determined and pushed by the past, but 'enticed' by the future. We do not live in a closed cosmos. His vision towards the close of his life was of 'the allure of the open future'. 'The world is no longer a causal machine. It can now be seen to be an unfolding process, realising possibilities and unfolding new possibilities' (Popper 1988). Social workers should pause if they are tempted to consign Popper to history's trash can. If evaluating is to play a part at the heart of an empowering social work practice it must be both critical and yet open to falsification.

Fourth, evaluating in practice must be for, by and with the service user – 'for' as to its purpose, and 'by and with' as to its process. Feminist standpoint theory applied to social work (Swigonski 1993), and participatory evaluation strategies hammered out in Third World development programmes (Edwards 1989, 1994) both pose major challenges to conventional evaluation strategies, and underscore the work that has yet to be accomplished if evaluating in practice is to be genuinely participatory. Although both have been criticised (Booth 1994; Hammersley 1995; Hawkesworth 1989), they offer much to social work practice and in the latter case far more than is usually recognised.

Understanding Evaluating Practices

I have begun an argument for an alternative groundwork for evaluating in practice, that places evaluation at the heart of direct practice and will challenge social workers to new understandings and new methodologies, yet one also which will recognise throughout the significance of social workers' existing evaluating practices. Recognising the significance of existing evaluating practices demands a different form of research to energise it and to set new agenda. Such research must be 'exploratory rather than confirmatory, building a model of evaluation from the practitioners' own accounts rather than superimposing an ideal model and testing for conformity' (Elks and Kirkhart 1993, p.555).

The evidence in the following paragraphs illustrates this inductive approach from a series of in-depth, unstructured interviews carried out with fifteen social workers practising in a wide cross-section of British public and voluntary agencies, including adult services in the community, child protection teams, and the probation service. Local agency practice teacher and social work course lists provided the ingredients of a sampling grid from which potential respondents were randomly drawn. All practitioners invited to take part in interviews which would explore their views about evaluating within their everyday practice agreed to participate. Experienced practitioners, accredited practice teachers and newly qualified social workers made up the sample. 'Qualitative research,' McCracken aptly remarks, 'does not survey the terrain, it mines it' (McCracken 1988, p.17). Consequently, potential research participants were selected from an intentionally wide compass of experience and presumed expertise, in order to allow a range of 'test cases' for analytic categories emerging during the research.

The heart of the interview involved the respondents talking about two recent examples of their work, one in which they thought they were doing the work well, and one in which they thought they were practising less well. They were asked to describe the work and to say how they knew whether it was going well or not. They were encouraged to identify the evidence specific to each instance of their work. In the analysis of the narrative accounts produced through these interviews I attempt to glimpse and systematically reconstruct aspects of practitioners' views of their world. Our interest is in what medical sociologists have called the 'clinical gaze' (Atkinson 1995, p.5). This research is reported elsewhere (Shaw and Shaw 1997a and b).

The general conclusions from listening to these social workers' accounts are threefold. First, almost all practitioners distinguish between 'evaluation proper', and their own evaluating practices with those service users for whose welfare they were responsible. Second, social workers typically found it possible to make explicit a more or less coherent set of normally tacit strategies which, in their view, make up real life, 'good' evaluating practice. In describing this as 'good' practice I make no judgement on whether it is good according to some professional yardstick. Third, practitioners are able to explicate ways in which they use these strategies in order to sort 'cases' according to whether they demonstrate evidence of 'good' or 'less good' practice.

Models of Evaluating

'Evaluation proper', called by someone 'Evaluation with a Capital E', was seen by almost all practitioners as part of a widespread culture of change in social work, the hallmark of which was an emphasis on performance and its measurement. It was experienced as coming from above in the form of a scrutiny which is planned, formal, and takes place occasionally rather than all the time. Hence, the agenda of Evaluation is believed to be driven by *service* level concerns and not by direct practice problems and opportunities. When it does happen it is relatively time consuming. But perhaps the most pervasive and frequently cited characteristic of Evaluation was that practitioners described it as measured quantitatively rather than qualitatively. 'I tend to think of evaluation proper, in inverted commas, as being more to do with facts and figures'.

Evaluating in action – the day-to-day, often tacit evaluating practices of social workers – was presented as being in tension at almost every point with this more formal model. It was repeatedly characterised as being about quality and worth, and not about quantity. Informal, partly private, subjective and crafted out of the personal immediacy of day-to-day work, it was sometimes described as 'on-your-feet evaluation'. However, it was seen by all social workers as being a troublesome part of social work practice, and that for several reasons. The language of evaluation was frequently talked about as 'foreign' to practice, and the practice of evaluation as not part of the centre of social work, but as a marginal 'add-on'. When social workers searched for ways of talking about their evaluating, they elicited a cluster of assumptions regarding how social work works. They described their efforts at evaluating as based on a belief that progress in social work practice is typically achieved by slow, incremental steps, where a long-term perspective and involvement is needed for results to be seen, and in which evaluation has to draw on complex evidence that is typically difficult to interpret.

'Real Life' Evaluating

Each of these two models of evaluating has its own hallmarks, which, apart from one or two important points of contact, together represent largely divergent sets of commitments, activities and attitudes. This becomes clearer when we outline the second conclusion from this evidence, that social workers typically found it possible to make explicit a more or less coherent set of hitherto tacit strategies which made up, in their view, good evaluating practice. Much of what practitioners had to say on this theme could be encapsulated in terms of three considerations: the exercise of a 'game plan'; having a good client; and recognising the part played by 'sheer luck'.

The possession of a 'game plan' entailed the ability to exercise 'control' in work with clients and other key actors, the exercise of a purposeful and constructive practice strategy, and playing within the rules of the game when it came to making decisions. Having this game plan provides a *general* strategy. However, this was not regarded as sufficient without an approach specific to the circumstances of a given 'case'.

All of this could be jeopardised by factors perceived to be beyond the social worker's control, above all else by whether the practitioner is working with a 'good' or 'bad' client, and the part played by 'luck'. A 'bad' client – someone typically with no motivation to change, a personal mistrust of the social worker, or an inability to change – would bring to nothing the efforts of the most streetwise social worker. Moreover, whatever game plan may be in place, and however wise and experienced a social worker may be, the majority of practitioners who told their evaluating stories believed there was an element of unpredictability near the heart of social work practice. Whether work went well or badly was not simply the product of rational or intelligent planning. Expressed at its simplest, in the words of one social worker, 'there's always an element of good fortune in these things'.

Evidence of 'Good' and 'Bad' Practice

Finally, practitioners were able to explicate ways in which they used these strategies in order to sort 'cases' according to whether they demonstrate evidence of good or less good practice. When talking about specific examples of where they felt their practice had gone well or less well, social workers illustrated ways in which good or bad practice was believed to depend on the answers they gave themselves to the following questions:

- Does the work produce emotional rewards or penalties for the social worker?
- Is the 'case' or problem 'stuck' or 'moving'?
- Did the intervention win steady, incremental change for the better?
- Did the social worker strike a moral balance? In so doing, did s/he avoid doing harm to the service user?
- Did the practitioner win disinterested, corroborating appraisals from fellow professionals?

Each of these informal 'quality criteria' can be illustrated from examples of work identified by social workers as having gone *badly*. Thus, one practitioner typically described negative emotional feedback as follows:

> I'm getting absolutely nowhere with her, and so it makes me feel quite frustrated, and I think that frustration shows...I don't get any satisfaction out of the interactions I have with her. It affects me as a worker I think.

Being 'stuck' in either an intractable or cyclical set of problems was frequently cited as evidence for work that had not gone well:

> She's ended up now having another baby and it feels like I'm on a treadmill for the second time around, because similar things are happening.

The complexity of evidence, and the inherent unpredictability of practice outcomes were, however, repeatedly offered as mitigating factors. It was these considerations, as much as any others, that appeared to explain why social workers mistrusted grand change as a social work project, and castigated themselves when they found they had slipped into that way of thinking and working.

> I got sucked into the idea of thinking 'This is a situation that can be cured', which I think was the wrong way to be looking at it. It should have been more, 'This is a situation which can be stabilised' rather than hoping that if I could put in some sort of basic practical support it was all going to go away.

Just as the medical doctor vows to do the patient no harm, so social workers – at least those to whom we spoke – are sensitive to the risk that engaging with welfare or correctional services may not simply fail to deliver change, maintenance or improvement, but may make matters worse.

> I felt like a total mug, certainly in terms of effectiveness. Not only totally ineffective but also possibly worsened a bad situation by colluding with this man in the belief that everything was all right, and wasted a good deal of time in supposed counselling sessions.

Corroboration from service users was valued but regarded as a rare red letter day. Indeed, evidence from elsewhere in the study, not reported here, suggested that practitioners frequently took it for granted that service users held a different view from themselves on whether practice had turned out well or not, and that the underlying criteria were often not shared between social workers and service user or carer. More commonly, social workers depended on the disinterested, corroborating assessment of fellow professionals. When this let them down it was regarded as clear evidence for bad practice.

We probably can conclude from this evidence that practitioners *do* evaluate their own practice, but that evaluation is a part of their practice which is experienced as inescapably troublesome. Furthermore it is at constant risk of being marginalised. These conclusions are consistent with, and go some way to elaborate, the limited evidence available from other research (Elks and Kirkhart, 1993; Humphrey and Pease 1992). Both agency-led 'Evaluation' and personal, day-to-day evaluating practices were probably in this probation officer's mind when she concluded:

You evaluate because you have to. It's not something that excites you in your work at all. If something is going well you enjoy evaluating and look back, 'Yeah, that had been great'. If it's not going well it's a burden because it's not very constructive.

A Manifesto for Evaluating in Practice

What are the practice implications of the 'floating stepping stones' and the evidence gleaned from social work practitioners? In the final part of this chapter I offer my own manifesto for practice (cf. Shaw 1997) and sketch out how one plank in this manifesto can be made to 'work'. My manifesto for evaluating in practice has six points.

First, social workers should reflect hard on their practice. This will include close attention to description and the relation of that description to planned and actual outcomes (England 1986). In social work education it will also include a full exploitation of the expectation that social workers should evidence practice, which is written in to the regulations governing social work training at qualifying and post-qualifying levels. Such reflection will also take into account the possibilities for inductive, 'grounded theory' (Epstein 1995).

Second, social workers must know what they know. By this I mean they must work to elicit their tacit, taken for granted knowledge, and assess the relevance, for good or ill, that their tacit knowledge has for their practice. This may include the reviewing of our own cultural knowledge in the way suggested by McCracken (1988), and also acting on the wider applications of the insistence of some black feminists that black women must 'learn to trust their own personal and cultural biographies as significant sources of knowledge' (Collins 1986, p.S29).

Third, social workers must begin with the knowledge that service users bring to them. This means more than listening to service user views, important and inescapably unsettling as that must always prove. It also includes an openness to a view of the world entirely at odds with our own preconceptions.

Fourth and fifth, social workers must engage in participatory evaluation with service users and cooperative inquiry with colleagues. Whitmore's compelling account of participatory inquiry with oppressed black women, Martin's review of feminist participative research, and Traylen's account of cooperative inquiry within a team of health visitors, together exemplify these two points (Martin 1994; Traylen 1994; Whitmore 1994).

Sixth, practitioners must exploit the implications of the analogue between some research methods and direct practice methods. In particular, they need to ground the development of evaluating as a direct practice competence in a rigorous 'translating' and 'colonising' of qualitative methodology. In these closing paragraphs of this chapter I sketch out how I believe this translating and colonising should be undertaken.

Qualitative Evaluating in Practice

Pleas are increasingly heard for social workers to recognise the lessons for practice offered by qualitative research (Everitt *et al.* 1992; Sheppard 1995; White, in this book, Chapter 9). There is, however, *some* force in the complaint of those working in a generally positivist tradition, that this plea has yet to be converted into good practice (Blythe 1992; Thyer 1989).

How does this translation work need to move forward? Certainly it is not sufficient for advocates of qualitative method simply to plead that social workers must 'apply' the lessons of qualitative research. Social workers need to cultivate a 'methodological imagination' which will rescue them from the present reliance on a very limited span of methods for learning about and understanding those for and with whom they work. Participant observation, interview methods, focus groups, life histories, and new developments using simulated clients, all offer the possibility of an enriched evaluating in practice.

The scope of *participant observation* as an agent for better action and understanding is extensive (Shaw 1996a, pp.135–141). Although observation methods pose ethical dilemmas (Bulmer 1982), it is the very sharpening of these dilemmas through participant observation that provides a pay-off for good practice. Ethical dilemmas are, of course, also present in slightly different guises in practice based on interviews. We are simply less aware of them by virtue – or vice – of over-familiarity.

Developments in social work practice with children suggest alternatives to accepted methods of *interviewing* which will generate an evaluative practice. Strongly and often unconsciously held beliefs about childhood as an unfolding of developmental stages have constrained the methods of researchers and social workers and led to a model of child interviewing which it is believed 'can help the clinician assess the developmental sophistication of the child's interpersonal style and social emotional reasoning' (Bierman and Schwartz 1986, p.276). However, interviewing strategies in inquiry with children recently have developed from this position in two directions (Shaw 1996b), both of which have good practice consequences for social work.

First, there has been a welcome and quite widespread acceptance of children as persons who have similar rights to those of adults in regard to giving informed consent to research access (Butler and Williamson 1994). The second development in interviewing with children and young people is, if anything, more far reaching. At its heart it involves a major reversal of how we view the interview, so that it is seen not simply as a source of information *from* young informants, but as evidence in and of itself. For instance, talking to adolescents is not a means of gaining information about socialisation processes but is itself an instance of socialisation. Baker's 'second look' at interviews with adolescents exemplifies this approach. She argues that 'the key to turning the interview into a resource is to view it as a real event in the real world – not only as a means of access to data but as data' (Baker 1983, pp.501, 508). This allows her to see the way the interviews display their character as adult–young person social encounters in which adults are questioning adolescents. The questions contain an implicit adult theory of adolescence and answers contain an implicit adolescent theory of adulthood. Interviews are an occasion for the management of identity. Baker's analysis is persuasive. 'Interviews are socialisation sites. In these interviews adolescents are invited to show membership in the adult language community by making sense of the questions and developing the discourse with the interviewer' (p.516–517; cf. Siegert 1986). Conclusions of this kind clearly have implications for problem-solving talk between adults and children in health, social work and educational settings.

One of the most promising developments in applying qualitative and participatory evaluation through groups has come through work on *focus groups* (Katz 1996; Kitzinger 1994; Kreuger 1994; Morgan 1988, 1993), almost to the extent that all group interviews become re-labelled to attract the *caché* of focus group. Focus groups take the form of group discussions organised to explore a specific set of issues. 'The group is *focused* in the sense that it involves some kind of collective activity – such as viewing a film, evaluating a single health education message or simply debating a particular set of questions' (Kitzinger 1994, p.159).

Focus groups have three particular advantages. First, the group interaction is itself the data – 'the interaction is the method' (Jarrett 1993, p.198).

Kitzinger says in summary that the method 'enables the researcher to examine people's different perspectives as they operate within a social network and to explore how accounts are constructed, expressed, censored, opposed and changed through social interaction' (1994, p.159). Second, focus groups are a form of participatory evaluation. They are valuable when there is a power differential between participants and decision makers, and hence have considerable potential for application within social work. Finally, they enable participants to learn the extent of consensus or disagreement on a particular issue. 'The co-participants act as co-researchers taking the research into new and often unexpected directions and engaging with each other in ways which are both complementary...and argumentative' (Kitzinger 1994, p.166).

Problem setting (Plaut, Landis and Trevor 1993, and present work by Shaw and Bloor on rough sleeping), empowering group participants (Jarrett 1993), service user involvement (Bond 1990–91), present work in Japan by Oka on self-help groups, and some applications to work with sensitive problems (cf. Zeller 1993), all illustrate ways in which focus groups have a potential application to evaluating in practice.

An important element of social work practice is the taking of 'histories', whether they be for assessment purposes, reports, or as part of practice interventions. Social work practitioners have tended to rely on an unduly narrow methodology of histories. The life-history work of the Chicago School in the 1930s, recent work on life-course sociology (Morgan 1985), and oral history methods (Samuel and Thompson 1990) all have the potential for 'translating' and thus for enriching evaluating in practice. Bowen's delightful essay on applying life-history methods to work with school non-attenders pointedly demonstrates the evaluative uses of a method chosen, in Bowen's own words, 'because it would make use of some of the skills I had learned and used as a practising social worker' (Bowen 1993, p.107). Martin's work on oral history in social work (Martin 1995), and applications of life-course sociology to social work and social welfare related problems (Clapham, Means and Munro 1993; Clifford 1994) also illustrate the potential of rethinking 'histories', although more work needs to be done on the specifically evaluative benefits of these methods.

In addition, sociological work on personal experience has potential uses for social work practice and especially evaluating in practice (Clandinin and Connelly 1994; Scott 1990). At present these applications are limited due to an apparent tendency to regard such methods as specialist, technical or even esoteric.

Qualitative methodologies also allow social workers to review areas of practice in which progress has become intractable. For example, the use of *simulated clients* in natural settings in order to identify variations in practice from one practitioner to another is presently being developed by Fran Wasoff and Rebecca Dobash (Wasoff and Dobash 1992, 1996; Shaw 1996a). The main value of the method is as a focus for practice development, rather than the evaluation of specific intervention. The use of simulated clients has several things going for it. First, social workers are familiar with the family of methods from which it is drawn, having used role plays and case vignettes. Second, simulated client methods overcome the ethical problems which arise if we wish to draw on the experience of service users for broader practice development purposes. Third, it makes practice visible. When significant changes are being introduced that need to be 'trialed', or when an agency or individual practitioner is stuck with this or that particular problem, then the use of simulated clients offers a new and promising method of developmental evaluation.

Conclusion

Evaluating in practice must be methodologically, rhetorically and professionally convincing. Methodologically, it must evidence, and make visible and open to inspection, the relationship between service user and provider. Rhetorically, it must assure the audience of other service users and social workers that the co-evaluators have walked in their shoes. It will be professionally convincing if it makes practice sense; 'sense' that is, not by the measure of conventionally received wisdom, but by forcing us to stretch out our minds and practice beyond the reach of the obvious.

I have profiled an argument that runs the risk of caricature by its very brevity. Yet the imaginative colonising of qualitative methods holds real promise for the evaluating of social work assessments, plans and interventions, and for the development of a reflexive, practitioner-led, falsifying and participatory evaluating in practice.

References

Altheide, D. and Johnson, J. (1994) 'Criteria for assessing interpretive validity qualitative research.' In N. Denzin and Y. Lincoln (eds) *Handbook of Qualitative Research*. Newbury Park: Sage.

Andrews, D. and Bonta, J. (1995) *The Level of Service Inventory – Revised.* New York: Multi-Health Systems.

Atkinson, P. (1995) *Medical Work and Medical Talk.* London: Sage.

Baker, C. (1983) 'A second look at interviews with adolescents.' *Journal of Youth and Adolescence 12*, 6, 501–519.

Besa, D. (1994) 'Evaluating narrative family therapy using single-system research designs.' *Research on Social Work Practice 4*, 3, 309–325.

Bierman, K. and Schwartz, L. (1986) 'Clinical child interviews: approaches and development considerations.' *Child and Adolescent Psychotherapy 3*, 4, 267–278.

Bloom, M. (ed) (1993) *Single-System Designs in the Social Services: Issues and Options for the 1990s.* New York: Haworth.

Bloom, M. and Block, S. (1977) 'Evaluating one's own effectiveness and efficiency.' *Social Work 22*, 2, 130–136.

Bloom, M. and Orme, J. (1993) 'Ethics and the single-system design.' In M. Bloom (ed) *Single-System Designs in the Social Services: Issues and Options for the 1990s.* New York: Haworth.

Blythe, B. (1992) 'Should undergraduate and graduate social work students be taught to conduct empirically based practice? Yes!' *Journal of Social Work Education 28*, 3, 260–264.

Blythe, B., Tripodi, T. and Briar, S. (1995) *Direct Practice Research in Human Services Agencies.* New York: Columbia University Press.

Bond, M. (1990–1991) '"The centre, it's for children": seeking children's views as users of a family centre.' *Practice 7*, 2, 53–60.

Booth, D. (ed) (1994) *Rethinking Social Development.* Harlow: Longman.

Bowen, D. (1993) 'The delights of learning to apply the life history method to school non-attenders.' In B. Broad and C. Fletcher (eds) *Practitioner Social Work Research in Action.* London: Whiting and Birch.

Broad, B. and Fletcher, C. (eds) (1993) *Practitioner Social Work Research in Action.* London: Whiting and Birch.

Bryman, A. (1988) *Quality and Quantity in Social Research.* London: Unwin Hyman.

Bulmer, M. (ed) (1982) *Social Research Ethics.* London: Macmillan.

Butler, I. and Williamson, H. (1994) *Children Speak: Children, Trauma and Social Work.* Harlow: Longman.

Cheetham, J., Fuller, R., Petch, A. and McIvor, G. (1992) *Evaluating Social Work Effectiveness.* Buckingham: Open University Press.

Clandinin, D. and Connelly, F. (1994) 'Personal experience methods.' In N. Denzin and Y. Lincoln (eds) *Handbook of Qualitative Research.* Newbury Park: Sage.

Clapham, D., Means, R. and Munro, M. (1993) 'Housing, the life course and older people.' In S. Arber and M. Evandrou (eds) *Ageing, Independence and the Life Course.* London: Jessica Kingsley Publishers.

Clifford, D. (1994) 'Critical life histories: key anti-oppressive research methods and processes.' In B. Humphries and C. Truman (eds) *Rethinking Social Research: Anti-Discriminatory Approaches in Research Methodology.* Aldershot: Avebury.

Collins, P. (1986) 'Learning from the outsider within: the sociological significance of black feminist thought.' *Social Problems 33*, 6, S14–S32.

Edwards, M. (1989) 'The irrelevance of development studies.' *Third World Quarterly 11*, 1, 116–135.

Edwards, M. (1994) 'Rethinking social development: the search for "relevance".' In D. Booth (ed) *Rethinking Social Development: Theory, Practice and Research.* Harlow: Longman.

Elks, M. and Kirkhart, K. (1993) 'Evaluating effectiveness from the practitioner's perspective.' *Social Work 38*, 5, 554–563.

England, H. (1986) *Social Work as Art.* London: Allen and Unwin.

Epstein, I. (1995) 'Promoting reflective social work practice.' In P. Hess and E. Mullen (eds) *Practitioner–Researcher Relationships: Building Knowledge From, In and For Practice.* Washington DC: National Association of Social Workers.

Epstein, I. and Grasso, A. (1992) *Research Utilisation in the Social Services.* New York: Haworth.

Erikson, E. (1959) 'The nature of clinical inference.' In D. Lerner (ed) *Evidence and Inference.* New York: Free Press.

Everitt, A. and Hardiker, P. (1996) *Evaluating for Good Practice.* London: Macmillan.

Everitt, A, Hardiker, P., Littlewood, J. and Mullender, A. (1992) *Applied Research for Better Practice.* London: Macmillan.

Fetterman, D., Kafterian, S. and Wandersman, A. (1996) *Empowerment Evaluation: Knowledge and Tools for Self-Assessment and Accountability.* Thousand Oaks: Sage.

Fischer, J. (1993) 'Empirically based practice: the end of ideology?' In M. Bloom (ed) *Single-System Designs in the Social Services: Issues and Options for the 1990s.* New York: Haworth.

Fuller, R. and Petch, A. (eds) (1995) *Practitioner Research: The Reflexive Social Worker.* Buckingham: Open University Press.

Gould, N. and Taylor, I. (eds) (1996) *Reflective Learning for Social Work: Research, Theory and Practice.* Aldershot: Ashgate.

Grinnell, R. (ed) (1993) *Social Work Research and Evaluation.* Itasca: F.E. Peacock.

Hammersley, M. (1995) *The Politics of Social Research.* London: Sage.

Hawkesworth, M. (1989) 'Knowers, knowing, known: feminist theory and claims of truth.' *Signs: Journal of Women in Culture and Society 14*, 3, 533–555.

Heron, J. (1996) *Co-operative Inquiry: Research into the Human Condition.* London: Sage.

Hess, P. (1995) 'Reflecting in and on practice.' In P. Hess and E. Mullen (eds) *Practitioner–Researcher Relationships: Building Knowledge From, In and For Practice.* Washington DC: National Association of Social Workers.

Hess, P. and Mullen, E. (eds) *Practitioner–Researcher Relationships: Building Knowledge From, In and For Practice.* Washington DC: National Association of Social Workers.

Hudson, W. (1988) 'Measuring client outcomes and their use for managers.' In R. Patti, J. Poertner and C. Rapp (eds) *Managing for Service Effectiveness in Social Welfare Organisations.* New York: Haworth.

Humphrey, C. and Pease, K. (1992) 'Effectiveness measurement in the probation service: a view from the troops.' *Howard Journal 31*, 2, 31–52.

Humphries, P. and Truman, C. (1994) (eds) *Rethinking Social Research: Anti-Discriminatory Approaches to Research Methodology*. Aldershot: Avebury.

Jarrett, R. (1993) 'Focus group interviewing with low income minority populations.' In D.L. Morgan (ed) *Successful Focus Groups: Advancing the State of the Art*. Newbury Park: Sage.

Jensen, C. (1994) 'Psychosocial treatment of depression in women: nine single-subject evaluations.' *Research on Social Work Practice 4*, 3, 267–282.

Katz, I. (1996) 'How do young Asian and white people view their problems? A step towards child centred research.' In I. Butler and I. Shaw (eds) *A Case of Neglect? The Sociology of Childhood*. Aldershot: Avebury.

Kitzinger, J. (1994) 'Focus groups: method or madness?' In M. Bolton (ed) *Challenge and Innovation: Methodological Advances in Social Research on HIV/AIDS*. London: Taylor and Francis.

Kreuger, R. (1994) *Focus Groups, a Practical Guide for Applied Research*. Newbury Park: Sage.

Lewis, (1988) 'Ethics and the managing of service effectiveness in social welfare.' In R. Patti, J. Poertner and C. Rapp (eds) *Managing for Service Effectiveness in Social Welfare Organisations*. New York: Haworth.

MacDonald, G. (1994) 'Developing empirically-based practice in probation.' *British Journal of Social Work 24*, 4, 405–427.

Martin, M. (1994) 'Developing a feminist participative research framework.' In P. Humphries and C. Truman (eds) *Rethinking Social Research: Anti-Discriminatory Approaches to Research Methodology*. Aldershot: Avebury.

Martin, R. (1995) *Oral History in Social Work*. London: Sage.

Meyer, C. (1984) 'Integrating research and practice.' *Social Work 29*, 4, 323.

McCracken, G. (1988) *The Long Interview*. Newbury Park: Sage.

McGuire, J. (ed) (1995) *What Works? Reducing Reoffending*. Chichester: Wiley.

McHugh, M., Koeske, R. and Frieze, I. (1986) 'Issues to consider in conducting non-sexist psychological research.' *American Psychologist 41*, 879–890.

Morgan, D. (1985) *The Family: Politics and Social Theory*. London: Routledge.

Morgan, D.L. (1988) *Focus Groups as Qualitative Research*. London: Sage.

Morgan, D.L. (ed) (1993) *Successful Focus Groups: Advancing the State of the Art*. London: Sage.

Nelson, J. (1993) 'Testing practice wisdom: another use of single-system research.' In M. Bloom (ed) *Single-System Designs in the Social Services: Issues and Options for the 1990s*. New York: Haworth.

Penka, C. and Kirk, S. (1991) 'Practitioner involvement in clinical evaluation.' *Social Work 36*, 6, 513–518.

Pitts, J. (1992) 'The end of an era.' *Howard Journal 31*, 2, 133–149.

Plaut, T., Landis, S. and Trevor, J. (1993) 'Focus groups and community mobilisation.' In D.L. Morgan (ed) *Successful Focus Groups: Advancing the State of the Art*. London: Sage.

Popper, K. (1979) *Objective Knowledge*. Oxford: Clarendon Press.

Popper, K. (1988) 'The allure of the open future.' Lecture to the World Philosophy Congress.

Reason, P. (ed) (1988) *Human Inquiry in Action: Developments in New Paradigm Research*. London: Sage.

Reason, P. (1994a) (ed) *Participation in Human Inquiry*. London: Sage.

Reason, P. (1994b) 'Three approaches to participative inquiry.' In N. Denzin and Y. Lincoln (eds) *Handbook of Qualitative Research*. Newbury Park: Sage.

Reid, W. (1988) 'Service effectiveness and the social agency.' In R. Patti, J. Poertner and C. Rapp (eds) *Managing for Effectiveness in Social Welfare Organisations*. New York: Haworth.

Reid, W. (1993) 'Fitting the single-system design to family treatment.' In M. Bloom (ed) *Single-System Designs in the Social Services: Issues and Options for the 1990s*. New York: Haworth.

Reid, W. (1994) 'The empirical practice movement.' *Social Service Review 68*, 165–184.

Robinson, E., Benson, D. and Blythe, B. (1988) 'An analysis of the implementation of single-case evaluation by practitioners.' *Social Service Review 62*, 2, 285–301.

Rotheray, M. (1993) 'The positivistic research approach.' In R. Grinnell (ed) *Social Work Research and Evaluation*. Itasca: F.E. Peacock.

Samuel, R. and Thompson, P. (eds) (1990) *The Myths We Live By*. London: Routledge.

Sayer, A. (1992) *Method in Social Science*. London: Routledge.

Schon, D. (1983) *The Reflective Practitioner*. New York: Basic Books.

Schon, D. (1992) 'The crisis of professional knowledge and the pursuit of an epistemology of practice.' *Journal of Interprofessional Care 6*, 49–63.

Scott, J. (1990) *A Matter of Record*. Oxford: Polity Press.

Seigal, D. (1984) 'Defining empirically based practice.' *Social Work 29*, 325–331.

Shadish, W., Cook, T.D. and Leviton, L. (1991) *Foundations of Program Evaluation*. Thousand Oaks: Sage.

Shaw, I. (1996a) *Evaluating in Practice*. Aldershot: Ashgate.

Shaw, I. (1996b) 'Unbroken voices: children, young people and qualitative methods.' In I. Butler and I. Shaw (eds) *A Case of Neglect? The Sociology of Childhood*. Aldershot: Avebury.

Shaw, I. (1997) *Be Your Own Evaluator*. Wrexham: Prospects Publishing.

Shaw, I. and Shaw, A. (1997a) 'Game plans, buzzes and sheer luck: doing well in social work.' *Social Work Research 21*, 69–79.

Shaw, I. and Shaw, A. (1997b) 'Keeping social work honest: evaluating as profession and practice.' *British Journal of Social Work 27*, 847–869.

Sheldon, B. and MacDonald, G. (1989–90) 'Implications for practice of recent social work effectiveness research.' *Practice 6*, 3, 211–218.

Sheppard, M. (1995) 'Social work, social science and practice wisdom.' *British Journal of Social Work 25*, 3, 265–293.

Siegert, M. (1986) 'Adult elicited child behaviour: the paradox of measuring social competence through interviewing.' In J. Cook-Gumperz, W. Corsaro and J. Streeck (eds) *Children's Worlds and Children's Language*. Berlin: Mouton de Gruyter.

Swigonski, M. (1993) 'Feminist standpoint theory and questions of social work research.' *Affilia 8*, 2, 171–183.

Thomas, E. (1978) 'Research and service in single-case experimentation: conflicts and choices.' *Social Work Research and Abstracts 14*, 4, 309–325.

Traylen, H. (1994) 'Confronting hidden agendas: co-operative inquiry with health visitors.' In P. Reason (ed) *Participation in Human Inquiry*. London: Sage.

Tripodi, T. and Epstein, I. (1980) *Research Techniques for Clinical Social Workers*. New York: Columbia University Press.

Thyer, B. (1989) 'First principles of practice research.' *British Journal of Social Work 19*, 4.

Thyer, B. (1995) 'Promoting an empiricist agenda within the human services: an ethical and humanistic imperative.' *Journal of Behaviour Therapy and Experimental Psychiatry 26*, 2.

Wasoff, F. and Dobash, R.E. (1992) 'Simulated clients in 'natural' settings: constructing a client to study professional practice.' *Sociology 26*, 2, 333–349.

Wasoff, F. and Dobash, R.E. (1996) *Working With the Public: Researching Bureaucrats and Professionals as They Work With People*. Aldershot: Avebury.

Whitmore, E. (1994) 'To tell the truth: working with oppressed groups in participatory approaches to human inquiry.' In P. Reason (ed) *Participation in Human Inquiry*. London: Sage.

Zeller, R. (1993) 'Focus group research on sensitive topics – setting the agenda without setting the agenda.' In D.L. Morgan (ed) *Successful Focus Groups: Advancing the State of the Art*. London: Sage.

Contributors

Andy Alaszewski is Professor of Health Studies at the University of Hull. He has a long-standing interest in work with people with learning disabilities and has conducted research in family care, institutions and community services, risk and multi-agency care.

Douglas Badger is Director of Social Work Studies at the University of Reading. His research interests are in social work education and in work with mentally disordered offenders.

Greta Bradley is Lecturer in Social Work and Director of the Master Social Work programme at the University of Hull. She has extensive practice experience in hospital-related social work and currently researches in areas of community care, social work education and European developments affecting the social professions.

Peter Burke is a Senior Lecturer in Social Work at the University of Hull. He qualified as a social worker in 1975 (CQSW), gaining his first degree from the Open University in the same year. Peter completed two further degrees by part time study; an MSc, and then an MPhil after entering academic life in 1983. His research interests include problem definition, practice issues and childhood disabilities. His book (jointly authored with Katy Cigno), *Support for Families*, is a study of families with children with learning disabilities, and was published by Avebury in 1996.

Juliet Cheetham was a probation officer before becoming a lecturer in applied social studies at the University of Oxford. In 1986 she became the first director of the Social Work Research Centre at the University of Stirling. She was the vice chair of the Social Policy and Social Work panel for the Higher Education Funding Council 1996 Research Assessment Exercise.

Monica Dowling practised as a social worker in Liverpool, Runcorn and Enfield. She left full time work to undertake a PhD at the University of Sheffield which she completed in 1992. Her current post as Lecturer in Applied Social Studies is at Royal Holloway, University of London, where she has recently completed a three-year research project on social service users' and carers' experiences of community care. Her research interests are concerned with social exclusion, poverty and community care and the experiences and views of social service users and carers.

Steve Farnfield is a half-time lecturer in social work at the University of Reading and a half-time psychiatric social worker with Portsmouth Social Services. At the university he teaches infant and young child observation and social work with children and families. In practice he is mainly concerned with play therapy for middle years children and he has a special interest in the attachment difficulties of children in care.

Sheila Furness has been a lecturer at Bradord and Ilkley Community College for the past three years; her main areas of teaching include community care, care management and social work practice. Prior to this she worked for a number of years as an inspection officer of residential homes employed by a metropolitan social services department. During this period she carried out her research into elder abuse as part of an MA course.

Mansoor Kazi is Senior Lecturer in Social Work and Applied Social Studies at the University of Huddersfield. He is also Director of the Centre for Evaluation Studies based at the University. Following graduation from the London School of Economics, he went to complete his MA in social work at the University of Hull. His previous position was Service Manager of Rochdale Education Welfare Service and team leader of the local education authority's Performance Review Team. He is currently involved in a number of evaluation projects in social work, health, probation and education settings in both public and voluntary sectors. He is writing a text on single-case evaluation to be published by Avebury.

Jill Manthorpe is Lecturer in Community Care at the University of Hull. She has particular interest in work with older people and has published widely in the area of risk, abuse and social care. Current research projects include local government reorganisation, students with mental health problems and professional decision making in areas of risk.

Ian Shaw is Director of Research and Senior Lecturer in Social Work in the School of Social and Administrative Studies, University of Wales Cardiff. He is presently working in the fields of evaluation, homelessness and child prostitution. He is writing a text on qualitative evaluation, and editing a reader on social work evaluation, both of which will be published by Sage Publications.

Nicky Stanley is Lecturer in Social Work at the University of Hull. She was formerly a practising social worker working in mental health and primary care settings and also trained approved social workers. She now teaches and researches in the areas of community care, mental health and child protection.

Bruce A. Thyer, PhD, is Research Professor of Social Work and Adjunct Professor of Psychology at the University of Georgia, and Associate Clinical Professor of Psychiatry and Health Behaviour at the Medical College of Georgia. He is the editor of *Research on Social Work Practice*, a quarterly peer-reviewed journal published by Sage Publications, Inc.

Susan White is a lecturer in the department of social policy and social work at the University of Manchester. She qualified in social work in 1984 working for ten years in statutory social services as a practitioner and as a manager. Her doctoral research was discourse analytic in focus and involved ethnographic fieldwork in a social services department. She is currently researching user perspectives in child adolescent mental health as part of a project funded by the Mental Health Foundation. She is also a part of a research team exploring Finnish and English child welfare practices.

Angela Williams is a qualified teacher and social worker and has worked with children and families in a variety of education and social services settings in England and abroad. Her interest in the evaluation of social work practice comes from her manager/practitioner role within Bradford Education Social Work Service and from practice teaching for Diploma in Social Work programmes in the area.

Subject Index

Name Index